KNOCK 'EM DEAD 2009

The Ultimate Job Search Guide

Martin Yate C.P.C.

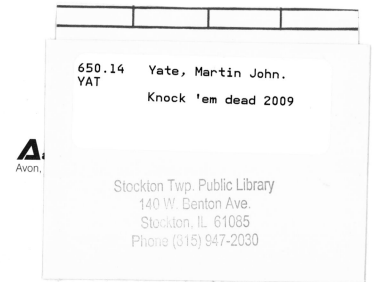

Avon,

To your successful job search

Published by
Adams Media, a division of F+W Media, Inc.
57 Littlefield Street, Avon, Massachusetts 02322 U.S.A.
www.adamsmedia.com

ISBN 10: 1-59869-672-6
ISBN 13: 978-1-59869-672-1

Printed in the United States of America.

J I H G F E D C B

Library of Congress Cataloging-in-Publication Data
available from the publisher.

This publication is designed to provide accurate and authoritative information with regard to the subject matter covered. It is sold with the understanding that the publisher is not engaged in rendering legal, accounting, or other professional advice. If legal advice or other expert assistance is required, the services of a qualified professional person should be sought.
— From a *Declaration of Principles* jointly adopted by a Committee of the American Bar Association and a Committee of Publishers and Associations.

Many of the designations used by manufacturers and sellers to distinguish their products are claimed as trademarks. Where those designations appear in this book and Adams Media was aware of a trademark claim, the designations have been printed with initial capital letters.

This book is available at quantity discounts for bulk purchases.
For more information, call 1-800-289-0963.

CONTENTS

Learning how to handle each of these interviewer types is key to turning job interviews into job offers. Learn how interviews are structured and what to do when interviewers don't ask the questions that allow you to promote your candidacy.

Your worst nightmare can come true at a stress interview, but once you learn that these questions are just amplified versions of much simpler ones, you'll remain cool and calm. Also: a vital discussion on handling illegal interview questions. What mock-meetings, role-playing, and in-basket tests are looking for, and how to handle them.

Learn the tips that will help you master job interviews in noisy, distracting hotel lobbies, restaurants, at poolside, and in other unusual settings. Includes an essential review of table etiquette.

For the recent graduate and entry-level candidate, here are some special interview questions specifically tailored to discover your business potential when real world experience is lacking.

Is parting such sweet sorrow? The end of a job interview will more likely mean relief, but here are eight dos and four don'ts to ensure that the lasting impression you leave is a good one.

Statistics show that the last person to get interviewed usually gets the job offer. Here are steps you can take that will keep your impression fresh in the interviewer's mind.

Don't let the interviewer forget you! Job interview follow-up is logical, and here are eight steps that guarantee the continuation of your candidacy.

Rejection? Impossible! Then again, you won't be right for every job. Here are some techniques that help you to create opportunity in the face of rejection.

The job offer finally arrives—they want you! Before you sign on the dotted line, however, you should be well schooled in the essentials of good salary and benefits negotiations; you're never going to have this much leverage again. Handling good job offers and poor job offers, negotiating future salary, and how to evaluate the salary and the job offer. Some great questions you can ask to make sure the job offer is one you want to accept; and essential information on reference questions, job offer letters, employment agreements, relocation, and stock options.

Relying on one interview at a time can only lead to anxiety, so you must create and foster an ever-growing network of interviews and, consequently, job offers. Implement the Knock 'em Dead job search plan and you will be able to both generate multiple job interviews and turn them into job offers.

Careful, psychological tests can be another hurdle in the interview cycle! Answering them casually can be hazardous to your professional health. The most common types of pre-employment tests, how to prepare for them, and techniques for answering correctly in the heat of the moment.

This section provides you with the skills you'll need to navigate specific crises.

Do whatever is necessary so that you don't get your walking papers before you decide to walk.

Continued employment no longer depends on company loyalty, but rather on your ability to change with the times. Becoming sensitive to imminent change.

How to make the best choices in tough times.

ACKNOWLEDGMENTS

Knock 'em Dead is now in its twenty-third year of publication and has become a staple for job searchers around the world. This is due to the ongoing support of my publisher, and the tireless encouragement of the Adams Media sales team. I would like to thank publishers past and present for their support of the *Knock 'em Dead* books, for giving me great editors over the years and especially for Peter Archer my current editor; please hang around, Peter ;-). I am also indebted to the many people at Adams Media whose hard work has contributed to the success of the series. It takes a team and I am grateful to be a part of this one.

WHY KNOCK 'EM DEAD?

You don't come to a book like this because everything is good in your professional life; you come here in times of crisis and change. So I'm not going to waste your time. You live in a global information economy, where corporate structures have flattened and downsized and outsourced work forces, where professional jobs get ever more complex and the competition for them gets ever greater. This is not an easy world in which to pursue a professional career—it requires serious attention.

You stand somewhere in the middle of a fifty-year career, and it is likely that you will change jobs every three or four years (not always by choice). You may have as many as three distinct careers over the span of this half-century work life. Your career is a marathon, not a sprint, and stamina and tactics count for a lot. This is probably not your first job search, and it almost certainly won't be your last.

Look at your current situation from this perspective, and commit yourself to carrying out this job search in a way that will leave you with a firm understanding of how to manage your career.

Knock 'em Dead: The Ultimate Job Search Guide will show you how to achieve this goal. I'll show you the best ways to research job opportunities, effectively turn them into interviews, and transform not one, but many of those interviews into job offers. I'll show you how to ace the aptitude tests and negotiate the best salary and benefit package for yourself. In these pages, you'll find a cohesive approach to job searching that will not only help you land jobs but will also supply you with the tools to make you successful once on the payroll.

Yet, because other job changes will come along in your life, sometimes unexpectedly, the greatest benefit you will reap from this book is preparedness for those future strategic career moves. If you follow my advice you will already have a plan of attack, a comprehensive job map of employers who want to hire you, and an almost inexhaustible supply of professionals with whom to network—all assets I'll wager you don't have today. In short, you will be in much greater control of your professional destiny.

I wrote *Knock 'em Dead* because too much of what I found in bookstores lacked practical advice about vitally important situations. Much of what I read was puerile at best and seriously detrimental at worst. I knew there was room for a different approach. Twenty-three years and millions of copies later, *Knock 'em Dead* has become a time-tested and proven commodity both here in America and around the world, effectively helping people with job change and career management in many different languages and cultures. This is only possible because the approaches you will find in these pages reflect a clear understanding of what it is that makes business tick. It couples that understanding with a unique, honest, and practical way of packaging yourself as a highly desirable professional.

Perhaps you are trying to land your first job or returning to the work force after an absence. Maybe you are a seasoned executive taking another step up the ladder of success. Wherever you are at this point in your career, this book can help. It will guide you through the job searching process and the toughest interview scenarios you will ever face.

The book is written in five interconnected parts. "The Well-Stocked Briefcase" gets you ready for the fray. Here, you will learn to build a résumé with broad appeal and use a unique customizing technique guaranteed to make your candidacy stand out.

Once you are ready for action, "Getting the Word Out" will show you just about every truly effective job search technique that exists and how to tap into thousands of opportunities that never reach the newspaper or your favorite Web site. You will learn simple and effective techniques for setting up multiple interviews and how to navigate through the intimidating telephone screening process.

The job interview is a measured and ritualistic mating dance in which the best partners whirl away with the glittering prizes. Learn the steps and you, too, can dance the dance. The "Great Answers to Tough Interview Questions" section gives you a comprehensive understanding of why interviewers ask the questions they do, what is behind them, and how to answer in a way that advances your candidacy. Your partner in the dance is the interviewer, who will lead with tough questions that contain subtleties hidden to the untrained ear. You will learn how to recognize these "questions within questions." You'll get hundreds of sneaky, mean, low-down trick questions beloved of interviewers. With each question, I will show you what the interviewer wants to find out and explain how you should reply. After each explanation, I'll give you a sample answer and advice on how to customize it to your individual circumstances. The examples themselves come from real life (I've been at this for thirty years)— they're all things that people like you have done on the job to get noticed. I'll show you how they packaged those responses and how they used their practical experience to turn a job interview into a job offer. With this knowledge you will be cooler, calmer, and more collected at your job interviews.

"Finishing Touches" assures that you will learn how to negotiate the best salary and benefits package for yourself once the offer is made, and even discover how to get a job offer after you have been turned down. Most important, the sum of all these techniques will give you tremendous self-confidence when you go to an interview: no more jitters, no more sweaty palms.

The final section, "In Depth," includes powerful ideas for long-term career survival, including understanding the need for enlightened self-interest and keeping your financial boat afloat in the tough times.

You can find lots more advice about job search and career management issues on the Web at *www.knockemdead.com*. This site includes articles about job search issues, on-demand workshops on networking, and an Internet resources database where you can link directly to more than 300 great job search resources. You can also ask me questions that may be unique to your situation. As you can imagine, I get more questions than there are hours in the day so, because of time constraints, I can't promise to answer every one, but I will do my very best.

No matter what questions or concerns you have, or what your particular situation is, the bottom line is this: If you want to land a *good* new job and get a better grip on the direction and trajectory of your career as you learn how to win over the interviewer *without lying*, then this book is for you. Now let's get to it!

—*Martin Yate*

THE WELL-STOCKED BRIEFCASE

THIS SECTION WILL show you how to discover, define, and package your skills, and to put together a comprehensive plan of attack that uses all the most effective job search techniques.

HAVE YOU HEARD the one about the man who wanted to be a bear hunter? Once upon a time, in a town ravaged by bears, there lived a man who spent his days watching life go by. He dreamed of traveling the world as a celebrity but had neither the right job nor the money. Nevertheless, he dreamed that if he could kill the bears, he could travel to other places plagued with bears and make his living as a bear slayer. Every day he sat on the porch and waited for a bear to go by. After many weeks of waiting, he thought he might go looking for bears. He didn't know much about them, except that they were out there.

Full of hope, he rose before dawn, loaded his single-shot musket, and headed for the forest. On reaching the edge of the forest, he raised the musket and fired into the dense undergrowth.

Do you think he hit a bear or, for that matter, anything else? Why was he bear hunting with a single-shot musket, and why did he shoot before seeing a bear? What was our hero's problem? He couldn't tell dreams from reality. He went hunting unprepared and earned what he deserved. The moral of this tale is: When you look for a job, keep a grip on reality, and don't go off half-cocked.

Out there in the forest of the professional world lurks an endless supply of companies and countless opportunities. These are major corporations, small family affairs, and many in between. They all have something in common: They have problems, and to solve those problems, they hire people. Think about your present job. What problems would crop up if you weren't there? You were hired to cope with certain problems: to anticipate them, prevent them from arising if possible, and solve them if not. At some elemental level, everyone, in every profession and at every level, is paid to be a problem solver. There are three lessons you should take away from this:

Lesson One: Companies are in business to make money. People have loyalty to companies; companies have loyalty only to the bottom line. They make money by sales and by being economical and saving money. They make money by being efficient and saving time. If they save time, they save money and have more time to make more money. Think productivity.

Lesson Two: Companies and you are exactly alike. You both want to make as much money as possible in as short a time as possible. That allows you to do the things you really want with the rest of your time. Think efficient systems and procedures, time management, and organization. Think of goals, rather than task orientation.

Lesson Three: There are buyer's markets (advantage: prospective employer) and there are seller's markets (advantage: prospective employee). Job offers put you in a seller's market and give you the whip hand.

Lesson One tells you the three things every company is interested in. Lesson Two teaches you to recognize that you have the same goals as the company. Lesson Three reminds you that anyone with any sense wants to be in a seller's market.

If you look for jobs one at a time, you put yourself in a buyer's market; if you implement my advice in *Knock 'em Dead*, you can generate multiple job offers (even in a tough economy) and put yourself in a seller's market. Operating in a seller's market requires knowing who your buyers are and what they're in the market for; it also requires that you be ready with a properly packaged product.

In this first part of the book, you will evaluate and package your professional skills in ways guaranteed to appeal to every employer. You will then discover how to identify *every* company in your target area that could be in need of your services; only when you know all the players and all the openings can you maximize your opportunities. I will then show how to get connected to the people in your profession, so that you'll have personal introductions at many prospective companies. It will take a couple of days' work to get focused and put your job search in gear, as you will probably need to refocus and update your résumé, generate cover letters, research potential employers, and create a comprehensive marketing plan.

While I cover each of these areas in sequence, I recommend that in the execution you mix and match the activities. In other words, when the direct research begins to addle the gray matter, switch to résumé enhancement; when the résumé starts to drive you nuts, switch to job research for a couple of hours. An hour of one activity followed by an hour of another will keep your mind fresh and your program balanced.

UNDERSTANDING THE REALITIES OF A JOB SEARCH

WHY SOME PEOPLE can't get a foot in the door, while others get more offers at better companies.

There used to be a stigma about changing jobs, but today we live in a different climate. Everyone you speak with during your job search has been through the same experience, so if you go about the process in the right way you will find many helpful hands and sympathetic ears. Strategic career moves and occasional unemployment are an integral part of modern working lives; consequently, the people you get to know over the years can be important to your long-term work life stability. You need to learn how to connect to both your profession and your local communities so that, during times of job and career change, you will have the support of relevant networks.

A while ago, I met an executive who was job searching for the first time in twenty years. He had been looking for seven months and wasn't the least bit concerned: "I've been told that it takes a month for every ten thousand dollars of salary, so I really have another eighteen months to go." He seemed to have this mistaken idea that after two years of unemployment, someone would magically appear with another executive job for him.

His method of searching was networking "because that is what I've been told is the best way to find jobs." It is if it works, but all too often people's networks lack the necessary depth and relevance.

There is no magic bullet when it comes to successful job search techniques, no single best approach. Of course, those special-interest gurus might tell you they have the magic bullet: the headhunter will say his way is the only way and that résumés never landed anyone a job; the résumé writer could tell you that direct mail and e-mail are the only ways to go. They are both wrong. The best technique—and there are a dozen different choices when it comes to job searching—is the one that unearths that perfect opportunity. The employment market varies from year to year—sometimes it's a buyer's market and sometimes a seller's—but regardless of the state of the economy, there are good jobs out there for the job searcher who employs a systematic and comprehensive approach.

When you implement a comprehensive plan of attack, you will generate plenty of interviews: that is when the second and third parts of *Knock 'em Dead* will prove invaluable. In those parts of the book I will take you behind the other side of the desk to show you what employers look for in their employees, the questions they ask to determine the best candidate, and the answers that convince them without making you sound like the proverbial snake–oil salesman.

Career Management for the Long Term

When you were born, there still existed a world of work in which hard work, dedication, and sacrifice led to long-term job security and a steady, predictable climb up the ladder of success. The world you now work in is entirely different. Companies still expect hard work, dedication, and sacrifice, but their only loyalty is to the bottom right-hand corner of the quarterly profit and loss statement.

Always the most productive nation on earth, the United States has lately seen technology make astounding productivity gains possible; in one quarter of 2003 our productivity leaped a staggering 9 percent. This does not, however, result in job opportunity and professional growth across the board, or even in substantial pay raises. Instead, it leads to automation and the outsourcing of jobs and whole industries, to other countries; different times require different strategies for long-term career success.

The job security and professional growth our parents were raised to expect as the norm is a thing of the past. As I mentioned before, over the course of a fifty-year work life you can typically expect to change jobs about every four years, and you may well have three or more distinct careers. In light of these realities, you must discard any vestiges of unquestioning corporate loyalty and replace them with a little enlightened self-interest. I am not suggesting you sacrifice your commitment to hard work and dedication in your professional life, just that you work quietly and privately with your own long-term economic survival in mind.

Why is this important? Because to accept these realities is to recognize that this job search is not your last. If you remember this and really pay attention to the letter and spirit of this book, you'll not only land a great new job, but you'll also have a firm grasp of a set of vitally important professional survival skills, skills that will serve you faithfully throughout all the job and career changes of your work life. Follow this advice right now and you will find, and land, a good new job. Integrate this advice into the long-term career management plan I outline in these pages, and jobs in the future may well come to you when you are not looking for them.

This will all become possible if you understand the recruitment process from the employer's side and implement these job search strategies in the way I advise, by customizing your approach to the preferences of the employer. Not surprisingly, it all starts with your résumé. The résumé creation process helps you focus on the job you want and learn to package your skills effectively. This is the first important step in turning your dreams into realities.

THE EFFECTIVE RÉSUMÉ

WHY AN EFFECTIVE résumé has a clear focus on a target job. Five exercises to help you build a strong résumé. Using a résumé information-gathering tool. Three types of résumés for different situations, and the rules for creating a powerful résumé.

When your résumé is built intelligently, it will open doors for you: it establishes a focus for your search, helps secure interviews, acts as a road map for interviewers, and serves as your champion long after you have left the interview.

Unfortunately, most résumés are not built intelligently. Most people feel that a good résumé is simply a recitation of all the things you have done in your work life. This can be a costly mistake.

The impact of technology on the workplace causes the nature of all jobs to change almost as rapidly as the pages on a calendar, so at worst a simple recitation of all the responsibilities held may leave your résumé filled with skills and duties that are no longer relevant in the workplace. At best, it may lead to a document that is fragmented and lacks focus; this can be deadly in the world in which your résumé now has to perform.

In the not-so-distant past, your résumé would have been immediately reviewed by human eyes. Today, résumés no longer go straight to a recruiter or manager's desk. They are more likely to be stored in a corporate or job site database. This means that before your résumé is reviewed by a human being, it must be chosen from that database as worth reviewing. Today, when some of those databases contain over 20 million résumés, this demands new strategies and tactics.

When recruiters access job site (or corporate) résumé databases, they always do so with a specific job description (JD) in mind. This is important: Job postings reflect the wording of job descriptions and consequently reflect the wording users feel best describes the talent they need. This is the wording they use in searching databases; it is familiar and has real meaning to the users.

Here's how the process works: You and I want to hire an accountant so, among other resources, we look in the CareerBuilder database. To access the database, we type "accountant" into the interface, specify geography, and click on the words (called descriptors or keywords) that we feel best describe that job. We can also add words of our own that do not appear in the dialog box choices. The CareerBuilder database contains over 25 million résumés, and with 25 million résumés there must be a few that match exactly what we need, so we can be fairly specific in our requirements.

Once programmed to search for a specific set of words, the software program scours the database and builds a long list of all the résumés that contain *any* of those descriptors or keywords. It then weights the list. Those résumés with the most frequent use *and* greatest number of keywords come to the top of the list. This is the *first* keyword test your résumé must pass: not enough relevant keywords means that no human will review it.

When your résumé gets to human eyes, the process is alarmingly similar. All too often the first person to see your résumé is a recruiter in HR who is probably recruiting for twenty to forty different jobs and cannot be expected to have an in-depth understanding of each one. Human Resources reviews the JD, then skims through the résumés looking for keywords from that JD. This skim takes between fifteen and forty-five seconds. No keywords means no second read. This is the *second* time your résumé must pass the keyword test. HR representatives typically plow through enough résumés to create a list of up to (but very rarely exceeding) twenty candidates.

If your résumé passes this hurdle, it may land in front of the manager who actually has the authority to hire you. Management hates reading résumés. Try reading twenty of them in a row, and see what your eyes and brain feel like at the end of your self-inflicted torture. So, any manager's first reading is also going to be a fifteen to forty-five second skim for those critical keywords. Only those résumés that pass this *third* keyword test will get a second reading, which more carefully evaluates the résumé against the JD's requirements, plus some other considerations we'll discuss shortly.

A résumé that tries to cram in everything you have done without any real focus is doomed to fail one or all of these three initial keyword hurdles, and failure at any of these hurdles means no interview, and therefore no job offer.

Fortunately, I have a practical—and, if you follow my guidelines, easy—solution for you: Before writing your résumé, get inside the employer's head and examine what he or she looks for when hiring.

Start with Simple Common Sense

Your résumé will always be more effective if it begins with a clear focus on, and understanding of, a specific target job. When you have this focus you can look backward into your work history for those experiences that best position you for the target job. This will enable you to tailor a killer résumé.

The big question is: How do you do this? With a series of simple steps I call the Target Job Deconstruction Process, TJD for short. Here is how it works:

Step #1

Focus on a specific and realistic target job, one in which you can succeed based on the skills you possess today. Some people think you change jobs to get a promotion, but this is largely incorrect. People get hired based on their credentials, not their potential. Most people don't get promotions to the next step up the professional ladder when they change jobs, because that would mean coming onboard as an unknown quantity in a job they've never done.

Typically, most professionals accept a position similar to the one they have now, but one that offers opportunity for growth once they have proven their mettle. The most common exception is an employee already doing that higher-level job but without the title recognition. Also, some executives combine experience and credentials from a number of jobs into a new configuration.

The most practical and effective way to find that next ideal job that will support your climb up the ladder of success is to decide on:

- A job you can do and that you can justify on paper
- A job you can convince others that you can do
- A job in which you can succeed once in the saddle

Let's look at "a job in which you can succeed." The ability to do 70 percent or more of the job will usually get you in the running for the interview cycle. You'll probably be able to do the job satisfactorily and have room for professional growth, making such a target job a good choice. Less than this and you may need to reconsider your target job or anticipate a longer job search to reach your goals.

If you have more than five to seven years of experience, there is probably more than one job for which you are qualified. More than fifteen years experience and there could be half a dozen jobs in which you could succeed. You should carefully evaluate and rank these jobs based on their availability, remuneration, fulfillment, and their potential for growth. This way you will target a "primary job" based on practicality and common sense. If you ultimately decide you want to go after that White Water Rafting Guide job because you own a canoe . . . well, at least you'll be doing it with your eyes open, knowing that you won't have most of the required skills, and consequently that your search might take considerably longer.

This does not mean you cannot pursue any of those other jobs for which you have the desire or some of the qualifications. On the contrary, I have an approach and a methodology in place for customizing your résumé for any job you wish to target. However, it is only sensible to create your primary résumé with a single "primary target" job in mind.

Once you have tailored a résumé to the most logical focus for your next job, tailor it to each of those other jobs for which you are qualified and/or interested. Often there is considerable overlap in the deliverables of the different jobs for which we are qualified. We can take that primary résumé, make a copy, re-title it, and make the necessary changes to give the secondary résumé a specific focus. You won't have to start from scratch, and you'll have customized résumés for each opportunity. In order to maximize the relevance—and thereby the impact—of all your résumés, go through a TJD process for each.

Step #2

Conscientious execution of the TJD procedure pays multiple dividends: aside from the added impact it gives your résumé, you will be surprised to find that it prepares you subconsciously for the interview and selection process. Your initial task is to surf job sites and collect a half-dozen job postings for your chosen primary target job. Want to save some time? Try one of these résumé spiders, which will search thousands of sites. Some are free, and some are for a fee. They all work similarly—the home page has a couple of dialog boxes: one for a job title and one for a geographic area. If you cannot find half a dozen jobs in your target geography just try another major metro area: For the purpose of TJD it doesn't matter where the jobs are located.

www.indeed.com　　　　　　*www.worktree.com*
www.jobbankusa.com　　　　*www.jobsearchengine.com*
www.jobsniper.com　　　　　*www.jobster.com*

From the collected JDs you will create your own TJD. The result will be a document that comprehensively describes your target job *the way employers themselves describe and think about it.*

Step #3

Deconstruct the collection of JDs in the following way:

1. Start a new Word document, and name it "Target JD" or something similar.
2. Under the subhead "Job Titles," list all the variations on the job title you are pursuing.
3. Look for those requirements that are common to all six, and highlight them. Choose one, then copy and paste it into your document. Underneath it list all the keywords used in the other five JDs to describe this skill, responsibility, requirement, or deliverable.
4. Repeat this process with requirements that are common to five of the six job postings then four of the six postings . . . and so on down the line.

At the end of this first part of the TJD process you will be able to read the document and say to yourself, *"When employers are looking for _____, these are the job titles they use; these are the skills, experiences, deliverables, and professional behaviors they look for; this is largely the way these needs are prioritized; and these are the words with which they commonly describe them."*

Step #4

The next step is to add to your TJD the list of skills and deliverables you have from your personal experience on the job. This is important, because job descriptions, helpful as they are, don't always tell the whole story. In many companies, job descriptions won't go into all the nuts and bolts of a particular job, because all JDs have to be approved by legal before seeing the light of day. This is part of an overall corporate cost-containment policy designed to protect against the release of job descriptions that might aid individual or class-action lawsuits brought on by disgruntled employees. How can I be sure of this? I used to be director of human resources at a substantial Silicon Valley technology company, and have overseen this process.

If you are new to the professional world and cannot bring personal awareness of a job's needs to the Target Job Deconstruction Process, you might want to do a little additional research to ensure that your résumé has the proper focus.

For further insight into a specific target job, visit the Occupational Outlook Handbook pages at *www.bls.gov/OCO*, which give detailed analyses of hundreds of jobs. After that, talk to people who are actually doing the work and have them deconstruct the job for you along the lines discussed.

Step #5

At some elemental level, all jobs are the same—they all focus on problem identification, avoidance, and solution. That's what we all get paid for, no matter what we do for a living.

Go back to your TJD and start with the first requirement. Think about the problems you will typically need to identify, solve, and/or prevent in the course of a normal work day.

Repeat this with each of the subsequent requirements by identifying the problems attendant on that particular responsibility, and then listing particular examples, big and small, of your successful identification, prevention, and/or solution to this problem. Quantify your results when possible.

Some examples may appear in your résumé as significant professional achievements, while others will provide you with the ammunition to answer all those questions that begin, "Tell me about a time when. . . ."

Step #6

Think of the *best* person you have ever seen doing this job and what made him or her stand out. Describe his or her performance, professional behavior, interaction with others, and appearance: "That would be Carole Jenkins, superior communication skills, a fine analytical mind, great professional appearance, and a nice person to work with." You are describing a model of what employers are seeking and a profile for your own professional development.

Now think of the *worst* person you have ever seen doing this job and what made that employee stand out. Describe his or her performance, professional behaviors, interaction with others, and appearance: "That would be Jack Hartzenberger, morose, critical, passive aggressive, always looked like he slept in his suit, and smelled like it too." You are describing a model that all employers want to avoid and a profile for your own professional suicide.

When you apply this understanding to your professional life it can only increase your job security as it opens doors to the inner circles at work and leads the way to plum assignments, raises, and promotions. Assuming you have an IQ above room temperature, you can see that apart from developing enormously valuable ammunition and insights into résumé creation and an awareness that can impact your ability to turn interviews into job offers, you are developing ways to impact your overall career success: You are learning about career management.

Step #7

Once you complete and review your TJD, you will have a clear idea of exactly what employers are seeking when they recruit for this position, the words they use to describe it, the specific skills (and the priority of those skills), and what you bring to the table in each instance.

If on reading this far in the chapter you realize that with the TJD process you can tune up your existing résumé, you can probably do so with the information I'll show you how to gather in the coming pages. If, on the other hand, you realize you need to start from scratch, complete this chapter and read *Knock 'em Dead Resumés.*

Résumé Building

Your job search will be most successful when it starts with a clearly defined target job, and when you understand the language that employers use to describe this job well enough to make your own background relevant and intelligible in their terms. The following questionnaire will help you assemble all the data you will need for a productive résumé.

> You can find an electronic version of this questionnaire at *www.knockemdead.com* on the résumé pages. An electronic document is expandable, so if you have had more jobs than are listed here, you can expand the document and list them all.

Résumé Information Gathering Tool

Save this questionnaire in a résumé development folder (within your career management folder) and back up this data to an external source. It will be a great time saver over the years. In answering these questions don't worry about grammar and perfect wording right now (that comes later), but do take the time to think about the issues. Be descriptive—don't just say you were a manger; say that you were a manager with fifty-five direct reports in Decatur and a further fifteen in Mumbai. Be specific whenever possible: Mention full budgetary responsibility (with dollar amount) plus selection, development, discipline, and termination responsibilities. Wherever you can, illustrate with real-world examples, and, wherever you can, quantify those examples in terms of money earned or saved, time saved, and productivity improved. Round these examples down, rather than up. Always identify your role as a team member when appropriate. This makes your claims more believable.

Contact Information

Name
Address
E-mail
Home Telephone (recommend alternate #) Cell
Current Job Title
Variations on this Job Title

Operational Area *(Sales, Finance, R&D, IT, Supply Chain, etc.)*
Industry/Market Sectors *(Technology, Pharma, Financial Services, etc.)*

Education and Skills

Post Secondary Education *(you might not use all this but do collect it)*

Degree	Concentration	Graduation date
Major		
Minor		
GPA		
GPA Major		
GPA Minor		
Ranking		
Honors, scholarships		
Special accomplishments		
International studies		
Degree	Concentration	Graduation date
Major		
Minor		
GPA		
GPA Major		
GPA Minor		
Ranking		
Honors, scholarships		
Special accomplishments		

Professional Education *(Ongoing professional education signals commitment to success)*

Course Name
Completion Date
Duration
Certification
Sponsoring Organization

Professional Credentials Not Covered Elsewhere

Professional Memberships and Affiliations *(American Management Association, American Marketing Association, etc.)*

Organization   Leadership Role

> Active membership in a professional association is a key tool for career resilience and success. If you don't know where to start, come to the association page at *www.knockemdead.com*.

Technological Skills *(List all that apply to you.)*

> **The Alphabet Soup of Technology**
> No one gets ahead today without technological competence. Capture your fluency here, and update regularly. That alphabet soup just might help your résumé's performance in database searches.

Corporate Accomplishments *(You can also include here your work on projects that resulted in copyright and patents, so long as you make clear your real contribution.)*

Awards and Recognition
Public Speaking/Presentations
Profession-Related Publications
Patents and Copyrights

Global Experience, Cultural Diversity Awareness

> In a global economy any exposure here is relevant, and it doesn't have to be professional in nature. That you were an Army brat and grew up in ten different countries can be a big plus. Just name the countries, not the circumstance.

Foreign Languages

Community, Civic Involvement *(List all organizations and any special projects/activities/leadership roles.)*

Other Avocational Activities

This should include all the activities with which you fill your out-of-work hours. Your résumé may include those activities that can say something positive about the professional you. For example, in sales and marketing just about all group activities show a desirable mindset. Bridge might argue strong analytical skills, and the senior executive who still plays competitive lacrosse and runs marathons is crazy not to let the world know.

Valuable Profession-Related Skills Developed Outside of Your Professional Work

Military
Service
Rank
Discharge
Promotions
Decorations
Honors

Professional Development Courses

Achievements

What professional capabilities/skills do you feel have most contributed to your professional success?

What professional behaviors (analytical or communication skills for example) do you feel have most contributed to your professional success?

Employment History

(To ensure a proper focus I strongly advise that you complete your target job deconstruction exercises before looking back at your work history.)

Current Position
Company
Employment dates
Location
Standing (division, public, private)
Industry/Market Sector
What does your company do?

Example

Squanto Corporation, Inc., Orlando, FL
1997 to Present
$500 million company
One of the largest resort and vacation sales/development companies in the United States.
In rapid growth through international expansion, strategic M&A, industry rollup, and IPO.

What were you hired to do?

Example

Worldwide Director of Operations, Entertainment Imaging 1998–2006
Selected to re-engineer and revitalize this $65 million business unit with accountability for thirty-two direct reports in four cities across the United States. Established strategic vision and developed operational infrastructure. Managed Supply Chain, Logistics/Distribution, Forecasting, System Integration, Project Management, Contracts Administration, and Third-Party Site Operations.

Or, more simply:

Example

DryRoc, Inc. Indianapolis, IN 2004–Present
Production Director
Drove production for world's largest wallboard plant, with 258 employees working in multiple shifts.

Title you report to

Your Title

Department/Unit
Leadership or Membership of Executive Teams, Project Teams, or Committees
Responsibilities/Deliverables
Quotes, Praise, and Endorsements from Management

When described by a professional colleague, how do you hope they would describe your most desirable professional qualities?

Having taken a first pass at the responsibility/deliverables area, take a few moments to review your Target Job Deconstruction. Identify the ways in which your department or unit is expected to contribute to the bottom line (making or saving money, improving productivity, and so on).

Example
Internal auditor: to contain costs by audits to ensure adherence to company policies and financial reporting procedures

Problem (and Opportunity) Identification and Solution

All jobs revolve around problem identification and solution.
At some level every job exists for four major reasons:

1. To identify potential problems and avoid them
2. To identify and solve the typical problems that arise daily as an integral part of the job
3. To identify and avoid or solve the major headaches that occur in every business on a regular basis
4. To identify opportunities for contributing to the bottom line

Develop examples of problem identification and opportunity initiatives, both small and large, for every job title you have held. The more you come up with the better, because they will add weight and reality to your résumé and show that you think with employers' needs in mind, which will boost your résumé's punch. All examples are valuable; those most relevant to your target job are most valuable.

To help you bring out the information that will be most useful to you in your résumé and in interview situations you can apply the PSRV process (you might know this as STAR—same process, different acronym).

- Identify a **Problem**.
- Envision your **Solution**, including strategy and tactics.
- Take note of the **Result** of your actions.
- Understand the **Value** of this to the company (usually in earnings or productivity enhancements).

Now describe four typical or notable problems with which you have been involved on your last (or current) job. Analyze each in terms of PSRV and include the following information:

Company
Employment dates
Location
Standing (division, public, private)
Industry sector
What does the company do?
What were you hired to do?
Title you report to
Your title
Department/unit
Leadership or membership of executive teams, project teams, or committees
Responsibilities/deliverables
Quotes, praise, and endorsements from management

Now you need to take what you have gathered and package it in a freshly tweaked résumé that focuses on your target job. There are three standard types of résumés:

Chronological: The most frequently used format. Use it when your work history is stable and your professional growth is consistent within a profession. The chronological format is exactly what it sounds like: It follows your work history backward from the current job, listing companies, dates, and responsibilities.

Functional: A functional résumé concentrates on the skills and responsibilities that you bring to the target job, and it de-emphasizes when, where, and how you got that experience. It is useful when changing careers, returning to the workplace or the profession after an absence, or when current responsibilities don't relate to the job you want. It is written with the most relevant experience to the job you're seeking placed first and de-emphasizes jobs, employment dates, and job titles by placing them toward the end.

Combination: A combination of chronological and functional résumés. Use this format if you have a steady work history with demonstrated growth and if you are continuing your progression within an industry or profession. It often starts with a brief performance profile, then lists job-specific skills relevant to the objective, and segues into a chronological format that lists how, where, and when these skills were acquired.

Each style emphasizes certain strengths and downplays certain weaknesses. In today's world, everyone needs a powerful résumé. It not only opens the door, but it remains with the interviewer long after we are gone, and will almost certainly be reviewed by him just before the final choice is made.

Check your revised résumé against these five essential rules:

Rule One: Use the most common job title for your target job, because different employers use different titles for the same job. You are, after all, hunting for interviews, not specific titles. Cast your net wide, using a title specific enough to put you in the running, yet vague enough to elicit further curiosity. One way you can make a job title "specifically vague" is to add the term specialist (e.g., Computer Specialist, Administration Specialist, Production Specialist). As discussed in *Knock 'em Dead Resumes*, you can also use a selection of two or three job titles.

Rule Two: If you state a specific job objective, couch it in terms of contributions you could make from that position. Do tell the employers what you expect of them—they are interested in their needs, not yours, at this point. It is best to start the résumé with a performance profile that captures the essence of the professional you as it relates to your TJD. This can be followed with a core competencies section and even a technology competencies section. These sections not only give the reader a helpful focus, but they also allow you to introduce relevant keywords that will be repeated in the body of your résumé. Use keywords in these sections that won't fit in the body of your résumé; this will result in better performance with the database spiders and bots.

CHRONOLOGICAL Résumé

Jane Swift, 9 Central Avenue, Quincy, MA 02169. (617) 555-1212 jswift@careerbrain.com

SUMMARY: Ten years of increasing responsibilities in the employment services industry. Concentration in the high-technology markets.

EXPERIENCE: Howard Systems International, Inc.
2004–Present

Management Consulting Firm
Personnel Manager

Responsible for recruiting and managing consulting staff of five. Set up office and organized the recruitment, selection, and hiring of consultants. Recruited all levels of MIS staff from financial to manufacturing markets.

Additional responsibilities:
- Coordinated with outside advertising agencies.
- Developed P.R. with industry periodicals—placement with over 20 magazines and newsletters.
- Developed effective referral programs—referrals increased 32 percent.

EXPERIENCE: Technical Aid Corporation
1996–2004

National Consulting Firm. MICRO/TEMPS Division

Division Manager	2001–2004
Area Manager	1998–2001
Branch Manager	1996–1998

As Division Manager, opened additional West Coast offices. Staffed and trained all offices with appropriate personnel. Created and implemented all divisional operational policies responsible for P&L. Sales increased to $20 million dollars, from $0 in 1990.

Additional responsibilities:
- Achieved and maintained 30 percent annual growth over seven-year period.
- Maintained sales staff turnover at 14 percent.

As Area Manager, opened additional offices, hiring staff, setting up office policies, and training sales and recruiting personnel.

Additional responsibilities:
- Supervised offices in two states.
- Developed business relationships with accounts—75 percent of clients were regular customers.
- Client base increased 28 percent per year.
- Generated over $200,000 worth of free trade-journal publicity.

As Branch Manager, hired to establish the new MICRO/TEMPS operation. Recruited and managed consultants. Hired internal staff. Sold service to clients.

EDUCATION: Boston University
B.S. Public Relations, 1995.

FUNCTIONAL Résumé

Jane Swift
9 Central Avenue
Quincy, MA 02169
(617) 555-1212
jswift@careerbrain.com

OBJECTIVE: A position in Employment Services where my management, sales, and recruiting talents can be effectively utilized to improve operations and contribute to company profits.

SUMMARY: Over ten years of Human Resources experience. Extensive responsibility for multiple branch offices and an internal staff of 40+ employees and 250 consultants.

SALES: Sold high-technology consulting services with consistently profitable margins throughout the United States. Grew sales from $0 to over $20 million a year.

Created training programs and trained salespeople in six metropolitan markets.

RECRUITING: Developed recruiting sourcing methods for multiple branch offices.

Recruited over 25,000 internal and external consultants in the high-technology professions.

MANAGEMENT: Managed up to 40 people in sales, customer service, recruiting, and administration. Turnover maintained below 14% in a "turnover business."

FINANCIAL: Prepared quarterly and yearly forecasts. Presented, reviewed, and defended these forecasts to the Board of Directors. Responsible for P&L of $20 million sales operation.

PRODUCTION: Responsible for opening multiple offices and accountable for growth and profitability. 100% success and maintained 30% growth over seven-year period in ten offices.

WORK EXPERIENCE:
2004–present HOWARD SYSTEMS INTERNATIONAL, Boston, MA
National Consulting Firm
Personnel Manager

1996–2004 TECHNICAL AID CORPORATION, Needham, MA
National Consulting & Search Firm
Division Manager

EDUCATION: B.S., 1995, Boston University

REFERENCES: Available upon request.

COMBINATION Résumé

Jane Swift
9 Central Avenue
Quincy, MA 02169
(617) 555-1212
jswift@careerbrain.com

OBJECTIVE:

Employment Services Management

SUMMARY: Ten years of increasing responsibilities in the employment services market-place. Concentration in the high-technology markets.

SALES: Sold high technology consulting services with consistently profitable margins throughout the United States. Grew sales from $0 to over $20 million a year.

PRODUCTION: Responsible for opening multiple offices and accountable for growth and prof-itability. 100% success and maintained 30% growth over seven-year period in ten offices.

MANAGEMENT: Managed up to 40 people in sales, customer service, recruiting, and adminis-tration. Turnover maintained below 14% in a "turnover business." Hired branch managers and sales and recruiting staff throughout the United States.

FINANCIAL: Prepared quarterly and yearly forecasts. Presented, reviewed, and defended these forecasts to the Board of Directors. Responsible for P&L of $20 million sales operation.

MARKETING: Performed numerous market studies for multiple branch openings. Resolved feasibility of combining two different sales offices. Study resulted in savings of over $5,000 per month in operating expenses.

EXPERIENCE: Howard Systems International, Inc.   2004–present
Management Consulting Firm
Personnel Manager

Responsible for recruiting and managing consulting staff of five. Set up office and organized the recruitment, selection, and hiring of consultants. Recruited all levels of MIS staff from financial to manufacturing markets.

Additional responsibilities:
- Developed PR with industry periodicals—placement with over 20 magazines and newsletters.
- Developed effective referral programs—referrals increased 320%.

COMBINATION Résumé page 2

Technical Aid Corporation 1996–2004
National Consulting Firm, MICRO/TEMPS Division

Division Manager	2001–2004
Area Manager	1998–2001
Branch Manager	1996–1998

As Division Manager, opened additional West Coast offices. Staffed and trained all offices with appropriate personnel. Created and implemented all divisional operational policies. Responsibilities for P&L. Sales increased to $20 million from $0 in 1990.

- Achieved and maintained 30% annual growth over seven-year period.
- Maintained sales staff turnover at 14%.

As Area Manager, opened additional offices; included hiring staff, setting up office policies, training sales force, and recruiting personnel.

Additional responsibilities:
- Supervised offices in two states.
- Developed business relationships with accounts—75% of clients were regular customers.
- Client base increased 28% per year.
- Generated over $200,000 worth of free trade-journal publicity.

As Branch Manager, hired to establish the new MICRO/TEMPS operation. Recruited and managed consultants. Hired internal staff. Sold service to clients.

EDUCATION: B.S., 1995, Boston University

✎**Rule Three:** Do not state your current salary. If you are earning too little or too much, you could rule yourself out before getting your foot in the door. For the same reason, do not mention your desired salary. If salary information is requested for a specific opening, put it in your cover letter and don't tie yourself to a specific figure; give a range. For details on developing a realistic salary range, see Chapter 20, "Negotiating the Job Offer."

✎**Rule Four:** The length of your résumé is less important than its relevance to a target job (you can always adapt your primary résumé to other target jobs). The rule used to be one page for every ten years of experience, and never more than two pages. However, as jobs have gotten more complex in their execution, they require more explanation. This can be turned to your benefit: a longer résumé provides you with that much more space in which to include and repeat relevant keywords from your TJD. You should still make every effort to maintain focus and an "if in doubt, cut it out" editing approach.

✎**Rule Five:** Finally, emphasize your achievements, problem-solving skills, and professional behavioral profile. Keep the résumé focused on a target job and make sure it has a core competencies section that will help an electronically stored copy of your résumé get dredged up from the database.

An excellent final test for your revamped résumé is to first re-read your TJD and then read your résumé from front to back. If it clearly echoes your TJD, then you are likely to have a productive résumé.

The Executive Briefing

Once you have a few years of professional experience, it is likely you will be qualified for more than one job. Because of this, it is a good idea to create one job-targeted résumé for the main attack of your job search, and then adapt different versions of it—also job-targeted—for those special circumstances as they arise. Ultimately, you could have three to five résumés for different opportunities. It's a smart step to take, because there is no such thing in life as "one size fits all." The less specific your résumé is to a target job, the less effective it will be.

Nevertheless, circumstances will arise where none of your résumés fits a particular opportunity, and there is no time to adapt the closest matching version. When this happens, you can employ the executive briefing—a useful tool even when your résumé *does* match.

An executive briefing enables you to customize your résumé quickly to any specific job and is especially helpful on the other side of the desk—for overworked administrative assistants and HR functionaries who may not understand all the niceties of a specific job function. Furthermore, the executive briefing allows you to update and customize that old résumé with lightning speed without delaying the rest of your research or missing out on the opportunity.

Like many great ideas, the executive briefing is beautiful in its simplicity. It is a cover letter on your standard letterhead (or e-mail) with the company's requirements for the job opening listed on the left side and your skills—matching point-by-point the company's needs—on the right. It looks like this:

Executive Briefing

From: A1coordpro@earthlink.net
Subject: Assessment Coordinator
Date: February 28th, 2008 11:18:39 PM EST
To: jobs@pepsi.com

Dear HR Staff,
Your advertisement on the *New York Times* Web site on February 27th, 2008, for an **Assessment Coordinator** seems to perfectly match my background and experience. As the International Brand Coordinator for Kahlúa, I coordinated meetings, prepared presentations and materials, organized a major off-site conference, and supervised an assistant. I believe that I am an excellent candidate for this position, as I have illustrated below:

YOUR REQUIREMENTS	MY QUALIFICATIONS
Highly motivated, diplomatic	Successfully managed project teams involving different flexible, quality-driven professional business units. The defined end results were achieved on every project.
Exceptional organizational skills and attention to detail	Planned the development and launch of the Kahlúa Heritage Edition bottle series. My former manager enjoyed leaving the details and follow-through to me. Coverdale project management training.

College degree and six years of experience	B.A. from Vassar College (1998). 6+ years relevant business experience in productive, professional environments.
Computer literacy	Extensive knowledge of Windows and Macintosh applications.

I'm interested in this position because it fits well with my new career focus in the human resources field. Currently, I am enrolled in NYU's adult career planning and development certificate program and working at Lee Hecht Harrison.

My résumé, pasted below and attached in MS Word, will provide more information on my strengths and career achievements. If after reviewing my material you believe that there is a match, please call me. Thank you for your consideration.

Sincere regards,
Jane Swift

An executive briefing sent with a résumé provides a comprehensive picture of a thorough professional, plus a personalized, fast, and easy-to-read synopsis that details exactly how you can help with current needs. Using the executive briefing as a cover letter for your résumé will greatly increase the chance that your query will be picked out of the pile in the human resources department and hand-carried to the appropriate manager.

The use of an executive briefing is obviously not appropriate for use when the requirements of a specific job are unavailable.

NETWORKING AND THE SUCCESSFUL JOB SEARCH

HERE'S HOW YOU can leverage a wide variety of networks and associations to get the referrals that lead to the perfect position.

As you tune up your résumé, simultaneously piece together a plan of attack for your job search. To make that plan of attack most effective, take a couple of minutes to understand how companies like to hire people. Understanding corporate recruitment preferences will help you fine-tune your job search approaches to maximize their productivity.

Hiring at most companies is planned up to twelve months in advance (apart from staff replacements due to employee turnover), so the interviews you go to this year were mostly planned and budgeted last year. Hiring budgets usually open at the start of the new calendar year with hires staggered through-out the balance of the year. The early part of every year usually has plenty of opportunity—so if you read this in November, you should be diligent about working on your job search right through the holiday season! It most certainly does not mean you can't find jobs at other times of the year; there are always jobs available, so long as you know how to find them.

The cost of hiring and training personnel runs into thousands and some-times tens of thousands of dollars, so the entire recruitment process is cost/productivity conscious (okay, so tell me something in business that isn't). The people involved in a specific search—the hiring manager and the assigned human resources people—all want the same thing: good hires, fast hires, and hires made as cheaply as possible. Understanding how and why things are done, and in what sequence they are done, will help you focus your efforts on the most effective job-finding techniques.

Put yourself on the other side of the desk for a few moments. Naturally, you would start the recruitment process by asking yourself, your peers, and your staff who within the company can do this job. If possible, you want to hire from within, because it's the cheapest way—you are dealing with known quanti-ties, and it is motivating to everyone to see internal promotion. Many jobs are filled this way, and this can give you a head start on the competition whenever you hear about internal promotions and transfers at your own or other compa-nies. Promotion also speaks of another opening created by that promotion or transfer.

This is reinforced by the next step taken in the recruitment process. When a hiring manager can't make an internal hire, he or she will logically ask, "Who do we know, and who do my people know?"

This goes beyond the casual inquiry. It includes all the résumés in the company's database, any promising candidates who have been interviewed in the past, internal posting of recruitment requirements (often tied to cash incentives for employee referrals), and people who might be known in the professional community. These approaches account for three out of every ten hires that are made externally. The questions you have to ask yourself are: How do I get better connected to my local profession? How do I get to know, and be known by, my peers? How do I become more visible in my pro-fessional community? We will answer all these questions in detail in the coming pages.

The next step—one slightly less reliable, as well as more expensive and time-consuming—is to look outside the company for people who have not been referred and who are unknown to the hiring managers. The first choice is often the Internet. As cost now becomes a serious consideration, it won't surprise you to learn that the majority of hires—38 percent, according to one estimate—come directly through the company's own Web site. Less than you might expect, 14.5 percent, come from the big three job boards (Monster, CareerBuilder, and HotJobs), while significantly more (17.5 percent) come from specialty sites that focus on a particular profession. After a little thought, the explanation is obvious: We don't pay fees when people come to our door on their own, so we naturally look more favorably on applicants coming to us through the company Web site. It is also logical to expect a better-qualified candidate to come from an advertisement placed, let's say, on the site of a professional association, because members of professional associations tend to be more professionally committed.

When it comes to advertising on the Internet and newspapers the picture gets murkier. While the Internet as a recruiting tool is shown in some studies to outperform newspapers by 8 to 1, the issue isn't quite as clear-cut as it might appear. For one thing, neither medium is able to objectively monitor who actually gets jobs as a result of seeing their advertisements. Additionally, recruitment advertising agencies encourage cross-media packages that include online and newspaper advertising; most newspapers post recruitment advertising on their own sites; and CareerBuilder, one of the big three job sites, is an agglomeration of 350-plus newspapers.

Beyond the Internet and newspaper advertising (which, by the way, has many job leads beyond the help wanted section), the balance of hires—about 30 percent—come mainly from on-campus recruitment and alumni associations, job fairs (both virtual and local), temp-to-perm hires, and headhunters.

So, the breakdown of effective recruitment strategies is very roughly split into thirds: one-third of hires comes from personal/professional networks and prior contacts, one-third from the Internet and cross-media advertising, and one-third from the remaining sources. We'll now put together a job search plan that reflects these realities.

The Hidden Job Market

On a radio talk show I listened to a caller's problem. She said, "I'm in the academic field, and I've been unemployed for two years, and I don't know what to do." I asked her how many employers she had contacted. She said about 200, so I asked her how many possible employers there were for her, and she said about 3,000. I thought of Goofy, the cartoon character, singing "Oh, the world owes me a living," and said, "Next caller, please." The world doesn't owe anyone a living. You have to go out and find that next job.

Around the same time I also heard from the producer of a national talk show on which I had recently appeared. She told me she used the techniques described in *Knock 'em Dead* and got thirty interviews in three weeks! I can't promise you those kinds of results, as that depends on your level of energy and commitment, but I can promise you that the following plan of attack really does work and that you won't find a more practical or comprehensive approach anywhere.

Anyone stumbling in a job search ten years ago was probably relying exclusively on the Sunday help-wanted ads; that same person stumbling today is probably relying on the modern-day equivalent, the big three Internet job boards: Monster, CareerBuilder, and HotJobs. Each is a valuable resource, so long as you know how best to use it to your advantage and integrate it into a comprehensive plan. Increasingly, job searches are also moving to more specialized sites such as healthcaresource.com, which posts health care jobs and saw a 36 percent increase in traffic last August; in the same month, dice.com, which is tech focused, saw a 34 percent jump, and CareerBuilder dropped 2 percent. Your goal is to land the best possible job for your professional needs. The problem is, you won't have the chance to pick the best job unless you check them all out. It is nothing short of arrogant to imagine that the only companies looking to hire are those who have posted advertisements where you happen to be looking this week.

Job hunters who go beyond scanning the want ads and posting a résumé on the big three job sites all too often fall back on applications to the well-known companies—the IBMs, AT&Ts, and Microsofts of the world. But 90 percent of the growth in American commerce is with small companies with fewer than 500 employees.

Did you know that average employee turnover from resignations, retirements, relocations, and terminations in the American workplace remains fairly steady at about 14 percent? In other words, just about every company in your target geographic area will be looking for someone during the year. You must make sure that you are aware of the opportunities as they arise and that the companies in turn are aware of you. This is where strategy comes into play.

You need to organize a comprehensive job search strategy that will give you maximum penetration in your target area, and track all the opportunities and potential employers you discover. I'm going to help you do this in three steps.

Remember that about one-third of hires come from employers' personal networks and prior contacts. In the following sections, I'll explain the very best networking techniques and how to leverage both professional and personal networks to give you the inside track on job openings. (By the way, if you would like to hear me talk about networking in person—in online person, at least—visit my Web site, *www.knockemdead.com*, and join me at the free networking workshop there.)

Another third of hires tend to come from Internet resources and cross-media advertising. Here I'll help you get the most out of posting résumés and leveraging your presence on Internet job sites. I'll show you how to find and use tools that will lead you directly to employers in your profession and target geography. Finally, I'll teach you how to use both online and print versions of newspapers and business and trade publications to locate local opportunities.

The balance of hires—again about one-third—come from job fairs; third-party employment suppliers including temporary help companies, employment agencies, headhunters, and what is quaintly referred to as "smokestacking"—that is, keeping an eye out for potential employers as you go about town on your daily affairs. It sounds quaint in this high-tech world, but it is still effective! I'll share all the most practical techniques to help you become maximally productive in these areas.

The New Networking

As you have probably figured out by now, choosing the best job search approach isn't as simple as choosing the Internet over your local newspaper: it is a matter, first, of understanding how companies set about finding employees, and then of implementing a plan that aligns your job search approach with corporate recruitment practices.

Employers favor hires from personal referrals above all other methods because they are easier, faster, and cheaper; and they are thought to result in an employee who is productive sooner and who stays with the company longer. All job hunters like the idea of networking, but for fully two-thirds of us it doesn't work as effectively as it should because our networks lack depth and relevance (employers strongly prefer to hire through this channel but they only make about one-third of their hires this way). It is also the most time-consuming job search approach to get up and running, and so for these combined reasons we'll handle the ways to build broad and relevant networks first.

Effective networking practices will help you land that next job, increase your visibility and credibility within your field, develop your skills, and forever enhance your employability and promotability; through networking you will find mentors and become a mentor yourself, further enhancing your abilities and your connectivity.

In the short term, getting personal referrals to job openings with area employers demands that you get connected to both your professional community and to the diverse networks that make up your local community. In some professions, as your career progresses further up the ladder of success, you may eventually need to become connected to your professional communities on a national level.

There is a whole section on this topic in a few pages.

When you connect with your professional community, beyond the people you work with, you get to know all the most dedicated and best-connected professionals in your area, and in turn you become known by them. You should think in terms of *networks*, rather than a single *network*. We all have a number of networks available to us, any of which may produce that all-important job offer. Here are the networks we all can and should tap into:

Professional Networks

- Other job hunters. Professionals seeking a position in the same profession or industry can be valuable resources; they don't have to be looking for the same type of position.
- Managers, past and present, and your references. They can be useful to you throughout your job search.
- Coworkers. This includes professional colleagues, past and present.
- Other professionals in your field. Professional associations are a good place to start in order to find these contacts.
- College alumni. Educational institution networks, from trade schools to the Ivy League, are a valuable job search resource.
- Company alumni associations. Companies increasingly see the value in maintaining contact with ex-employees.

Community Networks

- Family and relatives. This includes your spouse's family and relatives.
- Friends. This includes neighbors and casual acquaintances, and those you know through your personal interests.
- Service industry acquaintances. This includes your banker, lawyer, insurance agent, Realtor, doctor, dentist, hairdresser, and the like.
- Social, civic, and spiritual associations. This would include churches and temples, business groups, Little League, and so on.

- Hobbies. This includes everything from the golf club to chess club, and any activity you enjoy that involves a loosely knit group of similar people.

Networking Approaches

You will have networks of people you can approach now and networks you will have to build today for use tomorrow. Ultimately, the effectiveness of your networking will depend largely on the scope of your networks and their relevance to your life. Whatever the network—and we'll go into them all shortly—you have choices for making contact and nurturing those relationships:

- Electronically. By letter, over the telephone, and via e-mail, online chat, or message posting.
- In person. Conventions, association meetings, class reunions, fundraisers, continuing-education classes, community, religious groups, and events.

In practice, the professional who integrates intelligent networking into his or her professional life will use all of these approaches. Networking is a tremendously valuable survival tool in any career, but it is much more than a series of discrete events. It is a *process* of building relationships; your networks become more effective the more effort you put into their development. We are going to look at far more networks than any person could ever cultivate, so as you read this section, put all the suggested options through your personal lifestyle filters to judge which networks will best fit your life. If you can integrate networking into your life in ways that make it less of a chore and more a part of the joy of living, you will nurture those networks more assiduously and more honestly. Networking is an irreplaceable survival tool, and it needs to be incorporated into your professional life.

It is a bit like gardening: You plant the seeds when you initiate a new relationship, but you don't harvest immediately. Networking can and does bear fruit right away, but your harvest will get richer as time passes and you nurture your networking contacts. In the following section, you'll learn how to build and nurture networks in both your professional and personal lives.

Professional Associations

The best thing you can do for your career is to take a proactive approach to the management of it. That means grasping the underpinnings of career management by becoming an active member of a professional association or two. Joining and being active in a professional association is the best long-term vehicle for increasing your professional visibility to future employers. In fact, if you have heard disgruntled job hunters mutter, "It's not what you know, it's who you know," it probably means they are not members of a professional association and they don't understand networking.

Associations have monthly meetings in most major cities, plus regional and national get-togethers every year. The local meetings are of immediate interest, and, unless you work on a national level, membership in the local or state chapters of a national association will be quite adequate for your needs—and cheaper, too. When you join a local chapter of a recognized national association and attend the local meetings, you get to know and be known by the most committed and best connected people at all levels of your profession. Your membership will help you stay attuned to what is going on in your profession. These associations also offer training programs that make you a more knowledgeable and therefore a more desirable employee.

All industries and professions have multiple associations, any of which could be valuable depending on your needs. For example, if you are in retail, you could join any of some thirty national associations and fifty state associations. Together these associations represent employees of over 1.5 million retail organizations, which in turn provide employment for over 14 million people. Most other associations offer similarly impressive networking potential. Your membership becomes a link to millions of colleagues, most of whom will gladly talk to you, based on your mutual connectivity through the association. The professional association is a new "old boy/old girl" network for the modern world.

If you fit the profile of a special interest or minority group you will find professional associations that cater to another dimension of the professional you. These include—but are by no means restricted to—associations for African Americans, Latinos, Asian Americans, professionals with disabilities, and women. If you can find a niche association that's a fit, join it as well: it represents another, even more finely tuned network.

You can check out links to professional association resources in the Internet Resources section of the knockemdead.com Web site, or go to the library and check out the *Encyclopedia of Associations* (published by Bowker). It tells you about all the known associations for your profession and provides contact information and other relevant data. You can look at it in a print version or online, though the online access is restricted to your local library. Alternatively, you can try a Google search for relevant keywords. For example, "Asian" and "legal" and "association" will generate a listing of local associations specifically for Asian professionals working in the legal field.

If you are smart enough to join an association, you'll benefit greatly from attending the meetings, because this is where you will meet fellow dedicated professionals. But don't just attend the meetings; get involved. Associations always need someone to set out chairs or hand out paperwork and nametags. The task itself doesn't matter, but your visible willingness to be an active participant most certainly does and will get you on first-name terms with people you would probably never otherwise meet. Given the nature of association membership, you don't have to go straight from introductions to asking for leads on jobs. In fact, it can be productive to have initial conversations where you do not ask for leads or help in your job search, but where you make a contribution to the group; this is always preferable because others are more likely to help you when they see you making an effort toward the common good.

Of course, you will have to get to know people, which is easier than you might think, because all professional association members are there at least in part to advance their careers through networking. Once you have the lay of the land, volunteer for one of the many committees that keep associations running. It's the best way to meet people and expand your sphere of influence, as you can reach out to others as you engage in your volunteer association activities. Committee involvement doesn't take much time because they invariably employ the "many hands make light work" approach; they are structured to function with the help of full-time professionals like you, with mortgages to pay and families to support.

There is a good argument that, from a networking point of view, the bigger the committee the better. Membership and program committees are among the best to join. However, involvement in any committee will serve your needs, because being on one will enable you to reach out to those on other committees. If you join the membership committee, you can initiate contact with just about anyone in your professional world: "Hi, Bill Parsons? I'm Becky Lemon with the conference committee of the local association. I'd like to invite you as our guest to a meeting we are having next week."

Don't join committees for which you lack the experience to be a productive member, unless you make it clear that the reason you want to become a part of that team is for professional development—if this is the case, expect to become the designated water carrier for that committee, at least initially. If you volunteer and become active in an association, the people with whom you come in contact will begin to identify you as a team player, and this perception can be instrumental for landing that new job and surging ahead in your career.

The association directory, which comes with your membership package, provides you with a superb networking resource for verbal contact and e-mail networking campaigns. You can feel comfortable calling any other member on the phone and introducing yourself: "Hi, Brenda Massie? My name is Martin Yate. We haven't spoken before, but we are both members of the Teachers Federation. I need some advice; can you spare a minute?"

Your mutual membership, and the commitment to your profession that it bespeaks, will guarantee you a few moments of anyone's time, a courtesy you should always return when asked. Your association contacts will also feel more comfortable about referring you to others in their own networks and to employment needs at their own companies.

You can also use your association membership directory to generate personal introductions for jobs you have heard about elsewhere. For example, you might have found an interesting job posting on *www.careerbuilder.com*, or perhaps on a company Web site, with the request that you e-mail a résumé to some nameless entity in HR; this is where your networking can pay big dividends. Rather than apply cold, return to your membership directory and find people who work for that company. A judicious call or two will frequently get you a personal referral and some inside information on the opening. Once you have an interview scheduled, these same contacts can help you prepare for the interview with insider knowledge about the company, the department, and the hiring manager.

Professional associations all have newsletters, usually online and print. Many have a jobs section on the Web site or linked to the newsletter, where companies advertise because of the qualified response. Consequently, you will see recruitment ads that often don't appear anywhere else. You will also notice that association members write all the articles, as everyone likes to have their literary efforts appreciated; telling a member you have read an article that he or she has written gives you a great introduction to a networking call or letter.

Active association membership puts you on the radar of all the best-qualified and connected professionals in your area. You can also list it at the end of your résumé under a Professional Affiliations heading. This is guaranteed to get a second glance, as it signifies professional awareness. Employers and headhunters often use words like *association, club,* and *society* in their keyword searches, so association membership will also help get your résumé pulled up from the databases for investigation by human eyes.

Social Networking

A typical career spans half a century, and in that time you can reasonably expect the good, the bad, and the downright ugly to occur in your professional life. It's during the rough times that you need people, and networking, with its focus on talking to friends and colleagues, offers a great job searching technique that also eases the feelings of rejection everyone suffers on a job search. Nevertheless, it fails for many job searchers because those networks lack relevance and depth.

A new rage on the Internet that helps all of us to build deeper, more relevant networks is "Internetworking," or "social networking." It revolves around social and/or professionally oriented online networks that help you leverage your professional reach through connecting with others in your area, and through people with whom you share common experiences or interests.

Here's an example: A soldier who was cycling out of the military employed my help in her search for a new career. First, I plugged in the word *army* at linkedin.com, an online networking site to find other individuals with a similar background. I got more than 4,000 profiles of people who shared her military experience. We then tried a search using the phrase "information *technology*" (for her desired career change) and got 39,000 profiles. Both these potential networks would have relevance to her job search, but it got even better when we combined both the keywords as "information *technology and army*." This pulled up 908 profiles of people who shared her life experience and who had most probably already made the transition into her desired profession. You can almost guarantee that such a degree of initial connectivity will ensure her productive conversations with most of those 908 people, each of which is relevant to her job search. The whole process took about forty minutes. These professionally oriented sites allow you to post biographies that can include skills, employers, educational history, and any other information you think might be helpful to your professional goals; all as part of a profile that works just like a résumé but without that "I'm for sale" sign. For job hunters and career changers it is a genuinely new approach that you can network with and simultaneously be visible in places where employers and recruiters also happen to be swarming for recruitment purposes.

Online networking can get you useful introductions to people throughout the country and the world—people who might know of jobs at their own companies or who can introduce you to people at companies that do have openings. This new application of technology enables you to reach out into an endless horizon of relevant networking contacts.

It works quite simply: you join a social networking site (with a few like *www.linkedin.com* you have to wangle an invitation from an existing member, you fill out a profile, and you are ready to go. If you don't have a linkedin.com contact, e-mail me (*martin@knockemdead.com*) and as a member I'll immediately send you an invitation. You can network without the benefit of personal contacts, but if you in turn invite a selection of your own trusted contacts to join the same site, your connectivity grows exponentially. The inherent benefit of these networks is that if everyone invites just a few competent and trusted friends to join, the endlessly expanding network becomes a trusted resource.

For employers and recruiters, networking sites constitute a reliable pathway to the passive job seeker; for a job hunter or career changer, on the other hand, they constitute a reliable pathway to jobs through the people connected to them. You can search a site's database by Zip Code, job title, company, or other relevant keywords of your choice. The database will pull up the profiles of people who match your requirements and allow you to initiate contact directly, or through the chain of people who connect to you.

The Internet is global, so all sites have a global reach. Facebook and MySpace for example need no explanation, except perhaps to note that while these sites and others like them, while social in intent, are used for recruitment. If you want to be recruited as a result of your presence this will affect the content of your personal profile, which now may predominantly feature the content of your résumé; you will also be careful to remove anything that is less than professional in nature... like those shots of projectile vomiting from your college days.

Professionally focused sites such as Ryze claims members in 100 countries; Spoke attracts people in sales worldwide; and *www.linkedin.com* has half its members in the United States and the other half scattered around the globe.

This makes all the professional networking sites especially useful when searching locally or when you plan to relocate; you can search for contacts by specific Zip Code and make connections locally, or in any target geography. In a global economy, people with language skills have a special edge, so sites that encourage bilingual professionals can help you leverage those language skills with any global company searching for multicultural awareness in its employees.

You are also likely to find social networking sites especially valuable when you know a career transition is coming. If you know you are cycling out of one profession and into another, such as from the military into a career in technology, you will have time to build a global network of ex-brothers-in-arms, all of whom will be ready to extend a helping hand.

There are over 100 such sites catering to a number of different needs. You can see a comprehensive list of working sites at: *http://en.wikipedia .org/wiki/List_of_social_networking_website.*

Some professionally oriented networking sites are general in nature, like LinkedIn; others are profession-specific, such as Spoke, which caters to sales professionals around the world. These sites also offer an array of services useful to your networking activities:

- Job postings from employers and headhunters
- Reminders of when to follow up with a call or e-mail to nurture your relationships
- Message boards and forums for common-interest groups, such as women in business
- Links to job boards
- Offline social events to meet and mingle in person

When you register you create a professional profile, answering questions about your education, employers, dates of employment, responsibilities, and interests. Your answers will be published on the site as your profile. Since your profile is, in effect, your résumé, have your résumé handy to cut and paste some of the entries.

If you don't use your résumé to fill out your profile, take care to include the same keywords that appear on your actual résumé. Just as you will search for others on the site using keywords, those members who are hiring managers, HR pros, or headhunters will be searching for you through the site's search engine using keywords. When you search for contacts by keyword, you'll want to try job titles, company names, industries, and geographic locations just for starters.

Many sites allow you to identify topics that you would like to receive feedback on and discuss with others. For example: advice and information on hiring people, looking for job or business opportunities, and partnering opportunities in your area of expertise. The more areas of interest you check, the more options other people will have to contact you. You also have a choice of whether or not to allow direct contact.

With networking you aren't only looking to form relationships with people at your level: almost anyone in your industry or geography can be useful regardless of title or experience, as you'll soon see. The people of interest you find will likely fall into two categories: those who might hire you, and those who probably won't hire you but who have common experience or interests. With the first group, you will be more direct. You can initiate contact by sending an e-mail to introduce yourself, noting the recipient identifies herself as interested in hiring, and ask her to look at your profile. If this proceeds to a conversation and interviews, fine; if not, you can ask your contact to connect you to others in her network.

With the second group, it's best to build a relationship by finding common ground. You can initiate relationships by asking for advice, and many people will give you a few minutes of their time. You will develop the best relationships, though, by reaching out to others with help and advice, because when you offer good things, forging a relationship with you becomes important to the other person.

The challenge then becomes how to help, advise, or make a gesture that will encourage a relationship that shares introductions and job leads. The answer is logical and painless: use the job leads you hear about that are inappropriate for your own use.

It's a not-always-so-funny thing about job searching that you discover over the years: when you are fresh out of school no one is hiring entry-level workers; they all want you to call back in five years. Five years later when you happen to be engaged in a job search again, everyone wants either someone fresh out of school or someone with ten years of experience. In your job search activities you are constantly coming across needs that aren't right for you but that could be just what someone else is aching to hear about.

Take these leads and offer them to others as part of your introduction. Sometimes you have to send an e-mail stating why you want to make contact, and sometimes you can communicate immediately—it depends on the other person's privacy preferences. In the first instance you send an e-mail simply stating you have a job lead that he or she might find interesting. This is a nice gesture and will get you lots of introductions.

In the second instance, where you are actually in direct e-mail communication, you state your business: "I am involved in a strategic career move right now, and I have come across a job that isn't right for me but that could be just right for you. If you'd like to talk, let's exchange telephone numbers. I'll be happy to pass the lead on, and perhaps you have heard about something that would suit me. I am cycling out of the army and into the private sector and have been looking for jobs in IT in the South. . . ." Your job search will have you scouring the Internet job boards and newspaper ads for job leads, and now you have a use for all those positions that aren't quite right for you.

With the job opportunities that do seem appropriate, you are usually faced with mailing or e-mailing résumés to corporate HR departments, but your online networks give you an alternative. Somewhere on your networking site there may be people who work at that company now or have in the past. Search for them, using the company name in your keyword search, then contact them and explain that you have heard about an opening at the company and hope to get some inside information before you apply. If you make time to visit the company Web site before any conversation, you will be well-informed and make a good impression when you do talk.

With the exception of Ryze (which charges about $10 a month), just about all of the Internet working sites are free right now, but this will change as their validity is proven. LinkedIn has recognized that companies and entrepreneurs already pay for finding employees and business partners, so you can assume that sooner rather than later these sites will charge for membership and for some of their search services.

Networking takes time, but the more you reach out, the better your reputation becomes and the more others will reach out to you. One last word of caution: Online networking is a tool, a new and seemingly very attractive tool, but a single tool nevertheless. Use it in conjunction with a number of other job search approaches.

Alumni Associations

Almost every school, from Acme Welding to Wellesley College, has an alumni association, and being a member of your alma mater's association can have a pivotal role in your professional life when handled correctly. Going to the meetings, networking at the online site, and occasionally volunteering for some task are all activities that will ease you into collegial relationships with men and women on every rung of the corporate ladder—people who are in a position to boost your career.

The alumni association membership directory puts you in touch with the other graduates from your alma mater, and people like to extend their help to those with whom they share a background. Alumni associations all have newsletters (see how to leverage this tool in "Newspapers and Magazines," page 72), and many include information about job openings. Some alumni associations even have semi-formalized job-hunting networks in which alumni are encouraged to pass on their company's employment needs. As a member of an alumni association, you can also cultivate an informal relationship with the school's director of career services and get some inside knowledge of corporate hiring plans. Even when your school days are in the misty past, don't forget these people and the valuable resource they represent. Your alumni association is a valuable network just waiting for you to become involved and leverage its contacts.

If you don't know the URL (Web address) of your alma mater, go to *www.utexas.edu/world/univ/*; you'll find an excellent resource for community college URLs at *www.mcli.dist.maricopa.edu/cc/*. You could also try *www.classmates.com*.

Company Alumni Associations

Companies increasingly see the value in maintaining contact with ex-employees, through online corporate alumni associations, as a source for future hires and for leads on future hires. Go to *www.alumni.net* to find companies with established alumni networks.

Your Past Managers and Other References as a Networking Resource

As a rule, we are confident that our references will speak well of us. The fact is, however, that while some of them will, others, we might be surprised to hear, bear us no goodwill. It isn't wise to discover this by trial and error, as one potential offer after another bites the dust. Another mistake is not to speak to those references at all or only at the end of a job search when a job offer is imminent. (For a discussion of how to handle your references when you are under serious consideration for a position, see Chapter 20, "Negotiating the Job Offer.") If these are people you know well and whom you believe will speak well of you, why not leverage that goodwill throughout your job search?

At the very start of your job search you should identify as many potential references as possible. The more options, the better your likelihood of coming up with excellent references. With some experience under your belt you might be pursuing different job titles, and consequently different references might be appropriate for some of those jobs; of course, when employed, avoid using current managers and coworkers as references.

Yet at this point of the job search, excellent references, though important, are simply an added bonus. Your real agenda is to use these contacts as another aspect of your professional network.

The process is simplicity itself, starting with an introduction: "John, this is _____. We worked together at Citibank between 1998 and 2003. How's it going?" It is appropriate here to catch up on gossip and the like. Then broach the subject of your call.

"John, I wanted to ask your advice." (Everyone loves to be asked for an expert opinion.) "We had some cutbacks at Fly-By-Night Finance, as you probably heard," or "The last five years at Bank of Crooks and Criminals International have been great, and the _____ project we are just winding down has been a fascinating job. Nevertheless, I have decided that this would be a perfect time for a strategic career move to capitalize on my experience."

Then, "John, I realize how important references can be and I was wondering if you would have any reservations about my using you as one?" It's better to find out now rather than down the line when it could blow a job offer. The response will usually be positive, so you can then move to the next step.

"Thanks, John, I hoped you would say that. Let me update you about what I have been doing recently and tell you about the type of job I'm after." Give a capsule description of what you've done since you worked together and specifically what you are looking for. Also ask your contacts if they will keep an ear to the ground for you, and ask if they would mind giving you advice as situations arise during your job search. You'll also want to show courtesy by following your call with a thank-you letter.

With the scene set in this manner, you can network with each of these potential references every month or two, either for input on a particular opportunity or to ask who they know who might be looking to hire. With this approach you will have developed another small but very finely tuned networking resource for your job search.

Personal Networks

Personal networking means more than annoying the heck out of your friends until they stop taking your calls; it means using others within your personal sphere of influence to assist in your job search. Friends and acquaintances like to help, but as a group resource they can easily be exhausted. If you are like most people, your personal networks aren't going to be wide enough or relevant enough to support a job search on their own. The typical personal networks we can all tap into include:

- Family, relatives, and friends. This includes your spouse's family and relatives and their networks.

- Service industry acquaintances. Electricians, plumbers, carpenters, accountants, lawyers, hairdressers—anyone whose services you employ is a potential networking resource.
- Hobby and special-interest networks. This includes anyone with whom you share a common interest, whether fellow baseball or soccer team members, other parents involved in Little League, the girls at the knitting shop, or the gang at the gym.
- Religious and social community groups. This includes all the networks that become available to you when you reach out to help others.

We meet these people at conventions, association meetings, class reunions, fundraisers, continuing-education classes, and at community, religious, fraternal, and sporting events; and we are also likely to meet their friends and the friends of their friends.

While networking should become an integral part of your life, it will always move into a higher gear when strategic career moves are on your front burner. There are a wide variety of personal and community-based networks available to you, depending on your interests and your willingness to become an active member of your local community.

Some are personal: family, friends, and service industry acquaintances; these tend to be the people you see on a regular basis. Other, more formal, groups are socially oriented, such as religious, community, local business, and volunteer groups. Some are professional but not restricted to a specific profession, while others are community-based groups that focus on a common interest. You don't necessarily know the people in these groups but you do have a potential common bond based on community involvement.

Your personal networking efforts fall into two categories: those people you already know personally, and those you can meet through involvement in your community. With the first you can be direct, while with the second group you must be a little more patient and diplomatic. You might leverage some of these networks by phone or e-mail and some by both personal interaction and telephone or e-mail communication. But on the whole you'll do most of your personal networking, well, personally.

Family and Friends

The good news is that the people who know you best, your family and friends, will really try to help you. The bad news is that since most of them may have known you since you were a runny-nosed ten-year-old, you have been categorized, stereotyped, and pigeonholed. They might not really know—or might incorrectly guess—what it is you do. Odds are they don't know what you are capable of doing or what you want to do. Case in point: after ten books published around the world and millions of copies sold, my immediate family is still genuinely impressed that I know to come in out of the rain.

When job hunting, you tend to compound the overfamiliarity problem by tapping into this valuable network too soon and too often, before you have really thought out what your next job is going to be and what kind of leads will get you there. Still, you can get good mileage out of your family and friends network by retooling your approach.

Family and friends aren't stupid, but unlike the contacts you make in your professional networks, they probably don't have a full grasp of what you do for a living. On the other hand, they are highly motivated to help you and might know a lot of people. Many job hunters make the mistake of giving too much information about what they do professionally and in the process confuse those closest to them. With the right guidance, your immediate circle will cast a wide net and come up with leads for you, even if they have nothing to do with the professional world.

Here are the steps to help your loved ones help you:

1. Think carefully about what you do for a living and put it in a one- or two-sentence description that even Aunt Aggie can grasp: "I am a computer programmer; I write the instructions that help computers run."

2. Think carefully about the job you want, the kind of company you will work for, and the kind of people you need to talk to; condense it into a one- or two-sentence explanation: "I'm looking for a job with another computer company. It would be great if you or your friends know anyone I could talk to who works with computers."

3. Give them the information you need to get in touch with these people: "I am looking for the names and telephone numbers of anyone in these areas. I'm not looking for someone to hire me; I'm looking for people in my field with whom I can network."

This process of breaking your networking needs into three or four simple statements gives the people you know socially something they can easily remember and something they can really work with. You can do this with them one on one, or you can get everyone together for a barbecue and get the new program moving in one fell swoop.

Civic, Social, Volunteer, Religious, and Special-Interest Networking Groups

It's good to be involved in your local community, both for your own emotional health and the health of your community. Your involvement will provide you with a richer personal life, as well as a wide array of networking opportunities. You will find that effective networking with these groups is a little more time-consuming than with professional groups; after all, you have no prior professional relationships, and they don't have a familial "obligation" to help you out.

At the same time, you can't possibly join all the groups your community has to offer, so you will have to make some decisions about what is practical and which activities are going to be valuable to you in and of themselves; if the activity is personally fulfilling, you are more likely to stick with it over time and reap the rewards that come from that investment. Most people have time for no more than three ongoing social activities. These might comprise:

A religious or community volunteer group—Participation in spiritual and volunteer communities help us achieve a sense of meaning and balance in our lives, and such groups are especially helpful in the emotionally troubled times of job and career change. They get you involved with others who wish to make a difference in their lives by reaching out to others.

A hobby or special-interest group—This could be a chess club, a women's/men's group, a dance class, a philosophical discussion group that meets regularly at the local coffee shop, or any of the vast number of community-based special-interest groups. It doesn't matter so long as the activity is one that energizes the inner you, by taking you away from the worries of your professional world. The people you meet will all have professional careers and the common bond based on your special interests.

A business, professional, or civic group—All communities have networks of professionals joined together in formal groups: Rotarians, Chamber of Commerce, women in business, Kiwanis, and many more. These community-based associations, societies, and clubs are professionally oriented in membership, but they aren't focused on one profession; they straddle the line between your professional and community-based networking activities. Belonging to one will give you another angle of attack for your job search and perhaps improve your social life.

In all these groups your need for job leads must first take a back seat to becoming involved as a productive member. Soon enough you'll learn what people do for a living, while they learn about you both as a professional and as a human being. As opportunities arise you can talk about your job search needs; I'll talk about how to manage these conversations shortly. You can find out about these groups in your local newspapers, at the library, through your religious group, or by using your Internet browser.

Your Job Search Network

In your job search you will sometimes feel that companies are looking for every-one but you. The recent graduate is told to come back when she has experience; the experienced professional is told that only entry-level people are being hired. That's the luck of the draw, but one person's problem is another's opportunity. The solution is to join or create a support group and job search network with people in the same situation. While these can be online, many are local, community-based networks. The following advice largely applies to either.

Existing Support Groups

A number of national organizations and many communities support job search networks through religious or other social organizations. Members meet, usually on a weekly basis, to exchange ideas and job leads, and just as important to share and laugh with others in transition.

You can find groups in your area online at *www.careerjournal.com, www.job search.org,* or *www.rileyguide.com.* Your local state employment office also main-tains lists of job search support groups.

If you are a member of a job search support group and know of an upcom-ing job fair, you should go with a collaborative effort in mind. You may all be in different professions, but if you all make the effort to speak to other attendees and to collect a dozen business cards each regardless of the profession, you could come up with useful new leads to exchange at the end of the day.

Gathering Leads and Referrals from Networking Conversations

You get a personal referral to a professional colleague or find a suitable name from a professional association directory, or maybe you get a referral from a friend in your bowling league. You might need to follow up with people you have met briefly on some prior occasion. You never know who you are going to meet at the grocery store, coffee shop, hairdresser, or gym. For your networking in any of these situations to be maximally effective, you need a "networking headset" that you can apply as readily in person as you can over the telephone, when you have copious notes in front of you and all the time in the world to prepare.

A "networking headset" means you are always prepared to show an interest in others and speak to them in a friendly way, so that you won't let casual opportunities for expanding your networks slip by. With a networking headset, you will be surprised at the range of useful people you will meet. Even when those people know nothing about your profession, they might know someone involved in the same field as you. Everyone you meet has the potential to know someone who can be useful to your job search.

It's one thing to have an introduction and quite another to make the ensuing conversation productive. You can network with others in person at conventions, association meetings, class reunions, fundraisers, continuing-education classes, or at community, social, spiritual, and sporting events; or from a distance over the telephone, by letter, or via e-mail, online chat, or message posting. While the information-gathering aspects of these conversations will remain fairly constant regardless of the communication medium, there are one or two unique considerations about networking in person.

In-Person Networking

Always carry business cards. If your company doesn't supply you with cards, get some made at your own expense. Go to Google and type in "create business cards," and you will find suppliers and software for less than $20. When you attend social and professional events, keep those business cards handy (however, unless you are attending a job fair, leave your résumé behind, as thrusting your résumé at every new contact will be seen as overanxious and unprofessional).

You will need an introduction for yourself, which might vary slightly depending on the context, and while it's tough to do, you have to make the effort to reach out to others. Because everyone knows what it is like to be looking for a job, you will find the majority of people friendly and responsive. "Hello, I'd like to introduce myself. My name is Mark Germino. I'm in accounting/just started playing tennis; how about you?" Always try to end with a question that encourages your contact to introduce and talk about himself; it doesn't really matter what the question is. Once there has been a conversational exchange, you can begin to move forward with your networking agenda. (We'll go into a whole series of networking questions shortly.)

As you never know when you are going to make useful contacts, always maintain a well-put-together appearance when job searching. That doesn't mean that you always have to be dressed for the boardroom, just that you should give consideration to your appearance before leaving the house.

Even though gatherings of associations, clubs, and societies provide excellent networking opportunities, they are not scheduled specifically for that activity. The same goes for any type of casual interaction. Try to keep your initial in-person networking conversations to less than five minutes. You can end them gracefully with an offer of your business card. Similarly recognize that a request for yours is a signal for you both to move on. If someone you meet isn't carrying a card, have him or her write a name and contact information on the back of one of yours; always try to get both a telephone number and an e-mail address.

Whenever you meet someone in person, send an e-mail a few days later to thank him or her for any helpful information you may have gathered from the conversation; it also serves to keep you on that person's radar.

The Secrets to All Fruitful Networking Conversations

Your networks grow in proportion to the energy you put into them. That energy will express itself in the number of networking events in which you participate and how intelligently your networking conversations are structured. These "events" can occur in person or over the telephone. They can be conducted through e-mail as well, but actually talking with someone will generate the most consistently favorable results.

While your communication medium will vary, the agenda of your conversations will remain constant. Following are some ideas for the content of those in-person conversations, telephone calls, and e-mails. Obviously you will have to add the conversational context and rephrase the essence and intent of the words to make them your own. Show interest in your contacts as human beings, and then—and *only* then—move on with your agenda.

It's a good idea before leaving for an in-person event, or making a telephone call, to consider what information you want to gather and what messages you want to get across. Because we spend the majority of our waking hours at the office, most people are happy to talk about their work. Discovering what someone does for a living makes a useful opener, and if the answer puts the contact in your professional field, great; you can draw the connection and go from there.

If not, you should still show an interest in your contact's interests, because this person may well know some of the people you need to know.

If you have spoken to the contact before, recall the last memorable interaction you had with that person or mention someone you both know. Ask what is happening in that person's personal and professional life, and then listen to what is said and respond appropriately.

When it is time to move on to your information-gathering questions, prepare a statement that allows you to encapsulate your situation succinctly: "I just got laid off with 1,000 others" or "We have a baby on the way, and XYZ is a company where there just isn't room for me to grow professionally" or "My job just got sent to Mumbai, India, so I guess it's time for me to make a move."

When common professional ground exists through an association or other social network, you can assume that your listener will be well disposed toward you; you can repay this goodwill by showing respect for that person's time and politely cutting to the chase. You could also begin, "Brenda, I have been an accountant with Anderson for the last four years. I work in the small business area, and I'm looking to make a change." Rather than rambling, in less than ten seconds you have courteously provided a focus. It is here that you have the opportunity to avoid the next gaffe; don't say something like, "My ideal job would be. . . ." or "The next step I'd like to take is. . . ."

By describing an ideal job or your desired next step up the professional ladder, you make things more difficult for the listener, who thinks, "This guy is looking for something very specific, and any introductions I can make will probably be a waste of everyone's time." It is more productive to talk in terms of what you do day-to-day, or even just tell the contact in general terms the profession in which you work (I'm an accountant in retail) and that you are looking for a new opportunity.

(*Note:* The nature of these networking conversations assumes you are talking to professional colleagues and seeking leads on job openings, rather than talking to the managers, directors, vice presidents, and presidents who can make those hiring decisions. The conversations with anyone who has the potential to hire you are different because you are then making a marketing presentation; this will be handled later in this chapter.)

At this point, your conversation can move on to a discussion of the profession or industry, the areas of opportunity, and the direction you hope to pursue. If you handle yourself in a pleasant and professional manner, most people will try to be helpful. It helps to let your contacts know in general terms the job you intend to pursue, because while people usually want to help, they need a framework within which to target their efforts.

You can ask for general guidance about your tactics: "If you were in my situation, Charlie, what would you do?" You can ask if he or she has heard about local companies hiring. If appropriate, you can ask whether your contact would take a look at your résumé—because you'd appreciate an objective opinion from someone in the profession. These are all good questions, and they typically comprise the content of 99 percent of all networking calls, but you can achieve more.

We are now going to proceed with a comprehensive sequence of interview development questions that will lead you to a substantial number of jobs in the hidden job market. These are exactly the question sequences asked by the entire multibillion-dollar headhunting and employment services industry when prospecting for job openings.

The questions follow a logical sequence—but that order might not suit your needs. As you look at the questions, figure out what question you would ask if you had time for only one. Write it down, and repeat this process with the remaining questions on the list; the result will be a comfortably prioritized set of questions. During each conversation you will only have so much time to gather information, so avoid questions like "How's business these days?" Each question you ask should be specific. When you're satisfied with your list of interview development questions, print them out on a fresh sheet of paper and keep it by the telephone.

Questions for Leads at Your Contact's Company

You can ask if there are openings in the department or at the company and with whom you should speak about them. Don't ask, "Can you or your company hire me?" You can ask:

- "Who else in the company might need someone with my qualifications?"
- "Is the company/department planning any expansion or new projects that might create an opening?"
- "When do you anticipate a change in company manpower needs?"
- "Does your company have any other divisions or subsidiaries that might need someone with my attributes?"

Always ask about headhunters your contact might be in touch with, and whether he or she would be willing to pass on your name and contact information to them.

You might need to add some profession-specific questions. For instance, people in information technology might find questions about the operating systems, communication protocols, programs, and languages a company uses to be useful. In this instance, after receiving an answer, add a similarly focused follow-up question: "Thanks, Gail. Who else do you know who uses these configurations?" Be sure any question you add to your list is geared toward identifying people and companies in your areas of interest.

Even when an offer of introduction is made—"Let me speak to Charlene Howarth for you," (rather than being told to make direct contact yourself, "call Charlene at extension 912")—don't rely on your contact to get you into that company. If the door hasn't opened in a few days, it might not. You should execute your own plan of attack, seeking other personal introductions within the company from your networking resources and making direct application by telephone, e-mail, and snail mail résumé submissions.

Questions for Leads at Other Companies

When you are sure that no job openings exist within a particular department or company, move on to gathering leads in other companies: "Do you know of anyone at any other banks in town I might speak to?" or "Who do you know in the business community that might have a need for someone like me?"

If your contact can't think of a person, ask about other companies: "What companies have you heard about that are hiring now?" or "If you were going to make a move, what companies would you look at?" or "Which are the most rapidly growing companies in the area?"

Whenever you are offered a lead, say, "Hey, that's a great idea. I never thought of IBM," as your encouragement is positive reinforcement. Then after a suitable pause, ask for another company name, as in, "I really appreciate your help, Sam. I never thought of IBM. . . . Who else comes to mind?" When people see that their advice is appreciated, they will often come up with more helpful information. When you have gathered two or three company names, you can backtrack with a request for contact names at each of the companies: "Do you know of anyone I could speak to at _____?" and "Do you know anyone I could speak to at General Materials?"

You can also ask for leads at companies you plan to call, or even at those you have already called: "Jack, I was planning to contact _____, Inc. Would you happen to know anyone there who could give me a heads up?"

The extent of your questioning depends on the willingness of your contact to continue the conversation; I've known these conversations to run for fifty minutes. For example, when a conversation is going well, and if you are in a job search network, tacking on a last question that gives you job leads to trade with others can be a good idea: "John, I'm a member of a job search network. If you don't have a need for someone with my background right now, perhaps one of my colleagues could be just what you are looking for. Who are you guys looking for right now?"

If you are changing careers or considering a career change, your priorities might be different. In this case you can explain that you are considering a particular profession for a new career direction and ask what it is like working in the profession; what your contact likes least and most about the work; what education, experience, and professional behaviors help people succeed in the profession; who fails and why; and how one gets into and moves ahead in the profession.

What to Do When You Get a Referral

When you get leads on companies and specific individuals to talk to, be sure to thank your benefactor and ask to use his or her name as an introduction. "Thank you, Bill. I didn't know Wal-Mart was building a facility in town (duh!), and I appreciate getting Holly Barnes's name. May I use your name as an introduction, or would you prefer me to keep it confidential?"

Every time you get a referral be sure to ask whether you can use your contact's name as an introduction. The answer will invariably be yes, but asking demonstrates professionalism and will encourage your contact to come up with more names and leads. It is also quite acceptable to add afterward, "That's very helpful, Bill. Does anyone else come to mind?"

When you get permission to use your contact's name, use it in an introduction: "Jane, my name is Natalia Markowskiu. Our mutual friend Bill Smith suggested I call, so before I go any further, Bill has asked me to say hello." This is a bridge-building phrase and usually leads to a brief and complimentary exchange about your mutual contact before you go into your information-gathering agenda.

When you do get help, say thank you. If you do it verbally, it's a nice touch to follow it up with a note (see *Knock 'em Dead Cover Letters* for follow-up letter examples). The impression is indelible and might get you another lead, and it never hurts to include a copy of your résumé with the thank-you letter.

When your networking call comes to its natural conclusion, say your thanks, offer to return the favor, and leave the door open for future calls: "Jack, thanks so much for your help. I do appreciate it. You know, when you're job searching you realize how important your colleagues are, so I'd like to give you my telephone number and e-mail so that one day I might return the favor. Thanks for your time. Might I call you again sometime?"

Other statements that you might use at the end of your conversation include:

"I'll let you know how it pans out with Mary Chen."

"Might I get in touch in a couple of months to see if the situation has changed?"

When talking to a management contact in your profession, you might suggest, "Would it be worth my e-mailing a copy of my résumé for your personal management database?"

◆ ◆ ◆

You are going to get some pleasant surprises when you network, but also a few disappointments. You will be surprised at how someone you always regarded as a real pal won't give you the time of day and how someone you never thought of as a friend will go above and beyond the call of duty for you. So keep an open mind, and keep calling and e-mailing. Stay in touch with each of your networking contacts, but don't overdo it. It is better to invest your energies in developing the breadth, depth, and relevance of your networks, rather than just contacting people you already know.

Whether your contacts are able to help you or not, let them know when you get a job, and try to stay in contact at least once a year. A career lasts a long time, and it might be next week or a decade from now when a group of managers (including one from your personal network) are talking about filling a new position, and the first thing they'll do is ask, "Who do we know?" That someone is more likely to be you when you are connected to your profession and your local community.

MORE EFFECTIVE JOB SEARCH TACTICS

CHAPTER 4

IN A COMPETITIVE market, you need to make use of every tool that you can to land that ideal job; you cannot rely exclusively on networking, effective as it is.

In this chapter you will learn all the most powerful job search techniques, including ways to manipulate the job sites.

A man who goes fishing and puts one hook in the water has only one chance of catching any one of the millions of fish in the sea; a man with two hooks in the water has double the chances of getting a bite. The more hooks you have in the water, the better your chances of getting bites. All the job-hunting tools and approaches that we discuss in this section of the book—the Internet, newspapers and magazines, employment agencies, job fairs, and more—have proven effective, but no single one is a guaranteed silver bullet. Any one could turn up the ideal opportunity for you and your future, so your plan of attack should embrace as many of these approaches as is practical. Pursuing all of these avenues also allows you to leverage your networking efforts by going back to individuals with whom you have a connection and asking them for introductions to the right people in reference to specific jobs you have unearthed.

Using the Internet in Your Job Search

The rapid proliferation of online employment resources provides a daunting challenge: What is the best way to leverage the undoubted benefits of these resources without drowning in them? With such a wide range of choices, you could waste months just posting your résumé on the more than 5,000 job-related sites. Integration of these computer-based tools is perhaps the biggest problem in any job search.

It is all too easy to wile away the days noodling around from site to site. The potential for procrastination is enormous; you may tell yourself that you've spent the day job searching, but in the end you've only avoided the potential rejection that inevitably accompanies direct contact with potential employers.

More than anything, the Internet increases your ability to gather and disseminate information, which is a boon to any job searcher. I am now going to show you how to set up an effective job search/career management database, post a sanitized résumé (one that can't be traced back to you at your current employer) to job sites, seek out potential employers directly, and manage the inflow of job openings and supporting information that will come your way as the job search gathers momentum.

If you've been through a job search before, you are groaning at having to start all over again. The good news is that if you execute this job search as I recommend, apart from generating the widest possible choice of job opportunities, you will have the mechanisms in place to permanently keep an eye on job opportunities in your field. The next time you are considering a strategic career move, you will already have a database of thousands of appropriate employers, complete with contact information and some understanding of whom they hire. In other words, you will have a solid head start for a careful job search.

It can take a day or two to get organized and start the flow of outgoing résumés and incoming opportunities, but as you weave all these different activities together the time won't drag. If you don't organize properly, you can get buried in an avalanche of information and leads with no way to track them. Organization begins with setting up a career management base of operations for this job search, one you can continue to use for ongoing professional development and career-management activities.

Online Security and Confidentiality

The first step in organizing a base camp for your online operations is to create a secure online identity. Online privacy is an issue for everyone using the Internet, and this is especially important during a job search when a breach could cost you a current job.

I recommend you set up a separate e-mail account devoted exclusively to your job search. You should have an e-mail address that reflects the professional you, and unless you live alone, it can prevent an otherwise beloved rugrat inadvertently destroying valuable information.

If you have visited many online job sites, you have probably noticed they all promise you confidentiality. However, the blocking mechanisms don't always work, and you can inadvertently reveal your true identity through an inappropriate e-mail address or piece of information on your résumé. Creating a separate e-mail address, one reserved for your job searching and career management activities, is the equivalent of an espionage agent's drop box; it is one to which only you have the key. For anyone else, it leads nowhere. If you are employed, you do not want a headhunter or a recruiter from HR dredging up your résumé from a supposedly secure Web site and presenting it to your boss for review—now that could *really* ruin your day.

It isn't hard to set up a separate e-mail account, as your current ISP almost certainly allows multiple addresses. Earthlink, for example, allows up to eight different e-mail addresses for one monthly fee.

There are also free accounts offered through Yahoo!, Hotmail, and many other sites; just go to your browser and type "free e-mail" into the search engine. Go to the site of your choice, and follow the simple instructions for setting up an account.

Be sure to give yourself a professional address. Don't use something like *binky@yahoo.com* or *bigjoe@hotmail.com*, nor should you use abbreviations of your name like *martiny@yahoo.com*. Instead create an account name that reveals something about your professional profile, such as *systemanalyst@hotmail.com* or *topaccountant@yahoo.com*. Addresses such as these help recipients focus on your communication from the start, because they act as headlines for the reader. Many names like *topaccountant@yahoo.com* are long gone, and you will be encouraged to accept *topaccountant1367@yahoo.com*; before you accept this, try something like *top10accountant@yahoo.com*.

While you know better than to use your office e-mail for a job search, you should also never download your secure e-mail to your office e-mail inbox. Why? Three reasons:

1. Privacy issues within the workplace are in turmoil right now, so your company may be viewing your mail, and your inbox is a security breach because others can read it.
2. You could accidentally leave the browser open, and your secure e-mail could be accessed.
3. Companies can check Internet usage on your work computer through a variety of tracking tools. So play it safe; set up a secure e-mail address, and only access it from outside the workplace.

While setting up your e-mail and the career management database, you will also need to create an effective résumé (see *Knock 'em Dead Resumes*). Sanitize your electronic résumé by removing all contact information (name, address, phone, fax), and replacing them with your career management e-mail.

If you are currently employed, or if you want to create that impression, remove your current employer's name. Replace it with a generalized description of the company and location. For example, if you work for Pepsi-Cola in Chicago, Illinois, you could describe this as a "Midwestern *Fortune* 500 Beverage Company."

By disguising a current employer's name (potential employers understand the need for this), you can keep your job titles intact and protect your identity; it usually isn't necessary to sanitize prior employer contact information. However, if you have a senior title associated with a particularly visible company, it could be a clue as to who you are. In this case replace it with a more common but equivalent job title.

Remember to be careful. Many job sites will tell you their software creates the perfect résumé and protects it, but that is not always the case. Do not rely on these sites or the résumé distribution services to do what you need to do yourself. Taking the time to create a viable résumé is like a soldier cleaning his weapon before battle: it helps focus your mind for the task ahead.

How to Organize Your Job Searching and Career Management Database

To help you get a clear idea of how to set up an electronic home base for your job searching and career management activities, we are going to set up a database on Hotmail. You will see the screens you need to do this and the steps you'll have

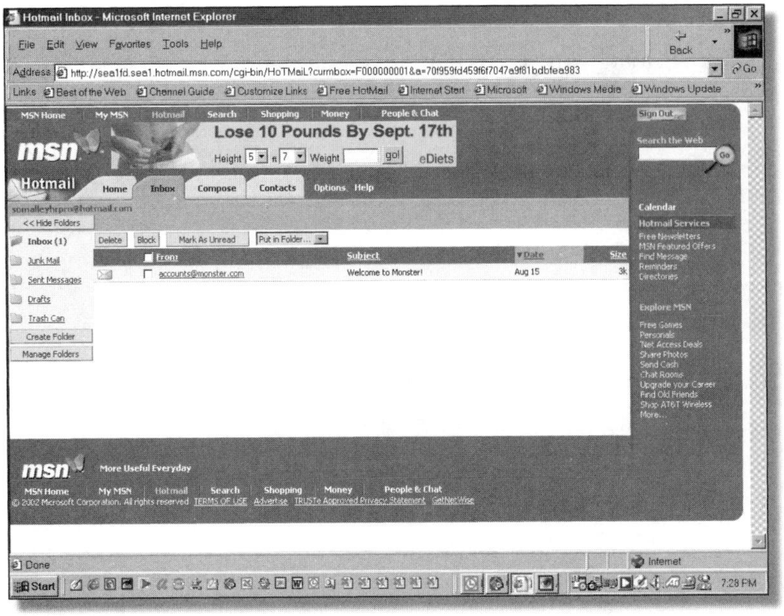

Fig 4.1. Managing folders

to take. In our example we will follow Susan, a technology professional, as she sets up her online database. We join the process just after our user has signed up for her e-mail account.

Focus on the "Create Folder" and "Manage Folders" buttons on the left-hand side of the screen. All major e-mail programs allow you to create and manage folders. Think of these electronic folders as you would paper folders and filing cabinets. What folders do you need? We should start with the two major sites where the user in our example knows she will be posting her résumé and searching for jobs, Monster and SHRM.org (the Society for Human Resource Management). Both of these sites offer a job delivery service, so when she signs up at either of these sites using her new e-mail account, she will be receiving new job postings via e-mail on a regular basis. With folders in place, she can file her e-mails appropriately for future reference (after a few weeks she'll be able to judge the relative value of the different sites on which she posts). She will also create a folder for leads; as leads mature into communications with specific companies and recruiters, she can design individual folders for each.

However, your organization does not end there. It is crucial for your career that you constantly and consistently build a database of job prospects, both of companies where you might want to work and of contacts within recruitment

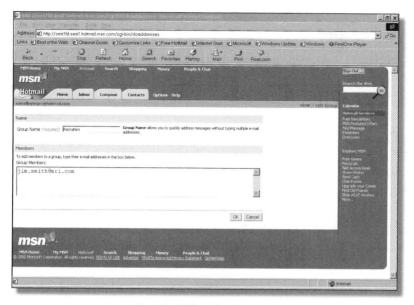

Fig 4.2. Address book groups

firms. Do this and you will be ten steps ahead of the game, during both this job search and any future strategic career moves.

You might choose to add a Job Leads folder. Into this you can put copies of all the e-mail postings you get from other sources.

On the screen, look up to the right, above the messages. There is a tab near the middle of the screen is labeled "Address Book." When you click on it you will be sent to another screen, where you are given additional options. This is the area where you can send and delete mail, view and edit messages, and, most important, create a new address book. You are going to want to create a whole new group, not just add an individual address. Each "group" will contain a separate set of related addresses.

The idea is to create separate groups that you can refer to in this or in any future job search. Typically these groups will fall into these categories: companies, recruiters, networking prospects, and professional colleagues. By creating an address book group for each of these categories you are creating a database for your work life. A professional colleagues address book will help you keep in touch with your immediate professional community in a more efficient manner, now and forever.

Additions to these groups do not need to be based on direct contact, interviews, or job offers. If you see recruiters that have a position within your industry of interest, put their addresses in that book; you'll know where to find them when you start getting the word out to the headhunters. If you find a company related to your function or geographic area, put the appropriate address in your book. You're creating a vehicle from which you can launch a massive career blitz tomorrow or six months from tomorrow. Organize yourself now, and you will be able to capture information today that you can use throughout your work life.

If you stay registered on the job boards while employed, you will always have a good idea of the skills that are in demand. This helps you stay abreast of the skills you will need to maintain your future employability.

We typically dump job postings or help wanted ads that don't turn into anything, or for other reasons aren't quite suitable. I don't want you to do this; a company that hires accountants today is just as likely to be hiring them three years from today. Knowing about the company and its contact information gives you a head start next time. This job searching and career management database is a tool you create for the benefit of your entire career; it is part of gaining control of your professional destiny.

Registering on Job Sites

Not all job sites and résumé banks work the same way. On some, you will copy and paste your résumé into dialog boxes as directed. On others, you will be completing a profile or questionnaire that the site has developed. This is where knowing the rules comes into play—knowing which to abide by and which to bend to your own best interests.

Job sites are usually free for you to use, but the employers are paying to post their job openings, just as they are also paying to search the résumé bank. These same paying customers want to control their search time, and the job sites work with them to develop ever more efficient screening tools. By making you, the job seeker, fill out profiles and answer questionnaires that ask for very specific information, you are helping them screen you in—or screen you out.

Whenever you are filling out a profile or questionnaire keep two things in mind:

1. Who will be reading this, and for what purpose?
2. What are they really asking me?

Let's look at the Monster résumé builder, because it is also a screening tool created to assist the employer.

In the following illustration we'll follow an applications programmer who has chosen to use the Monster site in her online strategy. Once on the site, she

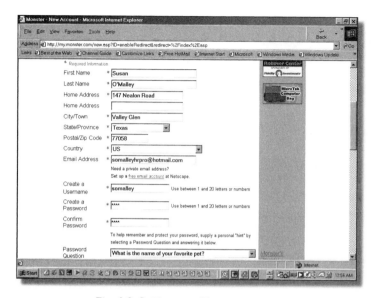

Fig. 4.3. Setting up a Monster account

follows buttons for new users and, like the millions before her, starts to set up her free My Monster account, filling out her name, address, career level, and degree, which are all required fields.

Now, one of the great features of Monster is that it will allow you to maintain five different résumés/profiles—this is useful for people competent in more than one professional area. When sites allow you to do this, take advantage of it. Make some of your profiles very specific and others very broad to increase your visibility.

The Monster résumé builder is typical in that it breaks up the résumé and profile into thirteen specific areas, including Career Objective, Target Job, Target Location, Salary, Work Status, Skills, References, and Education; you will have to address similar subject areas in most online profiles and registrations.

One of the first screens Susan is asked to complete includes her "Title" and "Career Objective." The site offers examples to help you answer these questions—but the advice is not in your best interest. Remember, employers pay Monster to save them time in the recruitment process by screening you out. Monster advises you to list a position title and to describe what type of position you are looking for under "Career Objective." You have to think beyond the question if you want to increase your visibility. Every field you fill out is a keyword opportunity. Instead of completing the "Title" field as "Applications Programmer," Susan uses the amount of space she has and makes a list of all the languages, software, and systems that she knows.

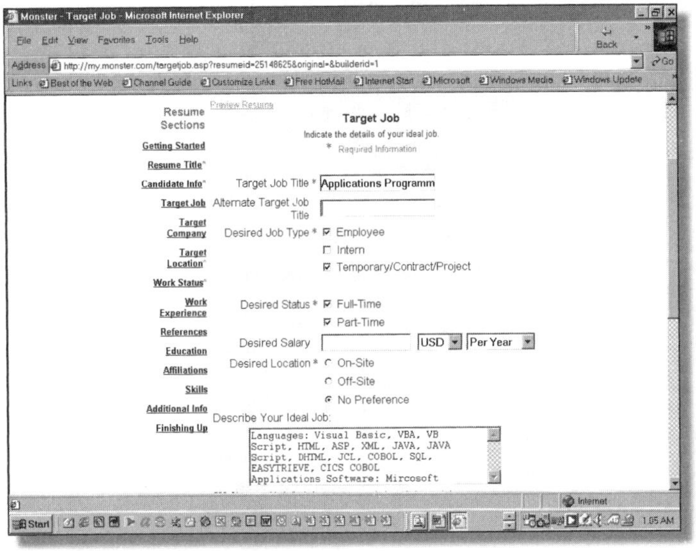

Fig. 4.4. Using the target job space

The "Objective" field holds up to 2,000 characters—that's half a résumé's worth of space for more of those valuable keywords! To follow the site's examples and list a two- or three-sentence objective would be a waste of this space. Instead Susan lists her professional profile, accomplishments, language, software, and systems expertise from her résumé. Understand that while answering these questions, you are really building your résumé again, so you must use plenty of keywords and highlight your past success stories. You will find a huge database of keywords in *Knock 'em Dead Resumes*.

The important point to remember is that you are not always limited to one answer—even in the case of check boxes. Always test the site to see if you can select more than one answer. Never assume you are limited—not even if the directions on the screen indicate that you are.

Susan was also asked about her salary requirements. We all dread this question, and as a pre-employment screening profile, nothing could be worse. But guess what? Although the salary question is sandwiched between "required" fields, it is not required. So Susan can, and should, leave it blank. In instances where you are forced to answer the question, use a salary range, not a single figure; I show you how to come up with an effective range in Chapter 20.

The last question on this screen asks Susan to describe her ideal job and allots her 500 characters with which to do it. Instead of answering the question, Susan uses this opportunity to add more keywords to her profile. Remember, the screener is searching and retrieving possible candidates from a list of keywords that they have put into the system. The more keywords that appear in your profile, the higher up on the list of matching résumés yours will appear—and the more likely it is to be read by a sentient human being. Write, "Job with opportunity to use: . . ." then follow this with a long list of relevant keywords.

When completing questions about relocation, don't jump to make a selection. Make sure you have to answer the question at all; and if you do, select the broadest option that you can. Even if you have the ability to list many preferred locations, don't. Instead, keep your response broad. Any company or recruiter only interested in local candidates will use the address on your résumé as the search parameter.

Although our user is madly in love with her fiancé and they both have family and friends in California, she should select "No preference." Here's the rule: You can always say "no," but you can't say "yes" unless you've been asked. For the right job, opportunity, and money, we would all move to Possum Trot, Kentucky. Besides, what isn't right for your career today may be tailor-made for a situation in the future. With your electronic career management database, you can store all these possibilities for future reference. Plus, any jobs you interview for but reject will only enhance your interviewing skills through experience.

The small print at the top of the page indicates that this screen is optional and may be skipped. Although the directions state that you can skip the entire page, they marked the "Company Category" field as "required" by using a red asterisk. Whenever completing online profiles and questionnaires, always read the small print.

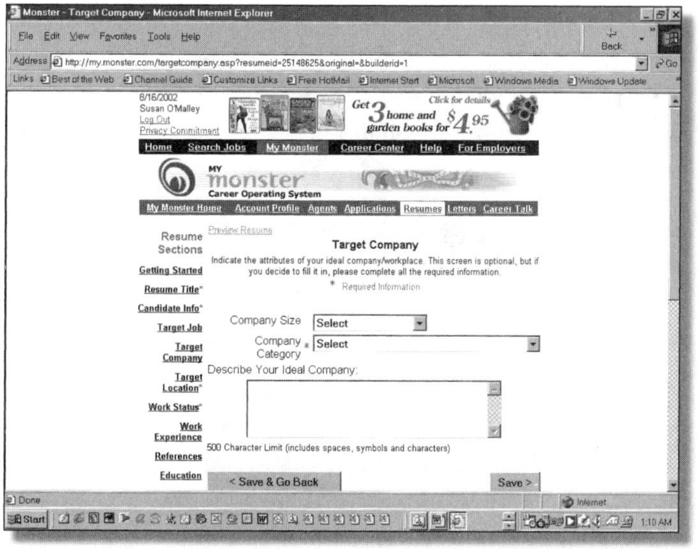

Fig. 4.5. Choosing a company

Another typical section on many questionnaires is about work experience. No doubt you will be given the opportunity and probably the instructions to list every job you've had in chronological order. Let's be clear on this issue. You are building your online résumé, not writing a chronological recitation of your work history.

Always use the work experience areas of questionnaires to put in illustrative stories about what you've done. Sometimes you are required to describe responsibilities. Detail your responsibilities and reporting relationships, then follow with accomplishments and keywords that apply within the context. You can test how much space is really available by pasting in blocks of dummy text and seeing how much the dialog box will accept.

Additionally, employers and recruiters are often looking for candidates who either are working for or have worked for certain companies or industry competitors. Take the time and space to list customers, partners, and companies you did business with. If you have sanitized your current employer, you can pop that information into this list. You are most likely to come across online questionnaires and profiles in these situations:

- Registering with a job site
- Posting a résumé to a job board
- Applying for a job with a company
- Registering with a recruitment firm

In each case, you must always consider who is asking you the question and why they are asking it. Each audience is trying to screen you in or out, so consider your responses carefully. Always read the screen instructions, avoid questions on salary and relocation if you can, and add as many keywords as possible.

These online questionnaires and profiles will affect your job search just as your résumé will. Treat this process with the respect it deserves—don't rush it. Make sure to proof and spell-check anything new that you compose, and only post to sites that will allow you to edit and update your material at any time.

Beyond the Monsters

The process of registering and loading your résumé will not be the same at every site you visit, but it will be similar. You should visit Monster, HotJobs, and Career-Builder and, having ascertained their suitability to your job search, register and post your résumé. However, as you will recall from earlier in the chapter, companies actually hire more people from smaller niche sites than they do from the big three. Seek out sites focused on your profession and geography. You can link automatically to all the sites from my Web site (*www.knockemdead.com*). Start with the resources I suggest, visit those sites, visit the sites they in turn are linked to, and, as you proceed, register (so that you can be sent notification of suitable jobs) and post your résumé on each one that seems relevant to your needs.

Make a folder on your career management database for each site, and as postings come in, store them in the appropriate folder. After a few weeks you will be able to see which sites are generating suitable openings and which you can drop.

With each site, I suggest you make your requirements broad to begin with. In some instances a particular site may inundate you with inappropriate jobs. When this happens, return to the site and redefine your needs more narrowly. On the other hand, you might not be getting enough responses from a particular site and might want to recast your needs in broader terms.

How to Approach Companies Directly

Companies now overwhelmingly prefer to have you approach them directly, and you can use the job sites you visit to identify companies in your area(s) of professional interest.

Go to any job site and search their posted openings by putting in minimal keywords and restrictions. For example, if a medical insurance sales manager goes to *www.6figurejobs.com* and does a simple keyword search for "insurance" she may get hundreds of results, and the vast majority will be for jobs that do not interest her. At the same time, those results will reveal recruiters and companies in her profession and target geography.

With the direct-research technique you can link directly to hundreds of employer Web sites. Visit these sites and see if they have suitable job openings posted there. Companies all use their sites as recruitment tools and usually have their open job requisitions posted there. When they do, you'll have additional information with which to customize your cover letter and résumé. Even if they do not appear to have an opening for someone like you, send them your résumé anyway. You don't really know what is going on at that company, and at the very least you will be in their database and therefore on their radar when a need arises.

Having visited the company Web site, add the link to the appropriate address book in your career management database. If you follow this procedure of identifying all profession-specific employers at all the job sites you visit, then visiting each of those employer Web sites and adding them to an address book, your hit list of potential employers will grow exponentially.

There are other Internet tools to help you find potential employers in your area. I went to Google and searched for "companies by industry and geography" and got a whole mess of resources. The first one I linked to was *www.searchbug.com*, a neat site that lets you find all kinds of things. I imagined for the moment that I was a dental assistant looking for a job in Little Rock, Arkansas. Working through the dialog boxes I keyed in "dental companies" and the town and state of my choice. It came back with over 600 companies!

Another useful site is *www.flipdog.com*, which finds job listings for you at company Web sites and with headhunters. At *www.superpages.com* you can search an industry category by city or company name. At *www.goleads.com* you can search a national database of companies by keyword, industry, geography, SIC code, or number of employees, and the results give you a contact name, which is always helpful. It costs $10 a month, but you can get a lot of mileage from a one-time thirty-day membership. The possibilities for making direct contact with suitable employers are endless.

Getting an Inside Track at Target Companies

This is where you can draw on those networks you've been building. You can use that association membership directory (and other networking resources) to get a personal introduction to the company—either a direct recommendation ("Hey, we should speak to this guy I know named Bill Hudson") or at least the name of someone you can call or to whom you can e-mail and mail your résumé.

Look in the membership directory for someone who works at the target company and call them. Your conversation, like those mentioned in our discussion of professional and personal networking, should run something like the following:

"Hi, Carole Mixon? This is Martin Yate. We haven't spoken before, but we are both members of the _____ association. Carole, I see that you work at Cybex Labs, and they currently have a job posted on the Web site for someone with my background. Could I ask you a couple of questions about the company?"

After a minute of conversation you can then ask for a name:

"Carole, rather than just send in my résumé blind, could you tell me the name of the person who this job reports to? I won't mention your name unless you want me to."

With a referral your résumé goes to a real person and not the database, again raising your visibility.

You can learn more about how to continue this conversation most productively by reviewing the networking conversations section on pages 50–57.

Getting the Scoop on Target Companies

If you want to do a little research on a particular company, perhaps to tweak your résumé, personalize your cover letter, or prepare for an interview, you can do this from your desktop too. Vault (*www.vault.com*) will tell you what past and current employees think about their employer, and WetFeet (*www.wetfeet.com*) will also give you great info about your target companies. Manufacturers' News, Inc. (*www.mniguide.com*) will give you information about almost half a million manufacturing companies. At Google's "News" link, you can search for press stories about the company. In the process the search engine spits out names of principals within the company, again giving you individuals to approach directly. An employer's own Web site is also a major source of information about the company and its management.

As your job search picks up steam, some employers will rise to the top as particularly desirable, and you will gradually build an information dossier on them. When you gather information about a company, create a company folder and paste the knowledge there; it will provide useful background information for interviews and show you have done your homework. This is flattering to the interviewer, who sees it as demonstrating effort and enthusiasm, both of which can end up being deciding factors in a tight job race.

All this effort has an obvious short-term value: it helps you land interviews and win job offers. It also has long-term value because you are building a personalized reference work of your industry/specialty/profession that will help you throughout your career.

I'd like to make a point about such "superdesirable" employers with a reference to the theater. I am sure you hear every year about the latest hit musical on Broadway, but I am not sure you realize these shows go through months of rehearsals, previews with selected audiences, and sometimes even road trips to try out the show in smaller, less important markets. They do this because they don't want to screw up when they hit the big time. The same applies to you. Most likely your résumé and interviewing skills (read: script and performance skills) are not up to speed at the very beginning of a job search. The last thing you need to do is fumble an opportunity to join the company of your dreams. It is better to hold off your approach until you know that your résumé is top-notch, you won't swallow your tongue in the first few minutes of an interview, and you've made a couple of inside contacts through professional networks.

Newspapers and Magazines

You can't spend your whole life sitting in front of the computer screen; it's bad for your health, and you'll miss important job leads by not integrating newspapers and magazines into your campaign.

Not all companies advertise on the Internet, and not all companies have Web sites. Especially for companies that rely on the local community for both customers and employees, the newspaper is still a major recruitment vehicle.

Virtually every newspaper has an employment edition each week, in addition to Sunday, when they have large selections of recruitment ads. Make sure you always get both these editions of the paper. Most companies still advertise in their local newspapers to ensure they are tapping into the local market and avoiding relocation costs whenever possible.

Your approach to mining the recruitment ads is similar to that used on Internet job sites. You will initially look for jobs relating specifically to your professional skill set, first focusing on those at your professional level, then looking at those above and below it. Following this you will look for other job titles that typically apply to your department or those that involve related functions; finally, you will look for ads from any employer in your line of work. You'll do this because employers don't always advertise exactly where you happen to be looking, and some don't advertise at all; they might use employment agencies or headhunters for that particular position. Finding jobs similar or related in function to yours tells you that there is hiring activity in your general area of expertise and that it might be prudent to throw your hat in the ring.

But cruising the want ads, however productive, is only part of your newspaper research. Read the business pages for both the advertisements and the articles. Regular display advertisements can lead you to employers you might not have considered before, and the editorial copy is full of opportunities:

- Always check out the promotions column. It will tell you about companies and give you the name of the person you can contact ("Congratulations on the promotion, Mr. Byrd. . . ."). Most important, if someone gets promoted or leaves one company for another, that leaves a job to be filled somewhere.
- The business news stories tell you about company success stories, new contracts signed, new products and services introduced, and companies coming to town.
- Industry overviews and market development pieces can tip you off to subtle shifts in your professional marketplace and thereby alert you to

opportunities—and provide you with the chance to customize your letters, calls, and résumé for specific targets.

- Business stories in city newspapers always quote local professionals. The person quoted might be someone in your field whom you can contact. Reminding that person of the article ("I saw you quoted in the *Argus* last week. . . .") is flattering and will get you a few minutes of that person's time to make a pitch, get an interview, or get some leads. (If you want to learn how to get yourself quoted in the press, examine the PR chapters in the companion e-book *Knock 'em Dead Communication* available at wowio .com, knockemdead.com and amazon.com.)

It is always a good idea to examine back issues of newspapers. These can provide a rich source of job vacancies unfilled from previous advertising efforts. I suggest working systematically through the want ads, going back twelve to eighteen months. While you obviously can't say you are responding to a position they advertised eighteen months ago, the odds are reasonable they could be looking for just such a person again, so do not refer to the advertisement in your call or cover letter.

Sound crazy? That's what a *Knock 'em Dead* reader said to me in a letter. He also said this technique landed him a $90,000-a-year job from a seven-month-old want ad. Sometimes the position was never filled and the employer despaired of getting someone through advertising. Sometimes the position was filled but the employee didn't work out. Perhaps they are only now starting to look for another person like the one they had advertised for earlier, or they might even be coming off a hiring freeze. Whatever the case, not every old ad you follow up on will result in an opening, but when one does, the odds can be short indeed. Smart money always goes on the short odds. You can pull the same results whenever Internet job sites have archives of old jobs you can access.

In addition to newspapers, keep an eye on the trade press: professional associations' periodicals, trade magazines, and the general business press. You can mine them all in a similar fashion. You will find a slew of articles written by industry professionals in these publications. Again, you can use these articles to find useful networking contacts and job leads. When contacting the author of an article, mention how much you agree with what was said, share a bit of your own information on the subject, or say something like, "It's about time someone told it like it is." Never say anything in the vein of, "Hey, the article is great but you missed. . . ." If an article mentions some special accomplishment of a particular person, you could send a copy of the article to that person with a note of congratulations and perhaps a copy of your résumé.

If you have ever tried your hand at writing, trade magazines offer a ready outlet for your efforts and can get you noticed by all kinds of people. You can also use your writing ability to create what are known as *special reports*, and use these in place of a résumé. I discuss this technique as a résumé alternative for the literary minded in *Knock 'em Dead Resumes*, and I discuss the nuts and bolts of business writing in *Knock 'em Dead Communication*.

It is a good idea to clip and keep all the articles that give you ideas. File them in some easily retrievable fashion, maybe pasted into a three-ring binder. That way, you will have the info where you can find and use it.

There are plenty of great job leads in newspapers and magazines, if you read them with a job search mindset. A good place to start online is at *www.newsdirectory.com*, which helps you identify and link to local and national publications in your area(s) of interest (they also have overseas press).

College Career Services

If you are in school, be sure to take advantage of this resource just as soon as you can, but remember the college placement office is not a substitute for your mother. It is not there to hold your hand or provide you with job offers. Career Services and their staffs are horrendously overworked, and they work hard merely to keep pace with the Herculean task of providing assistance to thousands.

Take the time to make yourself known here, and stress your willingness to listen to good advice. If you are then seen to act on that advice and come back for more, you will have earned the department's respect and will garner yourself extra attention and guidance. Treat your entire interaction with Career Services the same way you intend to treat the interview process. Make a real effort with your appearance and professional demeanor, and, of course, courtesy goes a long way.

The best way into corporate America is through internships and on-campus recruiters, who can recommend interns to the company as well as entry-level hires. Campus recruiters go to society and association meetings on campus all year long to see who is engaged, enthusiastic, and professional in their approach to life and career. When you take an active part in campus affairs, you will get to know many of these recruiters. If you are engaged with Career Services, they will usually know who is involved in which campus activities and why. You will also start to build a powerful network of peers for your whole career, because these are likely to be the most successful people in the professional world, as they are already engaged and committed. I know one campus recruiter for a major accounting firm who swears she has selected all her prime choices before the campus recruiting season even opens. How do such campus recruiters pick the winners from the also-rans? They all maintain very close working relationships with the Career Services office, so using this department as a first step in developing a sensible networking approach to your career will give you an inside track; most universities now also have a career services Web site with a database of both work-study and non-work-study jobs and internships.

Employment Services Organizations

These include state employment agencies, private employment agencies, contingency search and executive search, temporary help organizations, and career counselors.

People get very confused about who does what in this area and typically lump everyone under the term "headhunter." It can be frustrating if you confuse what each of these groups can do for you. So first, we'll clean up the definitions and terminology of the services that each group provides. Pay attention, because this is an area where there are few clear-cut lines of demarcation.

State employment agencies are staffed by government employees. Their job is to help you find a job; they are almost the only people whose focus is entirely on helping you. They are funded by the state labor department and typically carry names like State Division of Employment Security, State Job Service, or Manpower Services. The names vary but the services remain the same. They will make efforts to line you up with appropriate jobs and will mail résumés on your behalf to interested employers who have jobs listed with them. It is not mandatory for employers to list jobs with state agencies, but more and more companies are taking advantage of these free services. Once the bastion of minimum-wage jobs, these public agencies now list positions that can reach $100,000 a year or more, so they're a resource not to be ignored.

If you are moving across the state or across the country, your local employment office can plug you into the national job bank, or you can connect yourself online at *www.nationjob.com*, which can give you access to jobs all over the nation. This is the largest job bank in the world. They are not headhunters.

Temporary services companies also get their money from employers and are concerned with filling temporary assignments for those clients. They are not headhunters.

Private employment agencies are for profit, and their source of income comes either from the company (employer paid fee, or EPF), or from you (applicant paid fee, or APF). The first group always has the company's needs foremost in mind. They will search on behalf of employers, but typically only in their own databases, and they will market someone to employers only if that person is seen to be in high demand and can be used as a tool to develop other fee-paying assignments.

When working with an employment agency, choose your agent with the same care and attention with which you would choose a spouse or a lawyer. The caliber of the individual and company you choose could well affect the caliber of the company you ultimately join. Further, if you choose prudently, he or she can become a lifetime counselor who can guide you step by step up the ladder of success. They are not headhunters.

The other group in the APF category is by far the smaller of the two and is the only other resource that works entirely for you; it is also a grouping that does not have a particularly sterling reputation in the marketplace, based largely on incompetence and charlatan business practices. Almost any employment services company that asks you for money falls into this category, even when the company has plush carpets, caters to executives, and is part of a nationwide chain of offices. I urge you to steer clear of them. They are largely staffed by ex-executives who couldn't find themselves a job. They are not headhunters but may be after your scalp.

Career counselors and *job search counselors*, however, can be an exception. Their money comes from you, but while there are charlatans in the business, there are also exemplary, talented, and dedicated professionals in this group. Typically these people work alone or in very small companies, and they can help you with career choice, résumé preparation, job search, and interview preparation. How do you tell the difference between these and the disreputable APF crowd? Find out how many years they've been in business, what professional degrees they hold, their affiliations with professional associations, and their professional accreditations. Ideally, they should also have a background as contingency or retained recruiters. If you go to *www.knockemdead.com* you will find information on all the associations these people belong to, an explanation of the professional accreditations that matter, and a database of tenured, credentialed professionals in the field whom I know both professionally and personally. On the Web site I also recommend three organizations in this category, all of whose affiliates are tenured *and* credentialed, although some of these affiliates I do not know personally. They are not headhunters and would never tell you they were.

Contingency recruiters gain their income from employers and are largely involved with finding employed professionals for hard-to-fill positions. They do this on a contingency basis, the contingency being that they only collect a fee when they fill the position. Typically contingency recruiters will search their databases and actively recruit for a percentage of the openings they have to fill. Most contingency recruiters and some contingency firms will market an "in-demand" professional to target companies for a day or two and as a tool to develop other fee-paying assignments. Contingency recruiters are a hybrid, more professionally sophisticated than employment agency people but not working on a retainer basis. Some of these people can be called headhunters, some cannot.

Executive search firms are also employer paid. They are the only group entirely focused on the employer's needs, with absolutely no interest in you unless you fit an existing requirement. This is because they receive cash up front, more when a candidate/recruit is hired, and the final payment when that person starts work. They are almost exclusively interested in people currently successful in their jobs, not unemployed professionals looking for work.

These people rarely deal with salary levels under $100,000 per year. They are more interested in obtaining your résumé for their database than seeing you unless you match a specific job they are trying to fill for a client. They are more interested in the employed than in the unemployed, because an employed person is less of a risk (they often guarantee their finds to the employer for up to a year) and is a more desirable commodity. Executive recruiters are there to serve the client, not to find you a job. They neither want nor expect you to rely on them for employment counseling, unless they specifically request that you do so—in which case you should listen closely. These people are where the term *headhunter* originated.

The term *headhunter* is now applied to anyone who provides employment services, but in reality it only fits executive search consultants and a few contingency recruiters. A headhunter will have little interest in you unless you match an existing assignment.

Who to Work with, and How to Work with Them

What type of employment services company is best for you? Well, the answer is simple: the one that will get you the right job offer. The problem is, there are thousands of companies in each of these broad categories. How do you choose between the good, the bad, and the ugly?

Fortunately this is not as difficult as it sounds. A retained executive search firm is not necessarily better or more professional than a contingency search firm, which in turn is not necessarily better or more professional than a regular (EPF) employment agency. Each has its exemplary practitioners and its charlatans. Your goal is to avoid the charlatans and get representation by an exemplary outfit. Make the choice carefully, and, having made the choice, stick with it and listen to the advice you are given.

A company's involvement in professional associations is always a good sign. It demonstrates commitment and, through its use of extensive professional training programs, an enhanced level of competence. In the employment services industry, the high-end employment agencies and contingency search firms—as well as some retained search firms—belong to the National Association of Personnel Services (NAPS), the premier professional organization with state associations in all fifty states. The Association for Executive Search Consultants (AESC) is the premier organization for the retained executive search firms. Career Management Institute (CMI) is the leading association for job search and career management counselors, and NATS (National Association of Temporary Services) is the leading association for temp firms.

Involvement in independent or franchise networks of firms can also be a powerful plus for a job search. For example, an independent headhunter network like NPA (*www.npaworldwide.com*) has hundreds of member firms around the world. Membership in one of the leading franchise groups, such as Management Recruiters, Robert Half, or Dunhill likewise gives you access to a coordinated network of employment services professionals. These networks also have extensive training programs that assure a high-caliber consultant. Franchise offices can be especially helpful if relocation is in your future, as they tend to have powerful symbiotic relationships with other network members; in fact, this is often a primary reason for their being a member of that particular franchise or network. Members of the independent and franchise networks might also belong to the larger professional associations.

It is prudent to ask whether your contact has any additional accreditations. Most of the national professional associations have training programs that require accreditation, so possession of these is another sign that the agent is a committed and connected member of his or her profession. The most widely recognized of all these is the CPC designation. CPC (or its international equivalent, CIPC) stands for certified personnel consultant. The CPC and CIPC designations are recognized as a standard of excellence and commitment only achieved after rigorous training and study. You can find a comprehensive database of employment industry accreditation acronyms and their meanings at *www.knockemdead.com.*

CIPC designation requires that the holder has already achieved CPC designation, and it requires adherence to an international code of ethics as designated by the International Personnel Association (IPA).

Although certification can be applied for after two years of experience in the personnel consulting business, the studying involved usually means that even the newest holders of a CPC have five years of experience, while your average CPC probably has seven to ten years of experience and contacts with top-notch employers under his or her belt.

Qualified CPCs (like holders of the other accreditations) can also be relied upon to have superior knowledge of the legalities and ethics of the recruitment and hiring process, along with the expertise and tricks of the trade that only come from years of hands-on experience. All of this can be put to work on your behalf.

It makes good sense to have a friend in the business with an ear to the ground as you continue your upward climb. If you want my best advice: Find an NAPS member in good standing with CPC designation and listen to what she tells you, and if she has other accreditations, so much the better. You will find a listing of other relevant professional accreditations at *www.knockemdead.com.*

Finally, don't get intimidated. You are not obligated to sign anything, nor are you obligated to guarantee anyone that you will remain in any employment for any specific length of time.

It Finally Comes Down to the Individual

You can develop mutually beneficial relationships with employment professionals in all these categories; after all, their entire livelihood depends on their contacts—that is, the people they know in the professional world. Look at how many years of experience they have in employment services and how well they understand your profession. Look for involvement with their professional community and professional accreditations.

If a recruiter is interested in representing you, expect a detailed analysis of your background and prepare to be honest. Do not overstate your job duties, accomplishments, or education. If there are employment gaps, explain them. Be circumspect, because an unethical headhunter can create further competition for you when you share information about companies you are talking to. The details of your communications with a company are nobody's business but your own. If they ask who you are talking with, say your job search is confidential and you'd like to know whom they plan to speak with, in which case you will happily tell them if you are already in communication with that company.

Find out first what the recruiter expects of you in the relationship and explain what you expect. Reach commitments you both can live with, and stick with them. If you break those commitments, expect the representation to cease, as recruiters are far more interested in long-term relationships than passing nuisances. Keep the recruiter informed about all changes in your status: salary increases, promotions, layoffs, or other offers of employment.

Don't consider yourself an employment expert. You get a job for yourself every three or four years. These people do it for a living. Ask for their objective input and seek their advice in developing interviewing strategies with their clients.

Temporary Services Companies

Temp companies are a different kettle of fish. There are temporary help companies that provide employment services to companies in all industries and at most professional levels, from unskilled and semiskilled labor (referred to as *light industrial* in the trade) to administration, finance, technical, sales, and marketing professionals, as well as doctors, lawyers, and even interim executives up to CEOs.

Temporary help services can be a useful resource if you are unemployed. You can get temporary assignments, maintain continuity of employment and skills, and perhaps enhance your marketability in the process. If you are changing careers or returning to work after an absence, temporary assignments can help get new or rusty skills up to speed and provide you with a current work history in your field.

If you are unemployed and need the cash flow for bills, working with a temp company can supply that and expose you to employers in the community who, if you really shine, could ask you to join the staff full-time. This "temp-to-perm" hiring approach is increasingly popular with companies hiring at all levels, as it allows them to try before they buy. When "temping," you will also expand your networking contacts.

Here is some advice for working successfully with a temporary help company:

- Investigate the turnover of the temporary staff. If other temporaries have stayed with the company long-term, chances are that company does a good job and has good clients.
- Determine whether they are members of the National Association of Temporary and Staffing Services (NATSS).

- Select a handful of firms that work in your field; this will increase the odds of suitable assignments appearing quickly.
- Define the titles and the employment levels they represent, along with geographical areas they cover.
- Do not overstate your job duties, accomplishments, or education.
- Find out first what the temporary help professional expects of you in the relationship, then explain what you expect. Reach commitments you both can live with, and stick with them.
- Judge the assignments not solely on the paycheck (although that can be important), but also on the long-term benefits to your job search and career.
- Keep the temporary help counselor informed about any and all changes in your status, such as offers of employment or acquisition of new skills.
- Resolve key issues ahead of time. Should an employer want to take you on full-time, will that employer have to pay a set amount, or will you just stay on as a temporary for a specific period and then go on the employer's payroll?

Job Fairs

Job fairs (occasionally called career days) are occasions where actively hiring companies get together, usually under the auspices of a job fair promoter or local newspaper, to attract large numbers of potential employees to a one-day-only event.

Job fairs aren't regular events, even in metropolitan areas, so they won't take much of your time, but you should become an active participant when they do occur. They are always advertised in the local newspapers and frequently on the radio, so if you stay keyed in to the local news scene as part of keeping your job search antennae tuned you'll hear about them. Job fairs typically charge a small entrance fee, in return for which you get direct access to all the employers and formal presentations by company representatives and local employment experts. When you organize yourself properly, take the right attitude, and work all the opportunities, job fairs make for a great job searching opportunity.

When you attend job fairs, go prepared with:

- Proper business attire. You may be meeting your new boss, and you don't want the first impression to be less than professional.

- Business cards. If you are already employed, remember to request the courtesy of confidentiality in calls to the workplace.
- Résumés. You should take as many copies of your résumé as there are exhibitors, times two. You'll need one to leave at the exhibit booth and an additional copy for anyone you have a meaningful conversation with.
- Notepad and pen. Preferably, tuck them into a folder.

Job fairs are an opportunity for networking with other job hunters as well. If you know other people going to a job fair (perhaps you are a member of a job search support group), you should go with a collaborative effort in mind. You may be in different professions, but if you all make the effort to speak to other attendees and to collect business cards from other attendees regardless of their profession, you can help one another find more leads.

If you are attending solo, still make the effort to network with other attendees. Ask them to meet you later in the day to exchange leads that might be mutually beneficial. I have witnessed this in action at job fairs and seen a group of twenty who were total strangers in the morning happily exchanging handfuls of business cards at the end of the day.

It's easy to walk into a job fair and be drawn like a moth to the biggest and most attractive booths, sponsored by the largest and most established companies, and ignore the lesser ones. Remember that the majority of the jobs in America are generated by companies with less than 500 employees. You should visit every booth, not just the ones with the flashing lights and all the moths fluttering around. Also go with specific objectives in mind:

- Talk to someone at every booth. You can walk up and ask questions about the company activities, and who they are looking for, before you talk about yourself. This allows you to present yourself in the most relevant light.
- Collect business cards from everyone you speak to so you can follow up with a letter and a call when they are not so harried. Very few people actually get hired at job fairs; for most companies the exercise is one of collecting résumés so that meaningful meetings can take place in the ensuing days and weeks; nevertheless, you should be "on" at all times, because serious interviews do sometimes occur on the spot.

If you have a background and résumé that matches you for a specific opportunity, make your pitch. If, on the other hand, there's a job you can do but your résumé needs some adaptation to better position your candidacy, take a different approach. By all means pitch the company representative, but don't hand over a résumé that will detract from your candidacy (you can come up with a harmless pretext, such as having run out of copies). Instead, get the contact's business card and promise to follow up with a résumé, which you can then custom fit to the opportunity.

- Collect company brochures and collateral materials.
- Arrange times and dates to follow up with as many employers as possible: "Ms. Jones, I realize you are very busy today, and I would like to speak to you further. Your company sounds very exciting. I would like to set up a time when we could meet to talk further or perhaps set a time to call you in the next few days."

In addition to the exhibit hall, there are probably formal group presentations by employers. As all speakers love feedback, move in when the crush of presenter groupies has died down; you'll get more time and closer attention. You will also have additional knowledge of the company and the chance to spend a few minutes customizing the emphasis of your skills to meet the stated needs and interests of the employer in question.

Job fairs provide the best opportunities for administrative, professional, and technical people and those in the middle-management ranks. However, this doesn't mean the senior executive should feel such an event is a waste of time. Employers don't attend job fairs to attract senior executives, but it doesn't mean you can't gather information, collect cards, and generate leads.

On leaving each booth, and at the end of the day, go through your notes while everything is still fresh in your mind. Review each company and what possibilities it may hold for you. Then review what you have learned about the companies relevant to your profession to see what you might glean about industry trends, new skill requirements, marketplace shifts, and long-term staffing needs. Plan to send e-mails and make follow-up calls within the week to everyone with whom you spoke.

For more information you can go to Google and type in "job fairs."

Web-Based Résumés, e–Résumés, and Web Portfolios

Almost all job search activities take time and effort on your part, so when the opportunity comes along to utilize passive marketing, you should seize it. Here are passive marketing approaches to increase your professional visibility and credibility:

1. Keep your résumé posted and refreshed on a selection of job sites. Throughout a job search you need to keep your résumé visible on the job banks with which you have signed up. This sometimes takes a little maintenance, as typically job sites like to purge their résumé databases every ninety or 120 days so that their paying corporate customers will feel they are paying for fresh candidates. When you sign up at a particular site, make a note of their policy for purging their résumé databases, mark the "kill" date in your calendar, and go in a few days before and refresh everything.

   As almost all job sites use push technology as a means to tell you when openings matching your needs are posted, you can go to the site as needed during your job search, and maybe once a month while employed, to harvest the matching jobs and store them in your career management database.

2. Join social online Internetworking groups like Ryze and LinkedIn, and use your slightly adapted résumé as part of your profile.

3. Create Web portfolios and Web-based résumés. For some time now, artists and designers have been creating online portfolios for their work as a cost-effective marketing device. Now that the Internet has become ubiquitous, it is practical for you to establish an online presence as a career management tool. You can build what is variously called an e-résumé, a Web folio, or a Web portfolio for yourself, or have it built for you, costing anywhere from $40 up to $3,000.

Think of your Web résumé as a miniature Web site, and realize that establishing an online presence with one is a really useful passive marketing tool (once it is up and visible you are pretty much done), which gives you a marketing presence all the time. In the process it also extends your professional visibility and credibility in a couple of other ways:

- It can help in your current job search and during your tenure on the next job, as the responses it generates will extend your professional network, help you keep an eye on the marketplace, and identify new employers who could be interested in your services.
- Increasingly, professionals are doing Google searches on people before meeting them (23 percent, according to a Harris interactive poll), and a well-put-together Web résumé will enhance other people's perception of you before those initial meetings.

Better than a paper-based résumé, a Web résumé allows you to provide a multimedia proof of your achievements and strengths. With a traditional résumé, you have a page or two of text. With an e-mailable résumé, you have pretty much the same thing, but all too frequently you must cut and paste it into résumé templates on job sites like HotJobs or CareerBuilder—thereby destroying much of the impact of your work. With a Web-based résumé on its own site, you have the opportunity to expand beyond the immediate page, offering access to examples and supporting documents in other media.

For example, if you say that you have strong presentation skills, you can include a video or audio clip of a presentation; if you claim to be an authority in experiential marketing, you can feature the kinds of brand experiences you've created for your clients. Including articles, a list of awards, graphics, audio and video clips, blogs, and photos on your site are just some of the options you have to make your multimedia case. Prospective employers, headhunters, clients, and colleagues will get a far more comprehensive picture of the professional you, and because your e-résumé or Web portfolio looks so much better, its very existence speaks of a technologically adapted professional.

Marketing is about focus. Too many amateurish sites are not only ill-thought out, which reflects poorly on the creators, but also include a risky mix of personal information: religion, politics, lifestyle, and family photos along with the career-related content. The personal and professional you are separate entities, and it is best to keep them that way.

GETTING THE
WORD OUT

YOU HAVE TO get the word out and make contact with employers to land job interviews, and you make the most contacts in the shortest time when you make them simultaneously with e-mail, mail, and the telephone.

MAKING CONTACT

TO LAND THAT all-important first interview, you've got to be able to recognize the "buy signals" and make your way past the objections that can keep you from being considered for a job for which you might just be perfect.

While you are identifying opportunities with all the techniques we have just discussed, you need to make contact and pitch your candidacy. There are two commonsense approaches: pick up the phone and make a marketing call; or write, including a cover letter and résumé, and send it through e-mail or traditional mail, and often through both.

E-mail and mail are likely to be more appealing because there is less likelihood of direct rejection, yet at the same time you know that interviews don't get scheduled without telephone conversations—so you have to make calls, too.

In fact, you should make as many phone calls as you send letters and e-mails. As your job search picks up speed, you will see that both approaches are necessary steps in the same process. When you send out e-mails, letters, and résumés, you must follow up with phone calls, and when you make marketing calls (calling employers directly to present your credentials), you will often find yourself following up with e-mailed letters and résumés. Your plan of attack needs to maintain a delicate balance between the two approaches so your calls force you to follow up in writing, and your résumés and letters force you to follow up with phone calls. At the same time, circumstances will arise while networking that demand you switch from a networking presentation into a full marketing pitch, which as we noted earlier is a different type of conversation.

A balanced approach that uses phone calls, e-mail, and mail will generate the most interviews. When you have identified names of people to talk to within companies, it's common sense to start with a conversation; yet, there will be times, especially at the very start of your job search, when you are still developing your contacts.

With this in mind, first we are going to address launching the e-mail and traditional mail part of your job search campaign. Not because it is a more productive approach—it isn't—but because with e-mail you can get the word out without benefit of names to contact. If necessary, you can start things happening right now, in a town 1,000 miles away, by sending your résumé with the click of a button. At the same time it will help you get a career management database up and running on your desktop so that you never lose track of contacts once you've made them. This is not to say you won't be making networking calls and marketing presentations by phone whenever you have the opportunity. We are just going to talk about the e-mail/mail aspect of things first.

E-Mail and Letters

Must you send out hundreds or even thousands of e-mails and letters in the coming weeks? Yes and no. You should mail as much as you need and no more. Only if you approach and establish communication with every possible employer will you create the maximum opportunity for yourself. Two contacts a week is the behavior of the long-term unemployed.

On the other hand, I am not recommending that you immediately make up a list of 700 companies and contact them today. That isn't the answer either. Your campaign needs strategy, and without follow-up calls many of your letters will get lost in the shuffle, while a quick phone conversation could well get you an interview. Every job search campaign is unique; nevertheless, you should maintain a balance between the *number* of written pitches you send out on a weekly basis and the *types of people to whom they are sent*. Start off with balanced mailings and your phone contacts will maintain equilibrium, too.

The key is to send out balanced mailings representing all the different types of leads, and to send them out regularly and in a volume that will allow you to make follow-up calls. Many headhunters manage their time so well that they average over fifty calls per day, year in and year out. While you may aim at building up your call volume to this enviable number, I recommend that you start out with more modest goals. Send five to ten contacts per day spread across the following areas:

- In response to Internet job postings
- In response to newspaper advertisements
- To contacts in any of your professional networks
- To contacts in any of your personal networks
- To companies and contacts you identify from Internet, reference works, newspapers, and trade journal research
- To headhunters
- To job fair contacts

When you apply these approaches, you will discover that there are thousands of contacts waiting to be made, so this breakdown of contacts becomes a daily quota. If it seems a bit steep to begin with, scale down the numbers until they are achievable and gradually build up the volume. But remember—the lower your volume, the longer your job search. If you run your e-mail activities while you are on the Internet Resources page at *www.knockemdead.com*, you can link automatically to the sites of your choice in all these categories and many more.

Do you need to write more than one letter? Almost certainly. I have already made the case for having letters and résumés in more than one format, and there is no need to waste precious time crafting your written communication entirely from scratch. You can use the templates in *Knock 'em Dead Resumes* and *Knock 'em Dead Cover Letters*, where you will also find more information on creating and managing an effective direct-mail/e-mail campaign. The key is to do each variation once and to do it right, so make sure to save copies of your letters and résumés in separate subfolders within the career management database folder labeled "Communication Essentials."

Multiple Submissions

While you might start off making single submissions to companies, you will sometimes find it valuable to make a number of contacts within a given company, especially the larger ones, to assure all the important players know of your existence. Let's say you are a young engineer who wants to work for Last Chance Electronics. If you haven't been able to get a personal introduction through applying all the networking and direct-research approaches (unlikely but possible), it is well within the bounds of reason to mail or e-mail cover letters and accompanying résumés to any, or all, of the following people (each ideally addressed to someone by name, so your pitch has less likelihood of being lost): the company president, the vice president of engineering, the chief engineer, the engineering manager, the vice president of human resources, the technical recruitment manager, and the technical recruiter. Find names on the company Web site, in membership databases of all your formal professional networks, and in professional directories.

Keep a log of your mail and e-mail contacts so you will know when to follow up with a phone call—usually between two and seven working days after the intial contact; exclude Monday mornings from this count, as everyone is either in meetings or getting up to speed for the week.

Keep track of these contacts beyond the initial follow-up period. Résumés do get misplaced, and employment needs change. You can comfortably resend mail to everyone on your list every couple of months if necessary. Most recipients won't register that they heard from you two months ago, and of those who do, most won't take offense. Any who do are people who have no need for your professional skill set and whom you are therefore unlikely to run into anytime soon.

A professionally organized and conducted campaign will proceed on two fronts:

Front One: A carefully targeted approach to a select group of companies. You first identified these "superdesirable" places to work when you researched your long list of potential employers. You will continue to add to this primary target list as you unearth fresh opportunities in your day-to-day research efforts. While this may be your primary target list, at the beginning of the job search you are building both it and contacts within the company, so you may not be e-mailing to these companies initially. You will wait until you are comfortable with your developing skills—at least until you have finished reading the interview sections of this book.

Front Two: A carpet-bombing approach to every possible employer in your target area. After all, you won't know what opportunities exist unless you go find out, and you need to start generating activity.

Here you begin with an e-mail/mailing to one or two contacts within the company, then repeat the mailings to other contacts when your initial follow-up calls result in referrals or dead ends. Remember, just because Harry in engineering says there are no openings in the company doesn't make it so. Besides, any one of the additional contacts you make could well be the person *who knows the person* who is anxious to meet you.

Once your campaign is in motion and you start to receive responses to your mailings and begin to schedule interviews from your calls (how to make the calls is covered in the next chapter), your emphasis will change. Those contacts and interviews will require follow-up letters and conversation, and you will be spending time preparing for the interviews.

This is the point at which most job searches stall. We get so excited about the interview activity that we convince ourselves "this will be the offer." Experienced headhunters know that, thanks to Murphy's Law, the offer that can't fail usually does fail. The offer doesn't materialize, and we are left sitting with no interview activity. You have to keep that job search pump primed with ongoing activity to generate an ongoing flow of interviews, because you never know which one is going to generate the ideal opportunity.

The more contacts you make through mailings, the more follow-up calls you can make to schedule interviews. The more interviews you get, the more proficient you will become at them. The better you get at interviewing, the more offers you will get—and the *more* offers you get, the more choices you will have when making your decision.

Internet Résumé Distribution and Employment Services

I am not a big fan of résumé blasters (these sites will blast your résumé to thousands of companies for a fee, but the response odds aren't that good). However, when it comes to blasting your résumé to headhunters and their brethren, you should consider this option. On a site called *www.résumémachine.com*, you can target your résumé to suitable headhunters. This could be a timesaver, because there are so many recruiters, and each one represents a multitude of employers. This means that more companies will see your résumé with less effort on your part; and the résumés do get read. A cheaper option might be to do Google searches for relevant headhunters, such as "technology recruiters" and then to respond directly to them yourself; with this type of Google search you can fruitfully drill down and down until you find the level most responsive to you.

Direct-Marketing Calls

You must be clear in your mind that at the same time you are e-mailing and mailing résumés, you will pick up the phone and call people. This is the single most effective way of generating job interviews. I don't want you to think that you can execute a job search with just a mail and e-mail campaign; many people deceive themselves into thinking this is possible because they are terrified of picking up the phone to call strangers.

We have already talked about making networking presentations in person and networking calls over the telephone. Those discussions, however, focused on talking to peers, and getting leads on job opportunities and the names of hiring managers to contact. There is a difference between a networking call to a peer and a marketing call presenting the professional you to a potential employer. With your networking calls, getting leads on possible job openings and referrals or introductions to hiring managers were your primary objectives. With marketing calls, you directly target managers with the authority to hire. As those leads on managers, directors, and vice presidents begin to pile up, the time comes to make contact and introduce the professional you.

I'm going to show you how to build simple, sophisticated, and productive marketing presentations; how to navigate the ensuing conversations, recognizing and responding to the "buy signals" that denote interest; and how best to overcome objections to your candidacy.

Many years ago, in a past professional incarnation as a headhunter, I spent every day on the telephone talking to strangers. Even though I was quite good at it, I was also terrified at the prospect. You, too, might be a little nervous when confronted with the same challenge. One piece of advice helped me in my hour of abject terror: I was told I would never meet these people unless they were interested in what I had to offer, in which case they'd be happy I called. Also, because I was on the phone, no one would know who I was or how scared I looked. The other thing that helped was learning how to make almost every call successful, and as outrageous as that sounds, it can easily be done.

Most job hunters have but a single goal when they pick up the phone: "Get an interview." Naturally, this approach offers only one chance of success, but many more for failure accompanied by feelings of inadequacy and depression. You will multiply your marketing-call success rate when you have a multiple-goal strategy in place. When headhunters make marketing calls, for example, they typically have these five basic goals in mind to maximize the impact of every call they make:

- I will arrange an interview date and time.
- If my contact is busy, I will arrange another time to talk.
- I will develop leads on promising job openings elsewhere in this and other companies.
- I will leave the door open to talk with this person again in the future.
- I will send a résumé for subsequent follow-up.

Try to keep these commonsense goals in mind every time you talk with someone during your job search, because every conversation holds the potential for turning into an interview or leading you toward one that will generate first a phone interview then a face-to-face meeting. In the following sections you will learn to:

- Develop a concise word picture of your professional strengths.
- Be prepared for a telephone interview every time you pick up the phone.
- Recognize "buy signals" and objections as they crop up in your conversations, and learn how to turn them into interviews.
- Turn apparent dead-end conversations into live leads for interviews.

As you still may feel that making marketing calls is intimidating, let's take the sting out of them with an examination of their essential building blocks: what to say and how to say it.

The reason you might worry about calling people directly is that you are concerned they will be annoyed at the intrusion. This is a misconception. Remember, the first job of any manager is to get work done through others, so every smart manager is always on the lookout for talent. With a presentation that comes in at well under a minute, you can't be construed as wasting anybody's time. If that isn't enough to allay your fears, keep in mind that the person on the other end of the line has more than likely been in your position and is sensitive to how you feel.

Paint a Word Picture

The trick to turning marketing calls into interviews is to paint a convincing word picture of yourself. The marketing presentation you build should be short, to the point, and "specifically vague"—specific enough to make the listener prick up his or her ears with interest, and at the same time vague enough to encourage the questions that will kick-start the conversation.

Your aim is to paint a representation of your skills in broad strokes with examples of achievements that all managers like to hear. Brevity is required to avoid giving irrelevant or inappropriate information that might rule you out of consideration.

Your presentation should possess four characteristics to be successful, best remembered by an acronym from the advertising world: *AIDA*. You can apply this to your job search calls, and you can also use it at work when you have to present new ideas to colleagues or customers.

A—You must get the listener's **A**ttention.
I—You must generate **I**nterest.
D—You must create a **D**esire to know more.
A—You must encourage the employer to take **A**ction.

When you apply the concepts of AIDA to creating and making a marketing presentation, you will get attention. The interest you generate will be displayed by a desire to know more, so you'll hear questions like, "How much are you making?" "Do you have a degree?" "How much experience do you have?" By giving the appropriate answers to these and other questions (covered shortly), you can then parlay that desire into an interview.

The types of questions you are asked also enable you to identify the company's specific needs, and, once they are identified, you can customize any ongoing conversation toward those needs.

Here are the steps in building a marketing presentation. Notice the brevity as you read; this marketing pitch can be made in well under a minute.

Step #1

Your first step is to give the employer a snapshot of who you are and what you do; the intent is to give that person a reason to stay on the phone. You may sometimes have an introduction from a colleague, in which case you will build a bridge with that:

"Miss Shepburn? Good morning, my name is Martin Yate, and our mutual friend Greg Spencer suggested I call. . . ."

Or you may have gotten the name and contact information from, for example, a professional association directory, in which case you will use that as a bridge:

"Miss Shepburn? My name is Martin Yate. We haven't spoken before, but as we are both members of the _____ association, I hoped I might get a couple of minutes of your time for some advice. . . ."

Otherwise your introduction will cut right to the chase with a generalized job title (this increases the opportunity for positive response) and a brief description of your duties and problem-solving/bottom-line orientation.

Say enough about yourself to whet the listener's appetite and ignite a desire to know more. This is where the concept of the "specifically vague" comes in; so, for example, you might initially describe yourself as experienced, rather than identifying a specific number of years in your field. This encourages the listener to qualify your statement with a question: "How much experience do you have?" If you describe yourself right off as having four years experience, and the company is looking for seven, you are likely to be ruled out as underqualified before you are even aware that the company is hiring for a job that you have been doing in your sleep for the last two years. Therefore, never specify exact experience or list all your accomplishments during the initial presentation; your aim is just to open a dialogue:

"Good morning, Mr. O'Shea. My name is Cindy Steinmetz. I am an experienced office equipment salesperson with a track record selling to corporations, institutions, and small businesses. . . ."

By the way, if you want to ask the person on the other end of the line if he or she is free to talk, always ask, "Have I caught you at a good time?" Never ask if you have caught someone at a bad time; you are offering your contact an excuse to say they are busy. On the other hand, asking whether you have caught someone at a good time will usually get you a positive response; then you can go into the rest of your presentation. If at any point your contact says or implies that she is harried, immediately ask when would be a good time to call back.

Step #2

This is where you color in your word picture. Pull out a couple of items from your résumé asset-building exercises earlier in the book and follow your introductory sentence with a small selection. Keep them brief and to the point, without embellishments.

"As the number-three salesperson in my company, I increased sales in my territory 15 percent, to over $1 million. In the last six months, I won three major accounts from my competitors—a hospital, a bank, and a technology start-up."

Step #3

You have made the company representative want to know more about you, so now you "ask for the sale," stating the reason for your call and requesting to meet.

"The reason I'm calling, Mr. Grant, is that I'm looking for a new challenge, and as I know and respect your product line, I felt we might have some areas of common interest. Are these the types of skills and accomplishments you look for in your sales associates?"

Notice that your presentation is constructed to finish with a nonthreatening question (you aren't asking, "can you hire me?" instead you are looking for agreement about the desirability of your skills) that encourages a positive response, and also that the entire pitch can be spoken aloud in a conversational tone in well under a minute.

You should never make marketing calls without taking the time to construct a written presentation, because the self-analysis process involved makes you capture the essence of the "professional you." Read your pitch word for word the first few times, until you have the meat of it by heart, then keep it to hand as a safety net. Remember, though, that writing for the spoken word is very different from writing for the written word; it is less formal in grammar and syntax and more casually structured. When you have written it out, speak it aloud a few times to make it sound conversational and relaxed.

Knowing what you are going to say and what you wish to achieve—in other words, having a clear strategy—is the best way to generate multiple interviews and multiple job offers. When your presentation is prepared and polished, practice with a friend or spouse, or use a tape recorder or recording capabilities on your computer to critique yourself.

Once you have made a marketing presentation over the telephone, there will likely be a silence on the other end of the line. Be patient, as the employer may need a few seconds to digest your words. When the employer does respond, it will either be with a question, denoting interest (a "buy signal"), or with an objection.

Questions and Buy Signals

When the silence is broken by a question, you breathe a sigh of relief because any question denotes interest and is a buy signal. The employer can ask questions that show interest: "Do you have a degree?" "Have you done this kind of work?" "Have you done that kind of work?" Because any question denotes interest, every question is considered a buy signal.

Now, conversation is a two-way street, and you are most likely to win an interview when you take responsibility for your half. Just as the employer's questions show interest in you, your questions should show your interest in the work done at the company. By asking questions of your own in the normal course of conversation—questions usually tagged on to the end of one of your answers—you will forward the conversation. Also, such questions help you find out what particular skills and qualities are important to the employer. Inquisitiveness will increase your knowledge of the opportunity at hand, and that knowledge will give you the power to arrange an interview. If you leave all the interrogation to the employer, it will place you on the defensive, and at the end of the talk, you will be as ignorant of the real parameters of the job as you were at the start. As a result, the employer will know less about you than you might want.

Apply the techniques of giving a short reasonable answer, and of finishing your reply with a question to carry your call forward. In answer to your questions, the interviewer will explain the job's specifics, and as that happens, you will present your relevant skills and experiences; by asking questions of your own, you move the conversation toward an interview.

Joan Jones: "Good morning, Mr. Grant. My name is Joan Jones. I am an office equipment salesperson experienced in selling to corporations, institutions, and small business. As the number-three salesperson in my company, I increased sales in my territory 15 percent, to over $1 million. In the last six months, I won three major accounts from my competitors.

"The reason I'm calling, Mr. Grant, is that I'm looking for a new challenge, and as I know and respect your product line, I felt we might have areas for discussion. Are these the types of skills and accomplishments you look for in your staff?"

[Pause]

Mr. Grant: "Yes, they are. What type of equipment have you been selling?" *[Buy signal!]*

Joan Jones: "My company carries a comprehensive range from furniture through office machines and supplies; I sell according to my customers' needs. I have been noticing a considerable interest in— — — recently. Has that been your experience?"

Grant: "Yes, I have actually." *[Useful information for you.]* "Do you have a degree?" *[Buy signal!]*

Joan Jones: "Yes, I do." *[Just enough information to keep the company representative chasing you.]* "I understand your company prefers degreed salespeople to deal with its more sophisticated clients." *[Your research is paying off.]*

Grant: "Our customer base is very sophisticated, and they expect a certain professionalism and competence from us." *[An inkling of the kind of person the company wants to hire.]* "How much experience do you have?" *[Buy signal!]*

Joan Jones: "Well, I've worked in both operations and sales, so I understand both the sales and fulfillment processes." *[General but thorough.]* "How many years of experience are you looking for?" *[Turning it around, but furthering the conversation.]*

Grant: "Ideally, four or five for the position I have in mind." *[More good information.]* "How many do you have?" *[Buy signal!]*

Joan Jones: "I have two with this company, and one and a half before that, so I fit right in with your needs, don't you agree?" *[How can Mr. Grant say "no" to Ms. Jones?]*

Grant: "Uh-huh . . . What's your territory?" *[Buy signal!]*

Joan Jones: "I cover the metropolitan area. Mr. Grant, it sounds as if we might have something to talk about." *[Remember, your first goal is the face-to-face interview.]* "I am planning to take personal time off next Thursday or Friday. Can we meet then?" *[Make Mr. Grant decide which day he can see you, rather than whether he will see you at all.]* "Which would be best for you?"

Grant: "How about Friday morning? Can you bring a résumé?"

Your conversation should proceed with this kind of give-and-take. Your questions show interest, carry the conversation forward, and teach you more about the company's needs. By the end of the conversation you have an interview arranged and several key areas to promote when you arrive:

- The company sees growth in a particular area, so be sure you research where they stand in this area.
- They want both professional and personal sophistication.
- They ideally want four or five years' experience.
- They are interested in your metropolitan contacts.

The previous scenario was a simple one to show you ways to gather information as you answer questions. Occasionally your calls will go this smoothly, but not always. The example doesn't show you any number of other tricky questions that, inadequately handled, can rule you out of consideration. These include questions that appear to be simple buy signals, yet are in reality a part of every interviewer's arsenal of "knockout" questions—so called because they can save time by quickly ruling out certain types of candidates. Such questions often arise during a telephone interview, but can still occur during an initial face-to-face interview.

When it comes to conversation, we all come from different backgrounds. You and I will never talk alike, so don't think you have to learn the sample answers parrot-fashion. Instead, you should take the essence of the responses and personalize them until the words fall comfortably from your lips.

Buy Signal: "How much experience do you have?"

Too much or too little experience could easily rule you out. Be careful how you answer this question and try to gain time. It is a vague question, and you have a right to ask for qualifications. Employers typically define jobs by years' experience. At the same time there is a major move away from simple chronological experience, toward the more important concern about what you can deliver on the job. Managers and HR pros are now more open to thinking in terms of "performance requirements" and "deliverables" than ever before.

Here are a couple of ways to handle it:

"Could you help me with that question? If you give me a brief outline of the performance requirements, I can give you a more accurate answer." Or, *"I have _____ years' experience, but they aren't necessarily typical. If you'd give me a few details on the performance requirements I'd be able to give you a more accurate answer."*

The employer's response, while gaining you time, tells you what it takes to do the job and therefore what aspects of your experience are most relevant. Take mental notes as the employer talks—you can even write them down, if you have time. Then give an appropriate response.

You can move the conversation forward by asking a follow-up question of your own. For example: "The areas of expertise you require sound like a match to my experience, and it sounds as if you have some exciting projects at hand. What projects would I be involved with in the first few months?"

Buy Signal: "Do you have a degree?"

If your degree matches the stated requirements of the position, by all means go ahead and state it. If you don't have any degree and the position requires one, all is not lost. As Calvin Coolidge used to say, "The world is full of educated derelicts." You may want to use the "life university" answer. For example: "My education was cut short by the necessity of earning a living at an early age. My past managers have discovered that this in no way speaks of a lack of processing power. However, I am currently enrolled in classes to complete my degree."

It would cost you about $100 to enroll in degree-relevant classes and make this an honest answer, and in the process you'd be doing the right thing by your career. Ongoing education is important for your long-term career survival and economic success, and dramatically improves your earning and promotional potential, so enrollment in any and all career-relevant classes is to your benefit.

In a security conscious world, an increasing percentage of employers are verifying educational credentials and references. Do not lie about this during the interviews or on your résumé; it will cost you that job if you are found out, or if it comes out later, you could be terminated with cause—which can lead to further employment problems down the line.

Buy Signal: "How much are you making/do you want?"

This is a direct question looking for a direct answer, yet it is a knockout question, so you should proceed warily. Earning either too little or too much could ruin your chances before you're given the opportunity to shine in person. There are a number of options that could serve you better than a direct answer. First, you must understand that questions about money at this point in the conversation are being used to screen you in or screen you out. The answers you give now should be geared toward getting you in the door and into a face-to-face meeting. (Handling the serious salary negotiations that are attached to a job offer are covered in Chapter 20, "Negotiating the Job Offer.") For now, your main options are as follows:

- Direct answer: If you know the salary range for the position and there is a fit, give a straightforward answer.
- Indirect answer: "In the fifties." Or "in the 120s."
- Put yourself above the money: "I'm looking for an opportunity that will give me the opportunity to make a difference with my efforts. If I am the right person for the job, I'm sure you'll make me a fair offer. By the way, what is the salary range for this position?"

When you give a salary range rather than a single figure, you have more flexibility and have a greater chance of "clicking with" the employer's approved range for the position.

When you are pressed a second time for an exact dollar figure, be as honest and forthright as circumstances permit. If you have the skills for the job and you are concerned that your current low salary will eliminate you before you have the chance to show your worth, you might add, "I realize this is well below industry norms, but it does not reflect on my expertise or experience in any way. It speaks of the need for me to make a strategic career move, to where I can be compensated competitively and based on my skills."

If your current earnings are higher than the approved range, you could say, "Mr. Smith, my current employers feel I am well worth the money I earn due to my skills, dedication, and honesty. When we meet, I'm sure I can convince you of my ability to contribute to your department. A meeting would provide an opportunity to make that evaluation, wouldn't it?"

Notice the "wouldn't it?" at the end of the reply; this is known as *reflexive questioning*. A reflexive question such as this is a great conversation-forwarding technique because it encourages a positive response. Conservative use of reflexive questions can help you move things along. Watch the sound of your voice, though. A reflexive question can sound conversational, or it can sound pointed and accusatory; it's not what you say, but how you say it. Your goal is consensus not confrontation; an easy way to encourage the right tone in your voice is to smile as you speak, the simple technique will move your inflection toward the positive.

Such questions are easy to create. Just conclude with "wouldn't you?" "didn't you?" "won't you?" "couldn't you?" "shouldn't you?" or "don't you?" as appropriate at the end of any statement, and the interviewer will be encouraged to answer "yes." You have kept the conversation alive, and moved it closer to your goal. Repeat the reflexive questions to yourself. They have a certain rhythm that will help you remember them.

After you have answered one or two buy-signal questions, ask for a meeting. If you simply ask, "Would you like to meet me?" there are only two possible responses—"yes" or "no"—and your chances of success are about 50/50. When you suggest, however, that you will be in the area on a particular date or dates ("I'm going to be in town on Thursday and Friday, Mr. Grant. Which would be better for you?"), you have asked a question that moves the conversation along dramatically. Your question gives the company representative the choice of meeting you on Thursday or Friday, rather than meeting you or not meeting you. By presuming the "yes," you reduce the chances of hearing a negative, and increase the possibility of a face-to-face meeting.

How to Deal with Objections

By no means will every marketing presentation you make be met with a few simple questions and then an invitation to interview; sometimes the silence will be broken with an objection. This usually comes in the form of a statement, not a question: "Send me a résumé," or "I don't have time to see you," or "You are earning too much," or "You'll have to talk to personnel," or "I don't need anyone like you right now." Although these seem like brush-off lines, they don't have to be; frequently, objections like these can be parlayed into interviews.

Notice that all the following suggested response models have a commonality with buy-signal responses. They all end with a question, one that helps you learn more about the reason for the objection, perhaps to overcome it, and lead the conversation toward a meeting.

In dealing with objections, nothing is gained by confrontation, while much can be gained by an appreciation of the other's viewpoint. Consequently, most objections you hear are best handled by first demonstrating your understanding of the other's viewpoint. Try to start your responses with phrases like "I understand," or "I can appreciate your position," or "I see your point," or "Of course." Follow up with statements like "However," or "Also consider," or a similar line that allows the opportunity for rebuttal and to gather further information.

It's not necessary to memorize these responses verbatim, only to understand the underlying concept and then to put together a response in words that are sympathetic to your character and style of speech.

Objection: "Why don't you send me a résumé?"

The employer may be genuinely interested in seeing your résumé as a first step in the interview cycle, or it may be a polite way of getting you off the phone. You should identify the real reason without causing antagonism, and at the same time open up the conversation. A good reply would be, "Of course, Mr. Grant. Would you give me your exact title and the mailing and e-mail address? Thank you. So that I can be sure that my qualifications fit your needs, what skills are you looking for in this position?" or "What specific job title and opening should I refer to when I send it?"

Notice the steps:

- Agreement with the prospective employer
- A demonstration of understanding
- A question to further the conversation (in this instance to confirm that an opening actually exists)

Answering in this fashion will open up the conversation. Mr. Grant will relay the aspects of the job that are important to him, and you can use the additional information to draw attention to your skills in:

- Your executive briefing or cover letter
- A precisely customized résumé
- Your face-to-face meeting

Following Mr. Grant's response, you can recap the match between his company's needs and your skills; savvy headhunters follow this confirmation step with the following question, which you will also find very effective:

"Assuming my résumé matches your needs, as I think we are both confident that it will, could we pencil in a date and time for an interview next week? I am available next Thursday and Friday; which would be preferable to you?"

A penciled-in date and time very rarely gets canceled.

Objection: "I don't have time to see you."

If the employer is too busy to see you, it indicates that he or she has work pressures, and by recognizing that, you can show yourself as the one to alleviate some of those pressures through your problem-solving skills. You should avoid confrontation, however; it is important that you demonstrate empathy for the person with whom you are speaking. Agree, empathize, and ask a question that moves the conversation forward:

"I understand how busy you must be; it sounds like a competent, dedicated, and efficient professional [whatever your title is] could be of some assistance. Perhaps I could call you back at a better time to discuss how I might make a contribution in easing the pressure at peak times. When are you least busy, in the morning or afternoon?"

The company representative will either make time to talk now or will arrange a better time for the two of you to talk further.

You could also try, "Since you are so busy, what is the best time of day for you? First thing in the morning, or is the afternoon a quieter time?" Or you could suggest, "If you give me your e-mail address, you could study my background at your leisure. What's your e-mail address? Thanks, what would be a good time of day to call to follow up on this?"

Objection: "You are earning too much."

If the company representative brought up the matter, that's a buy signal. If the job really doesn't pay enough, and there will be openings for which you are earning too much, you've gotten (as the carnival barker says) "close, but no cigar!"

How to make a success of this seeming dead end is handled next. You should, however, follow the process through: "Oh, I'm sorry to hear that—what is the range for that position?" Depending on the degree of salary discrepancy you can reiterate your interest. You can also refer to Chapter 20, "Negotiating the Job Offer," where you will find further advice on dealing with this issue.

Objection: "We only promote from within."

Your response could be, "I realize that, Mr. Grant. Your development of employees is a major reason I want to get in! I am bright, conscientious, and motivated. When you do hire from the outside, and it must happen on occasion, what assets do you look for?" or "How do I get into consideration for such opportunities?"

The response finishes with a question designed to carry the conversation forward and to give you a new opportunity to sell yourself. Notice that the response logically presupposes that the company does hire from the outside, even though the company representative has said otherwise. You have called his bluff, but in a professional and inoffensive manner.

Objection: "You'll have to talk to Human Resources."

In this case, you reply, "Of course, Mr. Grant. Whom should I speak to in HR, and what specific position should I mention?"

You cover a good deal of ground with that response. You establish whether there is a job there or whether you are being fobbed off on HR to waste their time and your own. Also, you move the conversation forward again while modifying it to your advantage. Develop a specific job-related question to ask while the employer is answering the first question. It can open a fruitful line for you to pursue. If you receive a nonspecific reply, probe a little deeper. A simple phrase like, "That's interesting. Please tell me more," or "Why's that?" will usually do the trick.

Or you can ask, "When I speak to HR, will it be about a specific job you have, or is it to see whether I might fill a position elsewhere in the company?"

Armed with the resulting information, you can talk to HR about your conversation with Mr. Grant; remember to get the name of a specific person in HR with whom to speak, and to quote this prior contact by name.

"Good morning, Ms. Johnson. Cary Grant, over in marketing, suggested we should speak to arrange an interview for the open Sales Associate requisition."

This way you show HR that you are not a time waster, because you have already spoken to the person for whom the requisition is open.

Don't look at the HR department as a roadblock; it may contain a host of opportunities for you. In many companies different departments could use your talents, and HR is probably the only department that knows all the openings. With a larger employer you might be able to arrange three or four interviews with the same company for three or four different positions!

Objection: "I really wanted someone with a degree."

You should have learned the proper response to "Do you have a degree?" But in case you were abducted by aliens a few pages ago, you could respond by saying, "Mr. Smith, I appreciate your viewpoint. It was necessary that I start earning a living early in life. If we meet, I am certain you would recognize the value of my additional practical experience." If you have been smart enough to enroll in a course or two in order to pursue that ever important degree, you should add, "I am currently enrolled in courses to complete my degree, which should demonstrate my professional commitment, and perhaps that makes a difference?"

You might then ask what the company policy is for support and encouragement of employees continuing their education. Your response will end with, "If we were to meet, I am certain you would recognize the value of my practical experience, in addition to my ongoing professional commitment. I am going to be interviewing at the end of next week, and I know you will find the time to meet well spent. Is there a day and time that would be best for you?"

Objection: "I don't need anyone like you now."

Short of suggesting that the employer fire someone to make room for you (which, incidentally, has been done successfully on a few occasions), the chances of getting an interview with this company are slim. With the right question, however, that person will give you a personal introduction to someone else who could use your talents.

You can ask, "When do you anticipate new needs in your area?" or "May I send you my résumé and keep in touch for when the situation changes?" or "Who else in the company might have a need for someone with my background and skills?" or "Can you think of peers at other companies who might have a need for someone with my background?"

Live Leads from Dead Ends

There will be times when you have made a persuasive marketing presentation and made all the right responses to the questions you hear, but eventually the employer says, "I can't use anyone like you right now," and means it. Not every company has a job opening for you, nor are you right for every job; but you can still turn this rejection into a successful call.

Remember that networking calls have multiple goals: to arrange an interview, to arrange another time for a telephone interview, to send a résumé for future follow-up, and to develop leads on promising job openings elsewhere. The same applies to marketing calls. So far you have been piecing together a brief but powerful presentation, anticipating problems and preparing responses to common buy signals and objections. To this you can now add a series of job lead development questions. By adding these questions, you will achieve a measure of success from every marketing call you make, leaving you energized and with a feeling of achievement after every conversation.

The person on the other end of the line is a professional who knows other people in other departments, subsidiaries, and other companies, any of whom may have an interesting opportunity for you. If you ask the right questions you'll find that most professional colleagues, realizing they may well find themselves in your position one day, will be glad to advise you on who might have openings. While nearly everyone you call will be pleased to point you in the right direction, they can only be expected to do so if you ask, so don't be shy about asking interview development questions of any manager you speak to, either in person or over the telephone.

These are the seven categories of questions that you need to absorb so that you can move through them smoothly in person and over the telephone:

- Leads in department
- Leads in company
- Leads in other divisions of the company
- Leads to other companies
- Contacts in other companies
- Contact info exchange
- Open door to keep in touch

You will find the entire series of questions to ask in these categories in the section in Chapter 3 on questions to ask your contacts (starting on page 54). In fact, if you are paying attention to the *Knock 'em Dead* method, you will already have a list of personally prioritized job development questions prepared from the advice given earlier; if not, reread that section and develop your list. You can have one on your computer and one pasted up on the wall by your telephone ready for use at all times.

Most people labor over each call and agonize over its results. You are going to have plenty of calls to make, so your first job is to jump into the deep end and start swimming. When you have made thirty or forty marketing calls, you are going to feel like an old hand at the job, and what was once a nightmare will have become another professional survival skill. A very effective idea is to develop a list of ten or twenty calls where your presentation will be the same in each instance (for example, following up on a résumé you sent last week). Then write out a script for yourself, listing by bullets the points you want to make on each call. Then screw up your courage, and make those twenty calls one after the other without stopping to dwell on the rejection or even to do a jig when the call goes well. When you do this, you will make more calls, get more results, and get acclimated to using the telephone effectively as a job search tool.

Follow up on every lead you get. Too many people become elated at securing an interview for themselves and cease all efforts to generate additional interviews in the belief that a job offer is definitely on its way. Your goal is to have a choice of the best jobs in town, and, without multiple interviews, there is no way you'll have that choice. Asking interview development questions ensures that you are tapping all the secret recesses of the hidden job market.

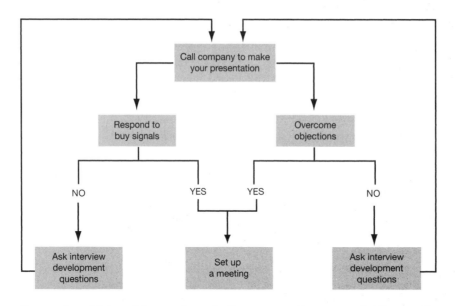

Remember: Networking and marketing are continuous activities, as shown by this chart.

Corporate Gatekeepers

When you are making marketing and networking calls, an overly officious clerical assistant will sometimes try to thwart you in your efforts to present your credentials directly to a potential employer—at least it might appear that way.

In fact, it is very rare that these "corporate gatekeepers," as they are known, are directed to screen calls from professionals seeking employment, as to do so only increases employment costs to the company. What they are there to do is to screen nuisance calls from salespeople and the like.

However, to arm you for the occasional objectionable gatekeeper standing between you and making a living, you might try the following techniques used by investigative reporters, private eyes, and headhunters.

Pre-empting Questions

Most gatekeepers are trained at most to find out your name and the nature of your business. But when they are asking the questions, they control the conversation. You can remain in control by pre-empting their standard script: "Good morning. I'm Mr. Yate. I need to speak to Nikki Jones about an accounting matter. Is she there?" Should a truly obnoxious gatekeeper ask snidely, "Perhaps I can help you?" you can effectively use any of the following options: "Thank you, but I'd rather discuss it with Ms. Jones." "It's personal." "It's a professional matter." Or you can blind them with science: "Yes, if you can talk to me about the finer points of *[some esoteric aspect of your profession]*." They invariably can't, so you're in like Flynn.

Diction, tone of voice, confidence, and clarity are all-important when dealing with clerical staff. They are trained to respect and respond to polite authority, so always demonstrate self-confidence in your manner. When you are clear about whom you want to speak to and can predict possible screening devices, you usually get through. With such gatekeepers you should also avoid using your first name in your introduction, as in "Martin Carlucci"; instead, try "Mr. Carlucci" or "Ms. Carlucci," which is always more authoritative.

When you have been given a name by a networking contact, you can use that introduction to get past corporate gatekeepers: "You can tell him Bill Edwards, a friend of his, suggested I call."

Go Up the Ladder

If you can't get through to the person you want to speak to, say the accounting manager, instead of wasting the call you can go up the ladder to the controller or the vice president of finance. Interestingly, the higher you go, the more accessible people are. In this instance the senior manager may well not schedule an interview with you but instead refer you back down to the appropriate level. Sometimes that VP will switch you directly to the person with whom you want to speak; even if that doesn't happen, the next time you call you have a nice, hefty name to drop when dealing with the pesky gatekeeper: "Mr. Craig Wilde, your divisional vice president of finance, asked me to call Mr. Jones. Is he there?" Even if you didn't speak directly to that VP up the corporate ladder, and VP Bigshot's secretary referred you back down the ladder, you can now say with all honesty, "Mr. Bigshot's office recommended. . . ." Then the conversation with your target can begin with your standard introduction, but be sure to mention first the name of the person who referred you.

If you haven't yet gleaned any names from a particular company through your networking activities and are being thwarted by a gatekeeper, try these approaches:

- On other networking or marketing calls, ask specifically for a lead at the leadless company: "Jack, I was planning to contact _____, Inc. Would you happen to know anyone there who could give me a heads up?" Over a couple of weeks you might develop a list of companies where you have no contacts and you can mention a list to your network contacts: "Jack, do you know anyone at Chase? Wachovia? How about Wells Fargo or Bank of America?"

- Check your association membership directories and your online networks, and look for members who work or have worked at your target company. Regardless of their titles, they can put you in touch with the right parties.
- Visit the company's Web site and look for names there; and don't forget to read the press clippings that always get posted, which invariably contain a quote or two from company representatives. You should also Google "news" searches for media coverage of the company and its executives.
- For especially desirable companies, check back with those people who know you well and respect your work: your references. They might know or be able to find out the names of people working within your target.

When none of your research, networking, or marketing activities has presented you with a name, try these techniques:

- Explain to gatekeepers that you need to send a letter to [whatever the person's title is] and ask for the correct spelling of the name. There is usually more than one person worth speaking to at any company, so ask for more than one name and title. In the finance area (and depending on your level), any or all of the following could provide useful contacts: the accounting supervisor, the accounting manager, the assistant controller, the controller, the vice president of finance, the chief financial officer, the executive vice president, the chief operating officer, the chief executive officer, and the chairman. Anyone who gives you one name will invariably give you more than one. Some years ago in Colorado I sat with a job searcher who used these techniques to gather 142 names from receptionists in one hour!
- In some companies where security is at a premium, gatekeepers are expressly forbidden to give out names and titles. In this case, you can use some side-door techniques: There are certain people in every company who by the very nature of their jobs have contact with people at all levels of the company and who are not given the responsibility to screen calls. These include people in the mailroom, maintenance, shipping and receiving, second-, third-, and fourth-shift employees, new or temporary employees, advertising and public relations people, sales and marketing people, travel center, Q/A, and customer service employees.

Another approach for getting by pesky gatekeepers is to vary the times when you call a target company; before 8 A.M., after 5 P.M., and during lunch hours, people often pick up their own lines and general lines coming into a department.

Voice Mail

Voice mail is on the increase. If the techniques I've mentioned don't do the trick for you, these will:

- When you have an introduction, you can use it to navigate voice mail systems and to leave as a teaser on your voice mail message: "Good morning, my name is William Powell. Cary Grant suggested I give you a call. He thought we might have something to talk about. You can reach me at 516-555-0501, and I'll try you later."
- When you lack a name, check to see if the system has a directory, and, if it does, take note of as many names and extensions as you can. If there is no directory, and the voice mail system tells you to enter an extension key, keep keying until you hit one that results in a human voice. It doesn't matter who answers as long as someone does. The conversation goes something like this:

  "Jack speaking."
  "Jack, this is Martin Yate. I'm calling from outside and I'm lost on this darned telephone system." This usually gets a smile. "I'm trying to get hold of [whatever the title is]. Could you check who that would be for me?"

Having left a message, don't sit anxiously waiting for the call back; get on with your job search and make another call. Most of all, don't leave endless voice mail messages, as it makes you look overeager. In cases where you don't get a response and need to call back again, do so, and if the person doesn't pick up and you get routed to the voice mail again, hang up and move on to your next call.

Stay the Course

No matter how many interviews your calls and mail campaigns are generating, you must continue to research potential job openings. While you have to maintain contact with interested companies, you must also make yourself maintain a daily marketing schedule, which includes making calls and sending e-mails and résumés to both nurture your existing contact base and expand it in each of the following areas:

- Internet job postings and the company Web sites you discover from them
- Newspaper ads and the other leads you identify in your print research
- Members of all your professional and personal networks
- Leads developed from job fairs and other research efforts
- Headhunters
- Follow-up letters to phone calls and from meetings

The balance you maintain is important because most job hunters are tempted to send the easy e-mails and make the easy calls (networking with old friends) and ignore the more challenging, more productive marketing calls. Don't stop searching even when an offer for a dream job is pending, and your potential boss says, "Robin, you've got the job, and we're glad you can start on Monday. The offer letter is in the mail." Never accept any "yes" as an absolute until you have it in writing, you have started work, and the first paycheck has cleared at the bank! Until then, keep your momentum building. It is the professional and circumspect thing to do, and as someone who has worked on the corporate side, I can tell you that job offers do get withdrawn for unfathomable reasons, and with not a whit of concern for the poor hunt.

It is easy to mail résumés and hope for calls, but you will always get more results if you make follow-up calls. However, if you are not getting a response with one résumé format, you might try changing from a chronological to a combination format, just as you would change the bait if the fish weren't taking what you had on the hook.

Also, try to keep things in perspective. Although your 224th contact may not have an opening for you, with a few polite and judicious questions he or she may well have a good lead. In the job search there are only two "yeses": Their "yes, we want you to work for us" and your "yes, I can start on Monday." Every "no" brings you closer to the big "yes." Never take rejections of your résumé or your phone call as rejections of yourself; just as every job isn't right for you, you aren't right for every job, and there is a great opportunity right around the corner, so long as you turn that corner by maintaining your forward momentum.

Stacking the Odds in Your Favor

We all have 168 hours a week to become bagmen or billionaires and to make our lives as fulfilling as they can be. For some of us this means a better job; for others it means getting back to work to keep a roof over our heads. How we manage these hours will determine our success. These job search commandments will see you successfully through the job change process and career transition:

- It has been said that in order to gain that next job it takes on average twenty-five conversations with men or women who have the authority to hire you. What do we learn from this? Make every effort to get into conversation with decision makers with hiring authority and sooner or later you will get that job offer you have been dreaming about. This may take twenty-five conversations or it may take 125, but the kernel of truth still holds: get into a conversation with enough hiring authorities and you will eventually get that desired job offer. To get into those critical conversations isn't easy; it might take you hundreds of contacts. So this is a task you must commit to every day of your job search.
- Work at getting a new job. Work at least forty hours per week at it. Divide your time between contacting potential employers and generating new leads; the Internet, networking, and all the other job search tools will generate plenty of leads for you.
- Research the companies you contact. In a tightly run job race, the candidate who is most knowledgeable about the employer has a distinct advantage; again, the Internet can be of immense help in becoming a knowledgeable candidate.
- Follow up on the résumés you send out with phone calls. Resubmit your résumé to identified openings after six or seven weeks. Change the format of your résumé and resubmit yet again. (See *Knock 'em Dead Resumes* for specific ideas on how to do this.)
- Stay in telephone contact with your job leads on a regular basis to maintain top-of-the-mind awareness. If you find yourself needing to call existing contacts more than every couple of months, you should be putting more emphasis on building your networks and doing direct research.
- Develop examples of your professional profile that make you special—and rehearse building these examples into your interview responses. You will learn all about developing a desirable professional profile in Chapter 11.
- Send follow-up notes with relevant news clippings, cartoons, and so on to those in your networks; it's a light touch that helps people keep you in mind.
- Work on your self-image. Use this time to get physically fit. Studies show that unfit, overweight people take longer to find suitable work. The more you do today, the better you will feel about yourself.
- Maintain a professional demeanor during the workweek (clothing, posture, personal hygiene).
- Use regular business hours for making contacts. Use the early morning, lunchtime, after 5 P.M., and Saturday for doing the ongoing research and writing projects that maintain momentum.

- Don't feel guilty about taking time off from your job search. Just do it conscientiously. If you regularly spend Saturday morning in the library doing research, you can take Wednesday afternoon off to go to the driving range once in a while.
- Maintain records of your contacts in the career management database. They will benefit not only this job search but also those in the future.
- Never stop the research and job search process until you have a written job offer in hand and you have accepted that job in writing with an agreed-upon start date; even then, continue with any ongoing interview cycles.
- Remember: It's all up to you. There are many excuses not to make calls or send résumés on any given day. There are many excuses to get up later or knock off earlier. There are many excuses to back off because this one's in the bag. But there are no real *reasons*. There are no jobs out there for those who won't look, while there are plenty of opportunities for those who work at it.
- Take off the blinders. We all have two specific skills: our professional/technical skills—say, computer programming; and our industry skills—say, banking. Professional/technical skills can be transferable to other industries; and industry skills can open other opportunities in your industry. For example, that programmer, given decent communication skills, could become a technical trainer for programmers or technophobes.

Using a Contact Tracker

As you get your job search up to speed, the number of baited hooks you have in the water will grow dramatically. The résumés you send out will require follow-up calls, and the networking and research calls you make to potential employers will create the need to mail out résumés, which in return will generate more follow-up calls.

Without tracking mechanisms in place this can quickly get out of hand. It would be crazy to make this effort to get your job search and career-management plan functioning, and then let important opportunities fall through the cracks for lack of attention to detail.

You can create a contact tracker on a spreadsheet program, with columns for company name, telephone number, contact name, e-mail address; the date you sent a résumé, and the date you should follow up with a call (or vice versa); and room for comments on the substance of conversations.

Follow-Up: The Key Ingredient

In theory, the perfect letters or e-mails you send cold or as a result of phone calls will receive a response rate of 100 percent. Unfortunately, there is no perfect letter, e-mail, or call in this less-than-perfect world. If you sit waiting for the world to beat a path to your door, you may wait a long time.

An IT executive of my acquaintance once advertised for a programmer analyst. By Wednesday of the following week he had over 100 responses. Ten days later he was still plowing through them when he received a follow-up call (the only one he received) from one of the respondents. The job hunter was in the office that afternoon, returned the following morning, and was hired before lunchtime.

The story? The candidate's paperwork was languishing in the pile, waiting to be discovered. The follow-up phone call got it discovered. The call made the interviewer sort through the enormous pile of paper, pull out the letter and résumé, and act on it. He wanted to get on with his work, and the job hunter in question made it possible by making himself visible on the employer's radar. Follow-up calls, and follow-up calls on the follow-up calls, do really work.

Make phone calls to initiate contact, and you'll get requests for résumés and requests to come right on over for an interview. Make follow-up calls on mailed and e-mailed résumés and you will generate further interviews.

No one is ever hired without passing through one or a series of formal interviews, and that is where *Knock 'em Dead* is headed next: toward an understanding of how to strategize about and execute those interviews that will ultimately lead to job offers.

Acing the Telephone Interview

6

INTERVIEWERS USE THE telephone to weed out applicants. Your goal is a face-to-face meeting, and these are the methods you must use to get it.

Some aspects of a job search are not clear-cut. For instance, a telephone interview for a job might be scheduled for a certain date and time, so you have plenty of time to prepare for it. Then again, a networking call can turn into a marketing presentation in a flash when you realize that the person on the other end of the phone line is in a position to hire you. Likewise, when that marketing presentation progresses past the initial "buy signs" and objections, it can suddenly become a telephone interview. These things happen, but as you understand the steps to take in order to move each of these situations forward, you must be sensitive to the possibility that while telephone interviews can be scheduled in advance, they are just as likely to occur on the fly.

Employers use the telephone as a time management tool; it is easier to cut to the chase on the telephone and weed out candidates quickly than in person. Your goal is a face-to-face meeting, so all you must do is convince the employer she will not be wasting time if she meets with you in person. Here are the techniques you should use to turn the phone conversation into a face-to-face meeting.

Organization for Marketing Calls and Telephone Interviews

Your first substantive contact with a potential employer will usually be by telephone; for entry-level professionals this first meeting will quite often take place at job fairs. We'll talk about job fairs a little later. For right now, let's concentrate on the telephone interview.

The phone interview happens in one of three ways:

- You are making a marketing or networking call, and the company representative goes into a screening process because you have aroused her interest.
- An employer calls unexpectedly as the result of a résumé you have mailed or e-mailed.
- You have arranged a specific time for a telephone interview.

Odds are good that you will experience plenty of telephone interviews during your job search. Whichever activities generate a telephone interview, you must think and act clearly to turn the opportunity into the real thing—a face-to-face meeting. The way you perform will determine whether you move ahead or bite the dust.

A few words about telephone services: call waiting might be nice to have for social use, but responding to its demands during a job search will only annoy the person you have on the line at the time. If you have call waiting, disconnect it or ignore it. More and more telephone companies are also offering additional lines with distinctive rings for your basic service and at no extra charge. With this facility you can have a permanent job search/career management line, and keep a constant eye on the job market without compromising day-to-day home life.

Perhaps the most important consideration about telephone interviews is that the employer has only his ears with which to judge you. If the call comes unexpectedly, and screaming kids or barking dogs surround you, stay calm, sound positive, friendly, and collected: "Thank you for calling, Mr. Wooster. Would you wait a moment while I close the door?" You can then easily take a minute to calm yourself, call up the company Web site, and get your paperwork organized without causing offense. If you need to move to another phone, say so; otherwise, put the caller on hold, take a few controlled, deep breaths to slow down your pounding heart, put a smile on your face (it improves the timbre of your voice), and pick up the phone again. Now you are in control of yourself and the situation.

If you are heading out the door for an interview, or if some other emergency makes this a bad time for an unexpected incoming call, say so straight away and reschedule: "I'm heading out the door for an appointment, Ms. Bassett. Can we schedule a time when I will call you back?" Beware of overfamiliarity: You should always refer to the interviewer by his or her surname until invited to do otherwise.

Allow the company representative to guide the conversation and to ask most of the questions, but keep up your end of the conversation. This is especially important when the interviewer does not give you the openings you need to sell yourself. Always have a few intelligent questions prepared to save the situation. The following questions will give you an excellent idea of why the position is open and exactly the kind of skilled professional the company will eventually hire:

- "What are the three major responsibilities in this job?"
- "What will be the first project(s) I tackle?"
- "What are the biggest challenges the department faces this year and what will be my role as a team member in tackling them?"
- "Which projects will I be most involved with during the first six months?"
- "Who succeeds in this job and why?"
- "Who fails in this job and why?"

When you get a clear understanding of an employer's needs with questions like these, you can seize the opportunity to sell yourself appropriately: "Would it be of value if I described my experience in the area of office management?" or "Then my experience in word processing should be a great help to you," or "I recently completed an accounting project just like that. Would it be relevant to discuss it?"

When you identify an employer's imminent challenges and demonstrate how your skills can lessen the load, you portray yourself as properly focused with a problem-solving mentality and immediately move closer to a face-to-face interview. Everyone hires a problem solver.

You can also keep up your end of the conversation by giving verbal signals that you are engaged in it; you do this with occasional short interjections that don't interrupt the employer's flow but let him know you are paying attention. Comments like "uh-huh," "that's interesting," "okay," "great," and "yes, yes" are verbal equivalents of the body language techniques you'll use to show interest during a face-to-face meeting.

Always speak directly into the telephone, with the mouthpiece about one inch from your mouth. Numbered among the mystical properties of telephone technology is its excellence at picking up and amplifying background noise. This is excelled only by its power to transmit the sounds of food and gum being chewed, or smoke being inhaled and exhaled. Smokers take note: nonsmokers instinctively discriminate, and they will assume that even if you don't actually light up at the interview, you'll have been chain-smoking beforehand and will carry the smell with you as long as you are around. Taking no chances, they probably won't even give you a chance to get through the door once they hear you puffing away over the phone.

You should take notes when possible; they will be invaluable if the employer is interrupted. You can jot down the topic under discussion, then when he or she gets back on the line, helpfully recap: "We were just discussing. . . ." This will be appreciated and show that you are organized and paying attention. Your notes will also help you prepare for the face-to-face meeting.

The company representative may talk about the corporation, and from your research or the Web site on your screen, you may also know something about the outfit. A little flattery goes a long way: admire a company's achievements, when you can, and by inference you admire the interviewer. Likewise, if any areas of common interest arise, comment on them, and agree with the interviewer when reasonably possible—people usually hire people like themselves.

On the 200 telephone interviews a year that I average (they are radio interviews, not job interviews, but I'm sure you can appreciate the similar level of nervous tension), I've found that standing for the interview calms the adrenaline a little, helps my breathing, and allows me to sound confident and relaxed. It might work for you, so give it a try.

Answering Questions

Beware of giving yes-or-no answers, as they give no real information about your abilities and do nothing to forward your agenda. At the same time, don't waffle; your answers need to be concise. Understanding someone over the telephone can sometimes be a challenge, so if you didn't hear or didn't understand a question, ask the speaker to repeat it. If you need time to think about your answer, and that is quite acceptable, say so: "Let me think about that for a moment."

Whenever possible, you should give real-world examples to illustrate your points: "That's interesting. I was involved in an audit like that a couple months back and it presented some interesting challenges."

It isn't a bad idea to prepare a brief potted history of your professional life, for when you are asked, "Tell me a little about yourself." At this point your answer can be fairly brief: "I have a bachelor's degree in Communications, and I've been working in pharmaceutical sales for three years. I am currently ranked fourth in the region. I have long competed against your company and know and respect your products, and your position in Chicago will help me get closer to family."

There are some 200 questions you are likely to be asked during an interview, which we'll cover in detail in the coming pages. Meanwhile, there are a handful of questions often asked during telephone interviews in addition to the ones that will come right after you make a marketing presentation. Let's look at them in light of your probable lack of information about the company and the job.

"What are you looking for?" With so little real knowledge about the company at this point, you need to be careful about specificity. Don't say, "I want to move into marketing," unless you know such opportunity exists. Otherwise keep your answer general.

"What are your strengths?" If you know about specific skill requirements, emphasize them; if not, stick to a brief outline of your professional behavioral profile (discussed on pages 161–165).

"What is your greatest weakness?" Don't throw the opportunity away before you even get in the door and have a real understanding of the job. Mention a brand-new technology/skill you have just developed, and say you have been working on it and try to keep abreast of the latest approaches in all aspects of your profession.

"I don't think you'll be suitable because you lack _____ skill." If the statement is true, acknowledge it, then follow with an example of a similar skill you picked up quickly and apply with consummate skill: "Yes, I understand. When I joined my current company I knew nothing about _____, but I studied on my own and with the help of a mentor within the department I was up to speed in a matter of weeks. Given my proven ability to learn quickly and my willingness to invest my own time, would you consider talking to me in more detail about this topic when we meet face-to-face?" With this type of response you are putting a positive spin on your shortcoming, which gives you a good shot at overcoming the objection. If you are successful in arranging a face-to-face interview, you'll now have time to bone up on the subject and identify a sensible self-development program before you meet with the employer.

Under no circumstances, though, should you ask about salary or benefits and vacation time; that comes much later. Your single objective at this point is to meet face-to-face; money is not an issue. If the interviewer brings up a direct question about how much you are earning, you can't get around it, so be honest. On the other hand, if you are asked how much you want, answer truthfully that at this point you don't know enough about the company or the job to answer that question; there is whole chapter on negotiation later in the book, which covers the money issue in some detail.

The telephone interview has come to an end when you are asked whether you have any questions—perhaps, "What would you like to know about us?" This is a wind-down question, so it is a good opening to get some specific questions of your own answered that can advance your candidacy:

- "What are the most immediate challenges of the job?"
- "What are the most important projects of the first six months?"
- "What skills and behaviors are most important to success on the job?"
- "Why do some people succeed and others fail doing this work?"

By discovering answers to these questions now, you will have time before the face-to-face meeting to package your skills according to the needs at hand and to create an appropriate executive briefing for distribution with your résumé to the different interviewers you meet.

If you have not already asked or been invited to meet the interviewer, now is the time to take the initiative.

"It sounds like a very interesting opportunity, Ms. Bassett, and a situation where I could definitely make a contribution. The most pressing question I have now is when can we get together?" (*Note*: Even though the emphasis throughout has been on putting things in your own words, phrases like "make a contribution" show pride in your work—a key professional behavior—and work as shorthand for "I'm a team player.")

When an invitation for an interview is extended, there are practical matters that you need to clarify with a handful of simple questions that address the when (date and time), and where (don't assume the interview will take place at a facility that you associate with the company). You will also want to inquire about the interview procedure:

- "How many interviews typically occur before a decision is made?"
- "Who else will be part of the selection process, and what are their roles within the department or company?"

- "What is the time frame for filling this position and how many other people are in consideration at this time?"

Follow with a casual inquiry as to what direction the meeting will take. You might ask, "Would you tell me some of the critical areas you will discuss on Thursday?" The knowledge gained will help you to package and present yourself, and it will allow you time to bone up on any weak or rusty areas. This is also a good time to establish how long the meeting is expected to last, which will give you some idea of how to pace yourself.

Once the details are confirmed, finish with this request: "If I need any additional information before the interview, I would like to feel free to get back to you." The company representative will naturally agree. No matter how many questions you get answered in the initial conversation, there will always be something you forgot. This allows you to call again to satisfy any curiosity—it will also enable you to increase rapport. Don't take too much advantage of it, though: one well-placed phone call that contains two or three considered questions will be appreciated; four or five phone calls will not.

In closing your conversation, take care to ascertain the correct spelling and pronunciation of the interviewer's name. This shows your concern for the small but important things in life—and it will be noticed, particularly when the interviewer receives your follow-up thank-you note. (See *Knock 'em Dead Cover Letters* for a comprehensive selection of samples.)

It is difficult to evaluate an opportunity properly over the telephone, so even if the job doesn't sound right, go to the interview; it will give you practice, and the job may look better when you have more facts. You might even discover a more suitable opening elsewhere within the company when you go to the face-to-face interview.

DRESSING FOR JOB INTERVIEW SUCCESS

WHEN YOU DRESS like a professional, you are likely to be treated as one, and that's a good head start without saying a word.

The moment you set eyes on someone, your mind makes evaluations and judgments with lightning speed. Potential employers also make the same lightning-speed evaluations when you first meet at the beginning of a job interview. It's a fair estimate that nine out of ten of today's employers will reject an unsuitably dressed applicant without a second thought.

"What You See Is What You Get!"

The initial respect you receive at the interview will be in direct proportion to the image you project. The correct professional appearance won't get you the job offer—but it will lend everything you say that much more credence and weight. Wearing a standard business uniform instantly communicates that you understand one of the paramount unwritten rules of professional life and that you have a confident self-image.

Employers rarely make overt statements about acceptable dress codes to their employees, much less to interviewees; instead, there is a generally accepted but unspoken dictum that those who wish to succeed will dress appropriately and those who don't, won't.

There are a few professions where on-the-job dress (as opposed to interview dress) is somewhat less conservative than in the mainstream: fashion, entertainment, and advertising are three examples. In these and a few other fields, there is a good deal of leeway with regard to personal expression in workplace attire. But for 95 percent of us, jobs and employers require a certain level of traditional professionalism in our wardrobes. While you need not dress like the chairman of the board (although that probably wouldn't hurt), adopting "casual Friday" attire on the day of your interview is not in your best professional interest. For a job interview, it is generally accepted that you should dress one or two levels up from the job you are applying for, while remaining consistent with the type of occupation it is within. To maximize your career options over the long haul of a career you must aim to consistently meet or exceed these standards.

Your Interview Advantage

Your appearance tells people how you feel about yourself as an applicant, as well as how you feel about the interviewer, the company, and the interview process itself. By dressing professionally, you tell people that you understand the niceties of corporate life, and you send a subtle "reinforcing" message that you can, for example, be relied on to deal one-on-one with members of a company's prized client base.

How you dress sends signals about:

- How seriously you take the occasion, and, by extension, how much respect you feel for your interviewers and all others whom you meet at the interviews.
- How well you understand the confidence a look of traditional professionalism gives clients, customers, peers, and superiors.

Yet no matter how important these concerns might be, they pale in comparison to the impact a sharp appearance can have on your own sense of self. When you know you have taken care of your appearance and that you look the best you can, you feel pride and confidence, your posture is better, you smile more, and you feel more "in control" of your destiny. In turn, others will respond positively to the image of professionalism and self-confidence that you present. Portraying the correct image at an interview will give you a real edge over your competition. You can expect what you say to be strongly influenced in the mind of your interviewer by the way you present yourself: Appearances count.

The Look

The safest look for both men and women at interviews is traditional and conservative. Look at investing in a good-fitting, well-made suit as your first step to a successful strategic career move. With your business clothes, quality matters far more than quantity; it's better to have one good outfit than two mediocre ones. Your professional wardrobe is a long-term career asset, so add quality items, and over time the quantity will come.

Up until recent years, this was fairly easy for men, as their professional fashions tended to remain constant. These days, men's fashions are experiencing a metamorphosis, with designers of high fashion offering affordable lines of updated, professionally acceptable looks. However, a man can always interview with confidence and poise in his six-year-old Brooks Brothers suit, provided it isn't worn to a shine.

For women, things are more complicated. Appropriate female attire for the interview should reflect current professional fashions if the applicant is to be taken seriously. Moreover, in selecting a current professional look, women must walk a fine line, combining elements of both conformity (to show she belongs) and panache (to show a measure of individuality and style).

The key for both sexes is to dress for the position you want, not the one you have. This means the upwardly mobile professional might need to invest in the clothes that project the desired image.

The correct appearance alone probably won't get you a job offer, but it does go a long way toward winning the attention and respect you need to land the offer. When you know you look right, you can stop worrying about the impression your clothes are making and concentrate on communicating your message.

Every interview and every interviewer is different, so it isn't possible to set down rigid guidelines for exactly what to wear in any given situation. However, there are a handful of commonsense guidelines that will ensure you are perceived as someone savvy, practical, competent, reliable, and professional.

General Guidelines

The right look varies from industry to industry. A college professor can sport tweed jackets with elbow patches on the job, and an advertising executive may don the latest designer dress or wear wild ties as a badge of creativity (that is what they are being paid for). Nevertheless, that same college professor is likely to wear a suit to an important interview, and even professional men and women in advertising and the media are likely to dress more conservatively for a job interview.

Most of us are far more adept at recognizing the dress mistakes of others than at spotting our own image failings. When you look for a second opinion, you often make the mistake of asking only a loved one. Better candidates for evaluation of your interview attire are trusted professional friends who have proven their objectivity in such matters.

Whenever possible, find out the dress code of the company you are visiting. For example, if you are an engineer applying for a job at a high-tech company, a blue three-piece suit might be overpowering. It is perfectly acceptable to ask someone in Human Resources about the dress code (written or informal) of the company. You may even want to make an anonymous visit to get a sense of the corporate style of the company; if that isn't practical, you can always visit the Web site to see how the company likes to be perceived by its public.

I have been asked, "If everyone wears sweaters at the company where I am interviewing, shouldn't I wear the same if I want to be seen to fit in?" In fact, very few companies allow a very relaxed dress code for all their employees all the time; an increasing percentage allow a somewhat relaxed dress code on a particular day (often Friday), when "casual professional" attire is allowed, if not always encouraged. Sometimes, some younger professionals mistake this to mean they can dress for the beach at all times. Even if the company is casual all the time for all its employees, do not dress casually for a job interview. There are two big reasons to avoid casual interview attire:

1. The company is considering an investment that will probably run into hundreds of thousands of dollars if the hire works out, and potentially as much as tens of thousands of dollars if it doesn't—hardly a casual event.

2. Companies sometimes allow casual dress at times and in circumstances that will not jeopardize business. They are comfortable doing this because they already know everyone on the payroll knows how to dress appropriately. The interview is where the company needs to know you appreciate the niceties of business dress; they already have a fair idea that you own a sweater and a pair of khakis.

Men

Following are the best current dress guidelines for men preparing for a professional interview.

Men's Suits

A *Wall Street Journal* survey of CEOs showed a 53 percent preference for navy blue and dark blue, while 39 percent favored gray or charcoal gray. Brown can be acceptable for subsequent interviews at some companies. In summer months, a lightweight beige suit is fine at second or third interviews; you would never wear a light-colored suit except during the warmer months. Ideally, wear a 100 percent wool suit, as wool looks and wears better than any other material. The darker the suit, the more authority it carries. (Beware: A man should not wear a black suit to an interview unless applying for an undertaker's job.) Pinstripes and solids, in dark gray, navy, or medium blue, are equally acceptable, although many feel a dark solid suit is the best option because it gives authority to the wearer and is seen as less stuffy than a pinstripe suit. Somewhat less common but also acceptable are gray-colored glen plaid (also called "Prince of Wales") or houndstooth suits.

A well-cut two-piece suit is preferable (with the standard two-button suit jacket, although the older three-button, single-breasted jacket is quite acceptable) to a three-piece suit that includes a vest or waistcoat. The three-piece is seen as ultraconservative, which might be a useful tool in some situations, but the extra layer of clothing brings in the heat and sweat factor, which argues against it for more practical reasons. Double-breasted jackets are seen as more edgy and you are more likely to wear them to an interview at an advertising agency than at the local bank.

Above all, it's the quality and fit of your suit that matters. Current fashions favor a slimmer cut, particularly in the trousers. However, the fit and cut must complement your own build. The leaner, tapered look elongates your appearance; the looser cuts add bulk. There should be no pull at the jacket shoulders and no gape at the back, and the jacket cuffs should break at your wrists. Your trousers should fit comfortably at the waist. A flat front is most flattering (unless you are enviably scrawny), and there should be only a slight break where the trouser hits the shoe; if your ankles are visible in the mirror, the pants are too damn short! Cuffed trousers add a very sophisticated and conservative look, but an important consideration might be that uncuffed trousers are seen to enhance your height.

Men's Shirts

The principles here are simple:

Rule One: Always wear a long-sleeved shirt.
Rule Two: Always wear a white, cream, or pale blue shirt.
Rule Three: Never wear a short-sleeved shirt.

By white, I do not mean to exclude, for instance, shirts with very thin red or blue pinstripes. Nevertheless there is a presence about a solid white shirt that seems to convey honesty, intelligence, and stability; it should be your first choice. It is true that artists, writers, software engineers, and other creative types are sometimes known to object to white shirts because they feel that it makes it look like "the suit is wearing them"; if this is you and you can't get over it, pale blue may be the best option. Remember—the paler and more subtle the shade, the better the impression you will make. Pale colors draw attention, and your collar is right next to your face, which is where you want the interviewer to stay focused.

While monograms are common enough, those who don't wear them may feel strongly about the implied ostentation of stylized initials on clothing. If you can avoid it, don't take the chance of giving your interviewer a reason to find fault in this area.

Cotton shirts look better and hold up under perspiration more impressively than their synthetic counterparts; if at all possible, opt for a cotton shirt that's been professionally cleaned and starched. A cotton and polyester blend can be an acceptable alternative, but keep in mind that the higher the cotton content, the better the shirt will look. While these blend shirts wrinkle less easily, you are advised to ignore the "wash-and-wear" and "no need to iron" claims you'll read on the front of the package when you purchase them.

Make sure your shirt fits the neck properly; the sleeve cuff should end at the wrist. Details such as frayed fabric and loose buttons will not go unnoticed when you are under professional scrutiny. It's best to choose your interview clothes well in advance, make any minor repairs, have them cleaned, and keep them ready.

Ties

While a cheap-looking tie can ruin an expensive suit, the right tie can do a lot to pull the less-than-perfect suit together for a professional look. When you can't afford a new suit for the interview, you can upgrade your whole look with the right tie.

A pure silk tie makes the most powerful professional impact, has the best finish and feel, and is easiest to tie well. A pure silk tie or a 50 percent wool/ 50 percent silk blend (which is almost wrinkle-proof) should be your choice for the interview. Linen ties are too informal, can only be tied once or twice between cleanings because they wrinkle easily, and only look right during warmer weather anyway. A wool tie is casual in appearance and has knot problems. Most manmade fibers are too shiny, with harsh colors that may undercut your professional image.

The tie should complement your suit. This means that there should be a physical balance: The rule of thumb is that the width of your tie should approximate the width of your lapels. The prevailing standard, which has held for over a decade now, is that ties can range in width between 2-3/4 and 3-1/2 inches. Wearing anything wider may mark you as someone still trapped in the disco era. Currently, ties are being worn narrower in the pages of the fashion magazines, but that really doesn't have to concern you.

While the tie should complement the suit, it should not match it. You would never, for instance, wear a navy blue tie with a navy blue suit. Choose an appropriate tie that neither vanishes into nor battles with your suit pattern. The most popular and safest styles are solids, foulards, stripes, and paisleys.

Do not wear ties with large polka dots, pictures of animals such as leaping trout or soaring mallards, or sporting symbols such as golf clubs or (God forbid) little men on polo ponies. Avoid wearing any piece of apparel that has a manufacturer's symbol emblazoned on the front as part of the decoration.

Other considerations include the length of the tie (it should, when tied, extend to your trouser belt), the size of the knot (smaller is better), and whether you should wear a bow tie to an interview (you shouldn't).

Men's Shoes

Shoes should be either black leather or brown leather. Stay away from all other materials and colors. Lace-up wingtips are the most universally acceptable. Slightly less conservative, but equally appropriate, are slip-on dress shoes—not to be confused with boating shoes. The slip-on, with its low, plain vamp or tassel is versatile enough to be used for both day and evening business wear. Those who are hyperconscious of fashion will say that a lace-up wingtip can look a bit cloddish at dinner; this may be true if you have a dinner interview with the senior law partner of a firm in Chicago, Los Angeles, or New York but otherwise don't lose sleep over it.

In certain areas of the South, Southwest, and West heeled cowboy boots are not at all unusual for business wear, and neither are those Grand Ole Opry versions of the business suit. But beware: outside of Dallas, Nashville, Muskogee, and similar municipalities, you will attract only puzzled stares—so try to be aware of the regional variations in professional dress.

Men's Socks

Socks should complement the suit. Accordingly, they should be blue, black, gray, or brown. When they match the suit color, they extend the length of your leg, giving more height and authority. They should also be long enough for you to cross your legs without showing off lots of bare skin, and should not fall in a bunch toward the ankle as you move. Elastic-reinforced, over-the-calf socks are your best bet.

Men's Accessories

The right accessories can enhance the professional image of any applicant, male or female, just as the wrong accessories can destroy it. The guiding principle here is to include nothing that could be misconstrued or leave a bad impression. For instance, you should not wear obvious religious or political insignias in the form of rings, ties, or pins, as they draw attention to matters that employers are forbidden to address by federal law. This does not necessarily apply when you are aware that a particular spiritual association will establish connectivity, such as wearing a cross when you interview with the Archdiocese.

The watch you wear should be simple and preferably plain, which means that funky Mickey Mouse is out. Sports- and Swatch-style watches, or digital monsters, are acceptable nowadays but aren't the best choice. Don't be afraid to wear a simple, slim analog watch with a leather strap; you will notice it is what the most successful and sophisticated business professionals wear.

A briefcase is always perceived as a symbol of authority and can make a strong professional statement. Leather makes the best impression, with brown and burgundy being the colors of choice. The case is best unadorned—embellishments can only detract from the effect of quiet confidence and authority.

It's a good idea to take a cotton or linen handkerchief on all interviews. Plain white is best because it looks crisp, but the color isn't really that important. You aren't taking a handkerchief to put in a breast pocket but for far more practical reasons. That handkerchief can be used to relieve the clammy-hands syndrome so common before an interview—anything to avoid the infamous "wet fish" handshake. Keep it in an inside pocket, avoiding the matching tie-and-pocket-square look of a dyed-in-the-wool doofus at all costs.

Belts should match or complement the shoes you select. Accordingly, a blue or gray suit will require a black belt and black shoes, while brown, tan, or beige suits call for brown. Wear a good-quality leather belt if you can. The most common mistake made with belts is the buckle; an interview is not the place for your favorite Harley Davidson, Grateful Dead, or Bart Simpson buckle. Select a small, simple buckle that doesn't overwhelm the rest of your look or make personal statements that you cannot be certain will resonate with an interviewer.

Men's Jewelry

Men may wear a wedding band, and cuff links are acceptable with French cuffs. Anything more in the way of jewelry can be dangerous. Necklaces, bracelets, neck chains, and earrings can send the wrong message, and tie tacks and clips are passé in most areas of the country. If you are contemplating a professional career, please understand that visible body piercings and tattoos will forever close many doors to your entry, and most of the rest to your ascent.

Men's Raincoats

The safest and most utilitarian colors for raincoats are beige and blue; stick to these two exclusively. If you can avoid wearing a raincoat, do so (it's an encumbrance and adds to clutter), but it is better to have a raincoat than to have your suit drenched.

Women

Following are the best current dress guidelines for women preparing for a professional interview.

Women's Suits

You have more room for creativity in this area than men do, but also more room for mistakes. Until recent years, your professional fashion creativity had to remain within certain accepted guidelines dictated not by the fashion industry, but by the consensus of the business world—which trails far behind the pages of fashion magazines. And while there are still the limits of good taste and necessary conservatism for the interviewer, the fashion designers have worked hard to create workable professional alternatives for the ever-growing female work force.

A woman's business wardrobe need no longer be simply a pseudo-male selection of drab gray skirts and blouses. With the right cuts, pinstripes and even ties can look both stylish and professional.

Wool and linen are both accepted as the right look for professional women's suits, but linen can present a problem. Linen wrinkles so quickly that you may feel as though you leave the house dressed for success and arrive at your destination looking like a bag lady. Cotton-polyester blends are great for warm climates; they look like linen but lack the "wrinkle factor." Combinations of synthetics and natural fabrics have their advantages: Suits made of such material will certainly retain their shape better. The eye trained to pay attention to detail, however (read: the interviewer's), may detect the type of fabric—say, a cheap polyester blend—and draw unwarranted conclusions about your personality and taste. The choice is up to you. If you do opt for natural fabrics, you will probably want to stay with wool. It provides the smartest look of all and is most versatile and rugged. There are wonderful, ultralight wool gabardines available now that will take you through the toughest interview on the hottest summer day.

Like her male counterpart, the professional woman should stick to solids or pinstripes in gray, navy, and medium blues. The ubiquitous Prince of Wales plaid (glen plaid) or houndstooth check can both look very distinguished on a woman as well. At the same time, a much wider palette of colors is open for consideration by the professional woman, from lilac to fire engine red. While there are situations where you will want to choose one of the more powerful colors, it might be best at one of the subsequent interviews, rather than the first.

A solid skirt with a coordinating subtle plaid jacket is also acceptable, but make sure there is not too much contrast or it will detract from the focus of your meeting: the interview. Colors most suitable for interview suits include charcoal, medium gray, steel gray, black (whereas a man is advised against black, the color is open and acceptable for the professional woman), and navy blue. Of all these looks, the cleanest and most professional is the simple solid navy or gray suit with a white blouse.

Jackets should be simple, well tailored, and stylish, but not stylized. This is probably not the time to wear a peplum-style jacket—a standard length that falls just at the hips is preferable. The cut and style should flatter your build and reflect your personal style, without detracting from what you have to say. Attention to details such as smooth seams, even hemlines, correctly hanging linings, and well-sewn buttons are essential.

How long a skirt should you wear? Any hard-and-fast rule I could offer here would be in danger of being outdated almost immediately, as the fashion industry demands dramatically different looks every season in order to fuel sales. (After all, keeping the same hemlines would mean that last season's clothes could last another season or two.) It should go without saying that you don't want to sport something that soars to the upper thigh if you want to be taken seriously as an applicant. Your best bet is to dress somewhat more conservatively than you would if you were simply showing up for work at the organization in question. Hemlines come and go, and while there is some leeway as to what is appropriate for everyday wear on the job, the safest bet is usually to select something that falls at or no more than two inches above the knee.

Increasingly popular is the one-piece business dress with a matching jacket. This outfit is particularly useful for the "business day into evening crowd," but can be perfectly suitable for interviews if it is properly styled and fitted. It is particularly important to stick with subtle solid colors for this look.

Blouses

Blouses with long sleeves will project a responsible and professional look. Three-quarter-length sleeves are less desirable, followed in turn by short sleeves. Never wear a sleeveless blouse to an interview; you may be confident that there is absolutely no chance that you will be required to remove your jacket, but why take the risk of offending someone with unexpected glimpses of undergarments?

Solid colors and natural fabrics, particularly cotton and silk, are the best selections for blouses—although silk is warm and therefore raises perspiration concerns for a nervous interviewee. Combinations of natural and synthetic fabrics are wrinkle-resistant but do not absorb moisture well, so with these choices you will need to take perspiration countermeasures into account.

The acceptable color spectrum is wider for blouses than for men's shirts, but it is not limitless. The most prudent choices are still white or cream or gray; these offer a universal professional appeal. Pale pink or light blue can also work, but should be worn only if it fully blends into your overall look. Light colors are "friendly" and draw attention to your face, yet will not distract the interviewer from what you have to say. The blouse with a front-tie bow has become dated; a classic softened shirt collar works best with a suit. The button-down collar always looks great, particularly if you are interviewing with a conservative company or industry.

Women's Neckwear

While a woman might choose to wear a string of pearls instead of a scarf to an interview, the scarf can still serve as a powerful status symbol. Opting to wear a scarf says something dramatic about you; make sure it's something positive. A pure silk scarf will offer a conservative look, a good finish, and ease in tying. Some of the better synthetic blends achieve an overall effect that is almost as good. While some books on women's clothing will recommend buying blouses that have matching scarves attached to the collar, there is an increasingly vocal lobby of stylish businesswomen who feel this is the equivalent of mandating that a man wear a clip-on bow tie. As with men's ties, the objective is to complement the outfit, not match it. Avoid overly flamboyant styles, and stick with solids or basic prints (foulards, small polka dots, or paisleys) in subtle colors that will complement—not compete with—your outfit or your conversation.

Women's Shoes

The professional woman has a greater color selection in footwear than does her male counterpart. The shoes should preferably be leather, but in addition to brown and black, a woman is safe in wearing navy, burgundy, forest green, or even, if circumstances warrant and it is not a first interview, red. The color of your shoes should always be the same or a darker tone than your skirt.

It is safest to stay away from faddish or multicolored shoes (even such classics as two-toned oxfords). First, all fashion is transitory, and even if you are up-to-date, you cannot assume that your interviewer is. Second, a good proportion of your interviewers might be men, who are less likely to appreciate vivid color combinations. As with the rest of your wardrobe, stay away from radical choices and opt for the easily comprehensible professional look.

Heel height is important, as well. Flats are fine; a shoe with a heel of up to about 2½ inches is perfectly acceptable. Stay away from high heels; at best you will wobble slightly, and at worst you will walk at an angle. The pump or court shoe, with its closed toe and heel, is perhaps the safest and most conservative look. A closed heel with a slightly open toe is acceptable, too, as is the slingback shoe with a closed toe. The toe on any style should not be overly pointed. Just think moderation in all things; the goal is to get hired, not dated.

Pantyhose

These should not make their own statement. Neutral skin tones are the safest, most conservative choice, though you are perfectly within the realm of professional etiquette when wearing a sheer white or cream if it complements your blouse or dress. You may be an exception if you are interviewing for a job in the fashion industry, in which case you might coordinate colors with your outfit, but be very sure of the company dress code that is already in place. Even in such an instance, avoid loud or glitzy looks.

As you well know, pantyhose and stockings are prone to developing runs at the worst possible moment, so keep an extra pair in your purse or briefcase.

Women's Accessories

Because a briefcase is a symbol of authority, it is an excellent choice for the professional woman. Do not, however, bring both your purse and a briefcase to the interview. (You'll look awkward juggling them.) Instead, transfer essential items to a small clutch bag you can store in the case. In addition to brown and burgundy (recommended colors for the men), you may include navy and black as possible colors for your case, which should always be free of personal, expensive, or distracting embellishments.

Belts should match or complement the shoes you select. A black or gray suit will require a black belt and black shoes; brown, tan, or beige suits will call for brown; and navy looks best with navy or burgundy accessories. In addition, women may wear snakeskin, lizard, and the like (though beware of offending animal rights activists). Remember that the belt is a functional item; if it is instantly noticeable, it is wrong.

Women's Jewelry

As far as jewelry goes, less is more. A woman should restrict rings to engagement or wedding bands if these are applicable, but she can wear a necklace and earrings, as long as these are subdued and professional looking. I should note that some men are put off by earrings of any description in the workplace, so if you wear them keep them small, discreet, and in good taste. Avoid fake or strangely colored pearls, anything with your name or initials on it, and earrings that dangle or jangle. A single bracelet on a woman's wrist is acceptable; anything around the ankle is not. Remember, too much of the wrong kind of jewelry could cost you a job offer or inhibit your promotional opportunities once on the team.

Makeup

Take care never to appear overly made-up; natural is the keyword. Eye makeup should be subtle, so as not to overwhelm the rest of the face. As a general rule, I advise very little lipstick at an interview because it can cause negative reactions in some interviewers, and because it can smudge and wear off as the hours wear on. (Who can say, going in, how long the meeting will last?) However, women tell me that as they advance into their thirties and beyond, the natural pinkness of the lips can fade; you might feel you look pale and washed out without lipstick. So if you feel "undressed" without your lipstick, use some but apply it sparingly and carefully, choose a neutral or subdued color, and, of course, never apply it in public.

For Men and Women: A Note on Personal Hygiene

Bad breath, dandruff, body odor, and dirty, un-manicured nails have the potential to undo all your efforts at putting across a good first impression. These and related problems all speak to an underlying professional slovenliness, which an interviewer may feel will manifest itself in your work. You want to present yourself as an appealing, self-respecting, and enjoyable professional to be around. You can't achieve this if the people you meet have to call on their powers of self-control in order to stay in the same room with you.

What was that old TV body odor commercial tag line: "What even your best friend won't tell you"? So don't ask yourself whether any friend or colleague has actually come out and suggested that you pay more attention to personal hygiene; it is such a touchy issue that most people will avoid you rather than discuss it. Ask yourself how you felt the last time you had to conduct business of any sort with someone who had a hygiene problem. Then resolve never to leave that kind of impression.

Personal grooming of hair, skin, teeth, and nails is easy and straightforward, but body odor is a different challenge. When it comes to body odor you are literally what you eat; onions, garlic, cilantro, and junk food can all give your bodily odors a distinctly unpleasant pungency. Because it takes time for your body to rid itself of such smells, the best advice is to start paying attention to diet as you begin to put your wardrobe together.

BODY LANGUAGE

LEARN TO CONTROL negative body movements and encourage positive ones. Discover the seven guidelines for good body language during your interview.

Given the awful choice of going either blind or deaf, which would you choose? If you're like most people, you would choose to go deaf. As human beings, we rely to a remarkable degree on our ability to gather information visually. This really is not all that surprising, because while speech is a comparatively recent development, humans have been sending and receiving nonverbal signals since the dawn of the species.

In fact, the language of the body is the first means of communication we develop after birth. We master the spoken word later in life, and in so doing we forget the importance of nonverbal cues—but the signals are still sent and received (usually at a subconscious level).

It is common to hear people say of the body language they use, "Take me or leave me as I am." This is all very well if you have no concern for what others think of you. For those seeking professional employment, however, it is important to recognize that your body is constantly sending messages, and to make every effort to understand and control the information stream. If your mouth says, "Hire me," but your body says, "I'm not being truthful," you are likely to leave the interviewer confused. "Well," he or she will think, "the right answers all came out, but there was something about that candidate that just rubbed me the wrong way." Such misgivings are generally sufficient to keep a candidate from making the short list. The interviewer may or may not be aware of what causes the concern, but the messages will be sent, and your cause will suffer.

Of course, interviewers can be expected to listen carefully to what you say, too. When your body language doesn't contradict your statements, you will generally be given credence. When your body language complements your verbal statements, your message will gain a great deal of impact, but when your body language *contradicts* what you say, the interviewer will be skeptical. In short, learning to use positive body signals and control negative ones during an interview can have a significant impact on your job search and on the new job.

Under the Microscope

The challenge for the interviewer is to determine, using every means at his or her disposal, what kind of an employee you would make. Your task as a candidate is to provide the clues most likely to prompt a decision to hire.

Let's begin at the beginning. When you are invited in to an interview, you are probably safe in assuming that your interviewer believes you meet certain minimum standards and could conceivably be hired.

In this context, the adage that actions speak louder than words appears to be something you should take quite literally. Studies done at the University of Chicago found that over 50 percent of all effective communication relies on body language. Since you can expect interviewers to respond to the body language you employ at the interview, it is up to you to decide what messages you want them to receive.

There are also studies that suggest the impression you create in the first few minutes of the interview is the most lasting. Since the first few minutes after you meet the interviewer is a time when he or she is doing the vast majority of the talking, you have very little control over the impression you create with your words—you can't say much of anything! It is up to your body to do the job for you.

The Greeting

For a good handshake:

1. Your hands should be clean and adequately manicured.
2. Your hands should be free of perspiration.

It is best to allow the interviewer to initiate the handshake. If, through nerves, you find yourself initiating the handshake, don't pull back, as you will appear indecisive. Instead, make the best of it, smile confidently, and make good eye contact.

Your handshake should signal cooperation and friendliness. Match the pressure extended by the interviewer—never exceed it. A typical professional handshake lasts for between two and five seconds, just two or three reasonably firm up and down pumps accompanied by a smile. The parting handshake may last a little longer; smile and lean forward very slightly as you shake hands before departing.

Certain professional and cultural differences should also be considered as well. Many doctors, artists, and others who do delicate work with their hands can and do give less enthusiastic handshakes than other people. If you work in media you'll notice that quite frequently on-air personalities don't want to shake hands at all; it's the easiest way to catch a cold and they depend on their voices and appearance more than most. Similarly, the English handshake is considerably less firm than the American, while the German variety is typically firm.

Use only one hand and always shake vertically. Do not extend your hand parallel to the floor with the palm up, as this conveys submissiveness. By the same token, you may be seen as too aggressive if you extend your hand outward with the palm facing down.

While a confident and positive handshake helps break the ice and gets the interview moving in the right direction, proper use of the hands throughout the rest of the interview will help convey an above-board, "nothing-to-hide" message.

Watch out for hands and fingers that take on a life of their own, fidgeting with themselves or other objects such as pens, paper, your tie, or your hair. Pen tapping is interpreted as the action of an impatient person; this is an example of an otherwise trivial habit that can take on immense significance in an interview situation. Rarely will an interviewer ask you to stop doing something annoying. Instead, he'll simply make a mental note that you are an annoying person, and congratulate himself for picking this up before making the mistake of hiring you.

Other negative hand messages include:

- Clasping your hands behind your head: You'll expose perspiration marks, and you run the risk of appearing smug, superior, bored, and possibly withdrawn.
- Showing insecurity by constantly adjusting your tie: When interviewing with a woman, this gesture might be interpreted as displaying something beyond a businesslike interest in the interviewer.
- Slouching in your chair, with hands in pockets or thumbs in belt: This posture can brand you as insolent and aggressive (just recall any teenage boy). When this error is made in the presence of an interviewer of the opposite sex, it can carry sexually aggressive overtones as well.
- Pulling your collar away from your neck: This may seem like an innocent enough reaction to the heat of the day, but the interviewer might assume that you are tense or masking an untruth. The same goes for scratching your neck during, before, or after your response to a question.
- Moving your hands toward a personal feature that you perceive as deficient: This is a common unconscious reaction to stress. A man with thinning hair, for example, may thoughtlessly put his hand to his forehead when pondering how to respond to the query, "Why aren't you earning more at your age?" This habit may be extremely difficult for you to detect in the first place, much less reverse, but make the effort. Such protective movements are likely to be perceived—if only on a subliminal level—as acknowledgments of low self-esteem.
- Picking at invisible bits of fluff on one's suit: This gesture looks exactly like what it is, a nervous tic. Keep your focus on the interviewer. If you do have some bit of lint somewhere on your clothing, the best advice is usually to ignore it until you can remove it discreetly.

By contrast, employing the hands in a positive way can further your candidacy:

- Subtly exposing your palms now and then as you speak can help demonstrate that you are open, friendly, and have nothing to hide. You can see this technique used to great effect by politicians and television talk show hosts.

- It can, very occasionally, be beneficial to "steeple" your fingers for a few seconds as you consider a question or when you first start to talk. Unless you hold the gesture for long periods of time, it will be perceived as a neutral demonstration of your thoughtfulness. Of course, if you overuse this or hold the position for too long, you may be taken as condescending. Steepling also gives you something constructive to do with your hands; it offers a change from holding your pad and pen.

Taking Your Seat

Some thirty inches from my nose
The frontier of my person goes.
Beware of rudely crossing it,
I have no gun, but I can spit.
　　　　　　　—W. H. Auden

Encroaching on another's "personal zone" is a bad idea in any business situation, but it is particularly dangerous in an interview. The 30-inch standard is a good one to follow: It is the distance that allows you to extend your hand comfortably for a handshake. Maintain this distance throughout the interview, and be particularly watchful of personal-space intrusions when you first meet, greet, and take a seat.

A person's office is an extension of his or her personal zone; this is why it is not only polite but also sound business sense to wait until the interviewer offers you a seat.

It is not uncommon to meet with an interviewer in a conference room or another supposedly "neutral" site. Again, wait for the interviewer to motion you to a spot, or, if you feel uncomfortable doing this, tactfully ask the interviewer to take the initiative: "Where would you like me to sit?"

The type of chair you sit in can affect the signals your body sends during an interview. If you have a choice, go with an upright chair with arms. Deep armchairs can restrict your ability to send certain positive signals, and encourage the likelihood of slumping. They're best suited for watching television, not for projecting the image of a competent professional.

Always sit with your bottom well back in the chair and your back straight. Slouching, of course, is out, but a slight forward leaning posture will show interest and friendliness toward the interviewer. Keep your hands on the sides of the chair; if there are no arms on the chair, keep your hands in your lap or on your pad of paper.

Crossed legs, in all their many forms, send a mixture of signals; most of them are negative:

- Crossing one ankle over the other knee can show a certain stubborn and recalcitrant outlook (as well as the bottom of your shoe, which is not always a pretty sight). The negative signal is intensified when you grasp the horizontally crossed leg or—worst of all—cross your arms across your chest.
- Some body language experts feel crossed ankles indicate that the person doing the crossing is withholding information. Of course, since the majority of interviews take place across a desk, crossed ankles will often be virtually unnoticeable. For women, some dress fashions encourage decorous ankle crossing. This body signal is probably the most permissible faux pas to erect; if you must allow yourself one body language vice, this is the one to choose.
- When sitting in armchairs or on sofas, crossing the legs may be necessary to create some stability amid all the plush upholstery. In this instance, the signals you send by crossing your legs will be neutral, as long as your crossed legs point toward, rather than away from, the interviewer.

Facial Signals

Once you take your seats, most often across a desk, and the conversation begins, the interviewer's attention will be focused on your face.

Our language is full of expressions testifying to the powerful influence of facial mannerisms. When you say that someone is shifty-eyed, tight-lipped, has a furrowed brow, flashes bedroom eyes, stares into space, or grins like a Cheshire cat, you are speaking in a kind of shorthand and using a set of stereotypes that enables us to make judgments—consciously or unconsciously—about that person.

Tight smiles and tension in the facial muscles often bespeak an inability to handle stress; little eye contact can communicate a desire to hide something; pursed lips are often associated with a secretive nature; and frowning, looking sideways, or peering over one's glasses can send signals of haughtiness and arrogance. Hardly the stuff of which winning interviews are made!

The Eyes

Looking at someone means showing interest in that person, and showing interest is a giant step forward in making the right impression. Remember: we are all our own favorite subjects!

Looking away from the interviewer for long periods while he is talking, closing your eyes while being addressed, and repeatedly shifting focus from the subject to some other point are all likely to leave the wrong impression.

Of course, there is a big difference between looking and staring at someone! Rather than looking at the speaker straight on at all times, create a mental triangle incorporating both of the eyes and the mouth; your eyes will follow a natural, continuous path along the three points. Maintain this approach for roughly three-quarters of the time; you can break your gaze to look at the interviewer's hands as points are emphasized or to refer to your notepad. This is the way we maintain eye contact in nonstressful situations, and it will allow you to appear attentive, sincere, and committed.

Be wary of breaking eye contact too abruptly and of shifting your focus in ways that will disrupt the atmosphere of professionalism. Examining the interviewer below the head and shoulders, for instance, is a sign of overfamiliarity. This is especially important when being interviewed by someone of the opposite sex.

The eyebrows send messages as well. Under stress, one's brows may wrinkle; this sends a negative signal about your ability to handle challenges in the business world. The best thing to do is take a deep breath and collect yourself. Most of the tension that people feel at interviews has to do with anxiety about how to respond to what the interviewer will ask.

The Head

Nodding your head slowly shows interest, validates the comments of your interviewer, and subtly encourages her to continue. Tilting the head slightly, when combined with eye contact and a natural smile, demonstrates friendliness and approachability. The tilt should be momentary and not exaggerated, almost like a bob of the head to one side. (Do not overuse this technique unless you are applying for a job in a parrot shop!) Rapidly nodding your head can leave the impression that you are impatient and eager to add something to the conversation—if only the interviewer would let you.

The Mouth

One guiding principle of good body language is to turn your mouth upward rather than downward. Look at two boxers after a fight: the victor's arms are raised high, his back is straight, and his shoulders are square. His smiling face is thrust upward and outward, and you see happiness, openness, warmth, and confidence. The loser, on the other hand, is slumped forward, brows knit and eyes downcast, and the signals you receive are those of anger, frustration, belligerence, and defeat.

Your smile is one of the most powerful positive body signals in your arsenal, and it exemplifies the up-is-best principle. Offer an unforced, confident smile as frequently as opportunity and circumstances dictate; avoid grinning idiotically, as this indicates that you may not be quite right in the head.

You should be aware that the mouth also provides a seemingly limitless supply of opportunities to convey weakness. This may be done by touching the mouth frequently; "faking" a cough when confronted with a difficult question; or gnawing on one's lips absentmindedly. Employing any of these "insincerity signs" when you are asked about, say, why you lost your last job, might instill or confirm suspicions about your honesty or openness.

Glasses

People who wear glasses sometimes leave them off when going on an interview in an attempt to project a more favorable image. There are difficulties with this approach. Farsighted people who don't wear their glasses will (unwittingly) seem to stare long and hard at the people they converse with, and this is a negative signal. Also, pulling out glasses for reading and peering over the top of your glasses—even if you have been handed something to read and subsequently asked a question—carries professorial connotations that can be interpreted as critical. If you wear glasses for reading, you should remove them when conversing, replacing them only when appropriate.

Wearing dark glasses to an interview will paint you as secretive, cold, and devious. Even if your prescription glasses are tinted, the effect will be the same. You might consider un-tinted glasses for your interview, or contacts. At the same time, glasses on a younger-looking person can add an air of seriousness and might be considered a plus.

Body Signal Barricades

Folding or crossing your arms, or holding things in front of the body, sends negative messages to the interviewer: "I know you're there, but you can't come in. I'm nervous and closed for business."

It is bad enough to feel this way, but worse to express it with blatant signals. Don't fold your arms or "protect" your chest with hands, clipboard, briefcase, or anything else during the interview. You can, however, keep a pad and pen on your lap. It makes you look organized and gives you something to do with your hands.

Feet

Some foot signals can have negative connotations. Women and men wearing slip-on shoes should beware of dangling the loose shoe from the toes; this can be distracting, and, as it is a gesture often used to signal physical attraction, it has no place in a job interview. Likewise, avoid compulsive jabbing of floor, desk, or chair with your foot; this can be perceived as a hostile and angry motion, and is likely to annoy the interviewer.

Some people (your author is included in the front ranks on this one) have an annoying habit of jiggling one leg up and down on the ball of the foot. Those of us who do this know it is a tic that says we are totally engaged and excited about some topic (and sometimes even the one under discussion), but those forced to endure it find it distracting and can interpret it as impatience. If you are a dreaded jiggler, you must get this under control for your job interviews!

Walking

Many interviews will require that you walk from one place to the next—on a guided tour of facilities, from one office to another, or to and from the table in a restaurant. (Of course, if you are interviewing in a restaurant, you will have to walk with your interviewer to and from the dining facility.) How long these walks last is not as important as how you use them to reinforce positive professional behaviors and impressions.

Posture is your main concern: Keep your shoulders back and maintain an erect posture. Smile and make eye contact as appropriate. Avoid fidgeting with your feet as you move, rubbing one shoe against the other, or kicking absent-mindedly at the ground if you stand to talk; these signals will lead others to believe that you are anxious or insecure. Crossing your arms or legs while standing carries the same negative connotations as it does when you are sitting. Putting your hands in your pockets or hands-on-hips or thumbs-in-belt postures are all to be avoided. These send messages that you are aggressive and dominating. It is better to hold a pad and pen, or keep your arms on the arms of the chair, which will also help you avoid slouching. Remember to show one or both of your palms occasionally as you make points, but do not overuse this gesture.

Putting It All Together

Now you have the big picture, and you can begin to be more aware of the signals your body can unwittingly send. Let's reduce all this information into a handful of simple recommendations. Positive signals reinforce one another; employing them in combination yields an overwhelming positive message that is truly greater than the sum of its parts.

So far we have focused primarily on the pitfalls to avoid—but what messages *should* be sent, and how? Here are seven general suggestions on good body language for the interview:

1. Walk slowly, and stand tall upon entering the room.
2. On greeting your interviewer, give a smile, make eye contact, and respond warmly to the interviewer's greeting and handshake.
3. As you sit, get your butt well back in the chair; this allows the chair back to help you sit upright. Increase the impression of openness ("I have nothing to hide!") by unbuttoning your jacket as you sit down. Keep your head up. Maintain eye contact a good portion of the time, especially when the interviewer begins to speak and when you reply. Smile naturally whenever the opportunity arises.
4. Use mirroring techniques to reproduce the positive signals your interviewer sends. Say the interviewer leans forward to make a point; a few moments later, you too lean forward slightly, demonstrating that you don't want to miss a word. Perhaps the interviewer leans back and laughs; you "laugh beneath" the interviewer's laughter, taking care not to overwhelm your partner by using an inappropriate volume level. This can seem contrived at first, but through observing those in your own social circle, you'll notice that this is natural behavior for good communicators.
5. Keep your head up and your eyes front at all times—and don't slouch in your seat.
6. Try to remain calm and do not hurry your movements; you'll look harried and are more likely to knock things over. Most people are more klutzy when they are nervous, and consciously slowing your body movements will lessen the chances of disaster and give you a more controlled persona.
7. Remember to breathe. When we are nervous we can forget to do this, which leads to oxygen deprivation and obviously screws up cognitive processes.

Open for Business

The more open your body movements during the interview, the more you will be perceived as open yourself. Understanding and directing your body language will give you added power to turn interviews into cooperative exchanges between two professionals.

Just as you interpret the body language of others, both positive and negative, your body language makes an indelible impression on those you meet. It tells them whether you like and have confidence in yourself, whether or not you are pleasant to be around, and whether you are more likely to be honest or deceitful. Like it or not, your body carries these messages for the world to see.

Job interviews are reliable in one way: They bring out insecurities. All the more reason to consciously manage the impressions your body sends. You will absorb the lessons in this chapter quite quickly if you take the time to observe and interpret the body signals of friends and family. When you see and can understand body language in others, you'll be more aware of your own, and more capable of controlling it.

THE CURTAIN RISES ON THE JOB INTERVIEW

FIRST IMPRESSIONS ARE the strongest. Here are the preparations to make before heading out to the interview.

Backstage in the theater, the announcement "Places, please" is made five minutes before the curtain rises. It's the performers' signal to psych themselves up, complete final costume adjustments, and make time to reach the stage. They are getting ready to go onstage and knock 'em dead. You should go through a similar process to get thoroughly prepared for your time in the spotlight.

Winning a job offer depends not only on the things you do well but also on the mistakes you avoid. As the interview approaches, settle down with your résumé and the exercises you performed in building it. Immerse yourself in your past successes and the professional behaviors that made them possible. Interview nerves are to be expected; the trick is to use them to your benefit by harnessing that nervous energy for your physical and mental preparation.

The company dossier: Always take a few copies of your résumé and executive briefing: one for you and one for each of the interviewers you might meet. Your main interviewer will invariably have a copy of your résumé, but you can't be certain of that with other people you meet. It is perfectly acceptable to have your résumé in front of you at the interview; it shows you are organized, and it makes a great cheat sheet. It is not unusual to hear, "Mr. Jones wasn't hired because he didn't pay attention to detail and couldn't even remember his employment dates"—just the kind of thing you are likely to forget in the nervousness of the moment.

A pad of paper and writing instruments: These demonstrate your preparedness, and they give you something constructive to do with your hands during the interview.

Reference letters: If you have reference letters from past employers, take them along. Some employers don't put much stock in written references and prefer a one-on-one conversation with past employers. Nevertheless, having them with you and getting them placed in your candidate file can't do any harm.

A list of job-related questions: The details of the job you already know are likely to be general in nature. Asking questions that give you the practical details of the activities you will be involved with in the first few months will make you think about your experience with a focus that is complementary to that of your interviewers. You might ask:

- "What are the most immediate challenges of the job?"
- "What are the most important projects of the first six months?"
- "What skills and behaviors are most important to success on the job?"
- "Why do some people succeed and others fail doing this work?"
- "Why is the job open?"
- "What is the job's relationship to other departments?"
- "How do the job and the department relate to the corporate mission?"

You can find more questions to ask at the end of Chapter 11, "How to Knock 'em Dead." (*Note:* In the early rounds of interviewing, stay away from questions about where the job can lead and what the pay and benefits are. It's not that these questions aren't important to you, just that the timing is wrong. It won't do you any good to know what a job pays when you aren't going to get a job offer. Instead, ask the questions that will lead to a job offer being extended, then ask the questions you need to evaluate that offer. For questions to ask during the negotiation phase, see Chapter 20, "Negotiating the Job Offer."

Any additional information you have about the company or the job: If time permits, visit the company Web site, review any company literature and research you might have, and do a Google search for news articles mentioning the company by name, and for articles that relate to your profession.

Directions to the interview: Decide on your form of transportation and finalize your time of departure, leaving enough time to accommodate travel delays. Check the route, distance, and travel time. If you forget to verify date, time, and place (including floor and suite number), you might not even arrive at the right place, or on the right day, for your interview. Write it all down legibly and put it with the rest of your interview kit.

To arrive at an interview too early indicates overanxiousness and to arrive late is inconsiderate, so arrive at the interview on time, but at the location early. This allows you time to visit the restroom (usually your only private sanctuary at an interview) and make the necessary adjustments to your appearance, review any notes, and put on your "game face." Remember to add contact telephone numbers to your interview kit, so if you are delayed on the way to the interview, you can call and let the interviewer know.

Your dress should be clean-cut and conservative. As you could be asked to appear for an interview at a scant couple of hours' notice, keep your best outfit freshly cleaned, your shirts or blouses wrinkle-free, and your shoes polished, and reserve them exclusively for interviews.

Visit the hairdresser once a month so that you always look groomed, and keep your nails clean and trimmed at all times (even if you work with your hands). While you will naturally shower or bathe prior to an interview, and the use of an unscented deodorant is advisable, you should avoid wearing after-shave or perfume; you are trying to get a job, not a date. Never drink alcohol the day before an interview. It affects eyes, skin tone, and your wits.

When you get to the interview site, visit the restroom to check your appearance and take a couple of minutes to do the following:

- Review the company dossier.
- Recall your commitment to the profession and the team, and the professional behaviors that help you succeed.
- Breathe deeply and slowly for a minute to dispel your natural physical tension.
- Review the questions you will need to identify first projects and initial needs.
- Smile and head for the interview—you are as ready as you are ever going to be. Afterward you will review your performance to make sure the next one goes even better.

Under no circumstances should you back out because you do not like the receptionist or the look of the office—that would be allowing those interview nerves to get the better of you. As you are shown into the office, you are on!

This potential new employer wants an aggressive and dynamic employee, but someone who is less aggressive and dynamic than he or she is, so take your lead from the interviewer.

Do:

- Give a firm handshake—respond to the interviewer's grip and duration.
- Make eye contact and smile. Say, "Hello, Ms. Larsen. I am John Jones. I have been looking forward to meeting you."

Do not:

- Use first names (unless asked).
- Smoke (even if invited).
- Sit down (until invited).
- Show anxiety or boredom.
- Look at your watch.
- Discuss equal rights, sex, race, national origin, religion, or age.
- Show samples of your work (unless requested).
- Ask about benefits, salary, or vacation.

Now you are ready for anything—except for the tough questions that are going to be thrown at you next. We'll handle those in the following pages.

GREAT ANSWERS TO TOUGH INTERVIEW QUESTIONS

IN THIS PART of the book you will learn why interviewers do the things they do. You'll also learn the formulas for answering tough interview questions without sounding like a snake oil salesman.

"LIKE BEING ON TRIAL FOR YOUR LIFE" is how many people look at a job interview. With the interviewer as judge and jury, you are at least on trial for your livelihood, so you must have winning strategies. F. Lee Bailey, one of America's most celebrated defense attorneys, attributes his success in the courtroom to preparation. He likens himself to a magician going into court with fifty rabbits in his hat, not knowing which one he'll really need, but ready to pull out any single one. Bailey is successful because he is ready for any eventuality and because he takes the time to analyze every situation and every possible option. He never underestimates his opposition, he is always prepared, and he usually wins.

Another famous attorney, Louis Nizer, successfully defended all of his fifty-plus capital offense clients. When lauded as the greatest courtroom performer of his day, Nizer denied the accolade. He claimed for himself only the distinction of being the *best prepared*.

You won't win your day in court just based on your skills. As competition for the best jobs increases, employers are comparing more candidates for every opening and becoming more skilled in the art of selection. To consistently win against stiff competition, like Bailey and Nizer, you have to be prepared for the questions that can be thrown at you, and that requires understanding what is behind them.

During an interview, employers ask you dozens of searching questions—questions that test your knowledge, skills, confidence, poise, and professional behaviors (we'll address this in some detail in a few pages). There are questions that can trick you into contradicting yourself and questions that probe your analytical skills and integrity. They are all designed so the interviewer can make decisions in these critical areas:

- Can you do the job?
- Are you motivated to take the extra step?
- Are you manageable and a team player?
- Are you professional in all your behaviors?
- Are you a problem solver?

Being able to do the job is only a small part of getting an offer. Questions of whether you are motivated to make an extra effort, whether you are manageable and a team player, and whether you think of yourself as a problem-identifier and problem-solver, are just as important to the interviewer. In this era of high unemployment and deep specialization, companies look more actively at the way you behave in the workplace and your professional behavioral profile. Specific desirable professional behaviors cannot be ascertained by a single question or answer, so the interviewer will seek a pattern in your replies that shows your possession of such behaviors—I discuss them in detail in Chapter 11.

You not only have to make a case for yourself in these five areas, you need to avoid these deadly traps that can damage your candidacy:

- Failing to listen to the question.
- Answering a question that was not asked.
- Providing superfluous, inappropriate, or irrelevant information.
- Being unprepared for the interview.

The effect of these blunders is cumulative, and each reduces your chance of receiving a job offer.

The number of offers you win in your search for the ideal job depends on your ability to answer a staggering array of questions in terms that have value and relevance to the employer: "Why do you want to work here?" "What are your biggest accomplishments?" "How long will it take you to make a contribution?" "Why should I hire you?" "What can you do for us that someone else cannot do?" "What is your greatest weakness?" "Why aren't you earning more?" and "What interests you about this job?"

The questions and answers in the following chapters come from across the job spectrum. Though a particular sample answer might come from the mouth of an administrator (while you are a scientist or perhaps an executive in one of the service industries), we all have a common ground in the ways we contribute to our respective bottom lines; this overlap guarantees their relevance to your concerns. I'll give you the question, then explain its motivation and the types of information the employer will be looking for in your answers.

Notice that many of the sample answers teach a small lesson in professional survival—something you can use both to get the job and to help you climb the ladder of success.

The answers provided in the following chapters should *not* be repeated word for word, exactly as they come off the page. You have to tailor them to your profession, illustrate them with examples from your own real-world experience, and, since you have your own style of speech, put the answers into your own words.

THE FIVE SECRETS OF THE HIRE

KNOWING HOW AN interviewer thinks is a critical element of the job search too frequently overlooked.

Every hire in every profession and every company, at every level, all over the world, was made based on the five criteria that unfold in this chapter, so you might want to read it twice—it's that important. Understanding these five secrets of the hire will revolutionize the way you perform at job interviews; they will also propel your climb up the professional ladder.

An employer never wakes up in the morning and says, "It's a wonderful day in the neighborhood; I think I'll go hire us an accountant." Employees never get added to the payroll for the fun of it; rather, they get added to the payroll to make a difference with their presence, to make a contribution to the bottom line (make money, save money, save time), and to solve and prevent problems in their area of expertise. You get hired to prevent problems and, when prevention isn't an option, to solve them as they arise in the daily discharge of your duties. In the process, you are also expected to make a contribution to the bottom line by contributing either to revenue generation or productivity. The following five criteria that employers apply to each and every hire they make all relate to this overriding "problem identification and solution" concern that gave rise to the job opening in the first place.

The First Secret: Ability and Suitability

Saying, "Hey, I can do this job—give me a shot and I'll prove it to you" is not enough. You have to prove it by demonstrating a combination of all the skills that define your ability to do the job in question and your suitability for the position. How well you program that computer, service that client, or sew up that appendix is part of the picture; but knowing the steps involved well enough to be able to explain them clearly and simply to others is equally important.

In this chapter we are going to deconstruct jobs and the selection cycle in a number of different ways to give you a complete understanding of how to ace job interviews. The first step we have taken is to recognize that all of our jobs are, at some level, those of problem solvers. Another way of distilling work down to its essence, in a way that will increase your understanding and interview performance, is to recognize that you bring two sets of skills to a job:

1. The professional/technical skills that allow you to be productive in your area of expertise and application.
2. The profession/industry knowledge that helps you understand "the way things get done in banking/agribusiness/pharmaceuticals." Those ways differ from one industry to the next.

For example, a computer programmer working in a bank has technical and professional skills; that is, he can write a program as requested by the employer, and at the same time he also has a knowledge of how to get things done in the industry in which he operates (in this case, understanding why the banking industry operates the way it does). Such professional or industry knowledge speaks to another level of awareness and suitability. Demonstrating both professional/technical and industry skills will help set you apart.

When you can explain the work you do in clear, simple terms and demonstrate how that role fits into the overall efforts of the department (and, in turn, the company), it helps your interview performance. An objective understanding of what employers are actually going to be looking for and asking you questions about during the interview to determine your ability and suitability, will also make a significant difference in your performance. Make sure that you go through the steps of Target Job Deconstruction described in Chapter 2. The information and understanding you gather through that process will really help you ace any job interview.

With this Target Job Deconstruction process, you learn both what employers will want to talk about and the nuts and bolts that will hold your answers together. In a few chapters we'll talk about handling different types of interviewers, one of which will be the one that doesn't know how to interview, and consequently doesn't ask the questions to allow you to shine. You've probably met these characters along the way and wondered how to deal with them. Now you have the tools: You know what they need to hear about even if they don't ask the right questions, and I'll show you how to get the information across in Chapter 13, "The Other Side of the Desk."

The Second Secret: Motivation

Employers are leery of people who can do the job but who want to do as little of it as possible. Identifying candidates motivated by a professional commitment to take the rough with the smooth, the rotten assignments with the plum ones is a major consideration for any employer.

Occasionally, you may find an interviewer asking you such questions as "Are you willing to make coffee?" The issue isn't whether you are prepared to do demeaning tasks. It is whether you are the kind of person who is prepared to do whatever it takes to help the team survive and prosper. Can you take the rough with the smooth? Are you prepared to go that extra mile? You are? Great. Think of a time when you did. Figure out how doing so helped your team and helped the company. Now rehearse the story until you can tell it in about 90 seconds. Show enthusiasm for your work and your profession, and show enthusiasm for the opportunity; it just might be the tiebreaker for your ideal job.

When it comes to a tightly run job race between equally qualified candidates, the offer will always go to the most enthusiastic contender. When you know a number of things about the company (and this is often easy to research on the Internet) and are clearly excited about the opportunity to become a member of the team, your visible motivation will tip the scales in your favor; this is because your enthusiasm is interpreted as an indicator of the energy you will put into your work.

The Third Secret: Manageability and Teamwork

There isn't a manager in the world who enjoys the challenges caused by an unmanageable employee. Avoiding such problems is a major concern for managers, who develop a remarkable sixth sense when it comes to spotting and cutting out mavericks.

Manageability is defined in different ways: the ability to work alone; the ability to work with others; the ability to take direction and criticism when it is carefully and considerately given; and, possibly dearest to the manager's heart, the ability to take direction when it isn't carefully and considerately given, perhaps because of a crisis. Equally crucial is a willingness to work with others regardless of their sex, sexual orientation, age, religion, physical appearance, abilities or disabilities, skin color, or national origin.

Such "manageability" considerations make a job interview tricky. Yes, you should certainly state your strongly held convictions—after all, you don't want to appear wishy-washy—but you should do so only as long as they are professional in nature and relate to the job at hand.

Let me give you an example of what I mean. Readers have asked me occasionally about what they perceive as discrimination as a result of their strongly held religious beliefs. Today's managers will usually go well out of their way to avoid even the perception of intolerance toward sincerely held spiritual beliefs. Yet, by the same token, they are deeply suspicious of any strident religious rhetoric that surfaces in a professional setting. (This also holds true of political, ethnic, and other inappropriate issues raised by a candidate during an interview.) The potential employer's caution in these circumstances, far from representing discrimination, is a sign of concern that the candidate might not be tolerant of the views of others—and might thereby become an obstacle to a harmonious work group.

The rules here are simple: Don't bring up religious, political, social, or racial matters during the job interview. If in doubt, ask yourself, "Is this topic relevant to my ability to do the job?" The interview is a potential paycheck—don't mess with it. You're a team player with a genuine liking for your fellow man. You are someone who gets along well with others, and because you have respect for other human beings, you have no problem tolerating the opinions or beliefs of others. Demonstrate this with your every word and action, and you will embody the spirit of decent people the world over.

The Fourth Secret: Professional Behavior

I emphasize professional behavior throughout this book because, to a large extent, the behaviors that are most desirable to employers are learned and developed as a result of our experiences in the workplace, not the behaviors we developed growing up. Remember that first day on your first job, when you eventually got up the courage to go forage for a cup of coffee? You found the coffee machine, and stuck on the wall there was a handwritten sign reading:

YOUR MOTHER DOESN'T WORK HERE
PICK UP AFTER YOURSELF

You thought to yourself, "Pick up after myself? Gee, I gotta learn a whole new way of behaving." So you started to observe and emulate the more successful professionals around you, and you slowly developed a whole slate of learned behaviors that help you succeed throughout your professional life.

An important component of your interview arsenal is the ability to show employers you are in possession of the full slate of professional behaviors they universally seek. These are the very behaviors that get you hired, get you noticed, land plum assignments, and generate promotions and raises—in short, they enable you to succeed in all your professional endeavors.

Showing possession of these universally admired professional behaviors, and exhibiting them in action with illustrative examples you give in answers to tough interview questions, is your passport to success at any interview. They will give your answers substance and a ring of truth. Going through the list of learned professional behaviors, you probably recognize that you apply many of them on a regular basis in your work; if not, they are readily learnable and you'll be able to begin developing these valuable career assets as soon as you recognize their importance. As you read through the list of behaviors, you'll see, for example, "determination," and think, "Yes, I'm a determined kind of gal." When this happens, try to come up with times when you used determination in the execution of your duties. You might also come across "time management and organization," and say, "*Oy vey*, now there's something I have to work on!" In this instance you have identified a key behavior that needs work, and you can immediately set about an improvement program.

The examples generated can be used in your résumé, in your cover letters, and as illustrative answers to questions in interviews. Then when you get asked, "So why are you different?" you will have something meaningful to say, and the illustrations that you provide will give that aura of truth to your claims.

Absorbing this list of learnable professional behaviors and making them part of the professional you will win you interviews and job offers, as well as provide the backbone of your long-term career success.

Communication and Listening Skills: The ability to communicate effectively to people at all levels in a company is a key to success. It refers to verbal and written skills along with technological know-how, dress, and body language. This is an especially important consideration when it comes to your cover letter and résumé, because these written documents are the first means an employer has of judging your communication skills. It means you must take the time to craft, edit, and re-edit your cover letter until it communicates what you want it to, including the fact that you have adequate communication skills.

I recently counseled an executive vice president in the $400,000-a-year range, and he was having problems getting in front of the right people. The first paragraph of his résumé stated that he was an executive with "superior communication skills"; unfortunately, the last twelve words of the sentence gave away his lie—they contained two spelling errors! In an age of spell checkers, this sloppiness isn't acceptable at any level.

Communication embraces *listening skills*: listening and understanding, as opposed to just waiting your turn to talk. Consciously develop your "listening to understand" skills, and the result will be improved and more persuasive communication abilities.

Goal-Orientation: All employers are interested in goal-oriented professionals: Those who achieve concrete results with their actions and who constantly strive to get the job done, rather than just filling the time allotted for a particular task. You might be able to include an example or reference to this behavior, or others, in your letters and résumé.

Willingness to Be a Team Player: The highest achievers (always goal-oriented) are invariably *team players;* employers look for employees who work for the common good and always keep the group's goals and responsibilities in mind. Team players take pride in group achievement rather than personal aggrandizement and look for solutions rather than someone to blame.

Motivation and Energy: Employers realize that a motivated professional will do a better job on every assignment. Motivation expresses itself in a commitment to the job and the profession, an eagerness to learn and grow professionally, and a willingness to take the rough with the smooth.

Motivation is invariably expressed by the *energy* someone demonstrates in their work, and is demonstrated by always giving that extra effort to get the job done and to get it done right.

Analytical Skills: This includes being able to weigh the short- and long-term benefits of a proposed course of action against all its possible negatives. We see these skills demonstrated in the way a person identifies potential problems and thereby minimizes their occurrence. Successful application of analytical skills at work requires an understanding of how your job and your department fit into the overall goal of profitability. It also means thinking things through and not jumping at the first or easiest solution.

Dedication and Reliability: Dedication to your profession, the role it plays in the larger issues of company success, and the empowerment that comes from knowing how your part contributes to the greater good are all desirable professional characteristics. Dedication to your professionalism is also a demonstration of enlightened self-interest. The more you are engaged in your career, the more likely you are to join the inner circles that exist in every department and company, enhancing opportunities for advancement. At the same time, this dedication will repay you with better job security and improved professional horizons.

Your dedication will also express itself in your *reliability*: Showing up is half the battle; the other half is your performance on the job. This requires following up on your actions, not relying on anyone else to ensure the job is done well, and keeping management informed every step of the way.

Determination: A determined individual is one who does not back off when a problem or situation gets tough. It's the one who chooses to be part of the solution rather than standing idly by and being part of the problem. Determined professionals have decided to make a difference with their presence every day and are willing to do whatever it takes to get a job done, even if that includes duties that might not appear in a job description.

Confidence: As you develop desirable professional behaviors, your confidence grows in the skills you have and in your ability to develop new ones, and with this comes confidence in taking on new challenges. You have the confidence to ask questions, the confidence to look at challenges calmly and at mistakes squarely, and the confidence to make changes to eradicate those mistakes. In short, you develop a quiet confidence in the ability of the professional you to deliver the goods.

Pride and Integrity: Pride in yourself as a professional means always making sure the job is done to the best of your ability; this means paying attention to the details and to the time and cost constraints. *Integrity* means taking responsibility for your actions, both good and bad, and it also means treating others, within and outside of the company, with respect at all times and in all situations. With pride in yourself as a professional with integrity, your actions will always be in the ethical best interests of the company, and your decisions will never be based on whim or personal preference.

When it comes down to it, companies have very limited interests: making money, saving money (the same as making money), and saving time (which saves money and makes time to make more money). Actually, you wouldn't want it any other way, as it is this focus that makes your paycheck good come payday. Developing these professional behaviors and maintaining sensitivity to the profit interests of any business endeavor is the mark of a true professional. To this end, behavior that demonstrates an awareness of the need for procedures, efficiency, and economy rounds out the profile of the consummate professional:

Efficiency: Always keeping an eye open for wasted time, effort, resources, and money.

Economy: Most problems have two solutions, and the expensive one isn't always the best. Ideas of efficiency and economy engage the creative mind in ways that other workers might not consider; they are an integral part of your analytical proficiency.

Ability to Follow Procedures: Procedures exist to keep the company profitable, so don't try to work around them. Following the chain of command, you don't implement your own "improved" procedures or organize others to do so.

Now, understanding what the desirable professional behaviors are and seeing that you possess them is only part of the secret. Let's talk about the importance of illustrating these behaviors at work.

Harry works in Shipping and Receiving. He reads the list of learned professional behaviors in the next chapter, comes across the category labeled "Determination," and thinks, "Yeah, that's me. I'm a determined kind of guy."

It's good for Harry to know this and be able to mention it at the interview, but how much better if he could give the interviewer a short movie to watch to illustrate his claim with a real-life work experience. So Harry recalls the time he came in over the weekend to clear the warehouse in time to make room for the twenty-ton press due in Monday morning at seven. When he tells this story to the interviewer, he gets a lot further than he would if he simply said, "Hire me because I'm determined"—a bland, unsubstantial claim that would be forgotten almost the instant it left Harry's mouth. Instead, the interviewer gets a mental image of Harry coming in on the weekend to make room for that press. Actually, the interviewer sees something much more important—namely, Harry applying the same level of determination and extra effort on behalf of the interviewer's company.

Simple statements don't leave any lasting impression on employers; anecdotes that prove a point do.

The Fifth Secret: Everyone Hires for the Same Job

Regardless of profession, at some level we are all problem solvers. This applies to any job, at any level, in any organization, anywhere in the world, and being aware of this is absolutely vital to job search and career success in any field.

Mr. Wanton Grabbit, eighty-year-old senior partner at the revered Washington law firm of Sue, Grabbit, and Runne, was looking for someone with five years of experience as an administrative assistant in a legal environment. He also wanted someone with experience in using his firm's state-of-the-art Bambleweeny 5000 computer network.

Grabbit interviewed seven candidates with exactly the experience his advertisement demanded. Each of them came away from the interview convinced that a job offer was imminent. None of them got the job. The person who did get the job had three years of experience and had never before set foot inside a law office.

Fiona Sneddon, the successful candidate, understood the fifth secret of the hire and asked a few intelligent questions of her own during the interview. Specifically, she asked, "What are the first projects I will be involved with?" This led Mr. Grabbit to launch into a long discourse on his desire to see the law firm rush headlong into the twenty-first century. The first project, he explained, would be to load the firm's entire filing system onto the Bambleweeny.

Although Fiona had never worked in a law firm before, she had handled these kinds of problems before. Having faced the problem before, even though it had not been in a legal environment, she demonstrated an understanding of the immediate problems the position had been created to solve. Furthermore, she could tell the illustrative stories from her last job that enabled Mr. Grabbit to see her, in his mind's eye, tackling and solving these immediate, specific, short-term problems successfully. The ability to handle immediate needs helps overcome problems caused by the absence of other qualifications.

Think of your profession in terms of its problem-identification/avoidance/solution responsibilities. Once you have identified the particular problem-solving business you are in, you've gone a long way toward isolating what the interviewer will want to talk about. Identify and list for yourself the typical problems you tackle for employers on a daily basis. Come up with plenty of specific examples. Then move on to the biggest, dirtiest problems you've faced. Recall specifically how you solved them.

Here's a technique used by corporate outplacement professionals to help people develop examples of their problem-solving skills and the resulting achievements (you went through a similar exercise while developing your résumé):

1. State the problem. What was the situation? Was it typical of your job, or had something gone wrong? If the latter, be leery of apportioning blame.
2. Isolate relevant background information. What special knowledge or education were you armed with to tackle this dilemma?
3. List your key qualities. What professional skills and professional behaviors did you bring into play to solve the problem?
4. Recall the solution. How did things turn out in the end?
5. Determine what the solution was worth. Quantify the solution in terms of money earned, money saved, or time saved. Specify your role as a team member or as a lone gun, as the facts demand.

With a subtle problem-identification/avoidance/solution orientation, you will be focused in a way that will appeal to any employer. If you follow the steps outlined here, you will develop a host of illustrative stories you can use to answer any of the interview questions you will face. Remember, stories help interviewers visualize you solving their problems—as a paid member of the team.

We get two very special benefits when we understand and apply the fifth secret. First, we show that we possess the problem-solving abilities of a first-rate professional in the field. Second, when we ask about the problems, challenges, projects, deadlines, and pressure points that will be tackled in the early months, we show we will be able to hit the ground running on those first critical projects.

◆ ◆ ◆

Integrate this awareness of why some people get hired over others as you read the following chapters in this section, and you will reap the rewards—while your competition resign themselves to harvesting sour grapes.

HOW TO KNOCK 'EM DEAD

CHAPTER 11

THERE ARE A couple of handfuls of learned professional behaviors that are catnip to all employers. Learn how to apply them during the interview process.

If you are like most people, you are terrified of job interviews, partly because you don't know exactly what questions are going to be asked. Even though there are questions you think the interviewer might ask, you have no idea how best to answer them. Even if you have an arsenal of rehearsed answers to likely questions, you know canned, slick answers are going to make you sound like an aluminum-siding salesman. Take a look at these scary questions: Do you know how to answer them?

- "Describe a situation where your work or an idea was criticized."
- "Have you done the best work you are capable of doing?"
- "What problems do you have getting along with others?"
- "How long will you stay with the company?"
- "I'm not sure you're suitable for the job."
- "Tell me about something you are not very proud of."
- "What are some of the things your supervisor did that you disliked?"
- "What aspects of your job do you consider most crucial?"

Can you answer all these questions off the top of your head? Can you do it in a way that will set your worth above the other job candidates? I doubt it—but after you have read this section you will be thoroughly prepared for these questions and hundreds more like them. You know it isn't enough to have slick, canned answers ready, because each answer you give must help satisfy one of those five secrets of the hire that employers apply to each candidate.

As you learned in the last few pages, an employer is looking for more than just the ability to flip a burger, write code, or balance a departmental budget.

Professional Behaviors

An important part of your interview weaponry is the ability to show employers you are in possession of a full slate of the professional behaviors—such as those described in Chapter 10—that are universally sought by all employers. These are the very behaviors that get you noticed, land plum assignments, and enable you to succeed in all your professional endeavors.

Showing possession of these universally admired professional behaviors, and showing them in action with the illustrative examples you give in answers to tough interview questions, are your passports to success at any interview. They will give your answers substance and a ring of truth. Going through the list of learned professional behaviors in Chapter 10, you will probably recognize that you apply many of them on a regular basis in your work; if not, they are all readily learnable and you'll be able to begin developing these valuable career assets just as soon as you recognize their importance.

As you read through the list of behaviors, try to come up with times when you used determination in the execution of your duties. The examples you generate can be used in your résumé, in your cover letters, and as answers to questions in interviews. Then when you get asked, "So why are you different?" you will have something meaningful to say, and the stories you provide will give that aura of truth to your claims. Absorbing the list of learnable professional behaviors and making them part of the professional you will win interviews and job offers and provide the backbone of your long-term career success.

The reason these learnable behaviors are so universally admired is that they relate to profit and the ongoing competitiveness of a company. Using examples of them in your answers to interview questions (as well as in your résumé and cover letters) will make you stand out as someone worthy of special consideration.

Get Ready for the Tough Questions

We are now going to look at all those sneaky, dirty, mean, lowdown trick questions that can be thrown at you in the course of an interview. I will help you understand what is behind each question, the kind of information an employer is likely to be seeking, and give an example of the kind of points you might want to make in your answers. The examples should be used as a starting point; you'll look within your own experience for the responses to use at an actual interview.

As the requirements of the job unfold for you at the interview, meet them point by point with your qualifications. If your experience is limited, stress the appropriate professional behavior (such as energy, determination, motivation), your relevant interests, and your desire to learn. If you are weak in a particular area, keep your mouth shut—perhaps that dimension will not arise. If the area is probed, stress skills that compensate or demonstrate that you are a fast learner.

Do not show discouragement if the interview appears to be going poorly. You have nothing to gain by showing defeat, and it could merely be an interview tactic to test your self-confidence by putting you under stress (we'll be handling stress techniques in Chapter 14).

If for any reason you need time to think, say, "Let me think about that for a moment. . . ." If you get flustered or lost, gain time to marshal your thoughts by asking, "Could you help me with that?" or "Would you run that by me again?" or "That's a good question; I want to be sure I understand. Could you please explain it again?"

When studying the tough questions that follow, remember to use the information you have gathered about your professional self from exercises earlier in the book to create the examples and explanations that reflect your skills, experiences, and professional behaviors.

> ### *"What are the reasons for your success in this profession?"*
> With this question, the interviewer is not so much interested in examples of your success—he or she wants to know what makes you tick. Keep your answers

short, general, and to the point. Using your work experience, personalize and use examples from your professional behavior profile.

In the following suggested answer, and in those for the next few questions, the most important words to include in any answer are italicized (words like *solution*, *problems*, and *contribution*). You might answer the question this way: "I attribute my success to three things: First, I've always received support from coworkers, which encourages me to be *cooperative* and look at my job in terms of what *we* as a department are trying to achieve. That gives me great *pride* in my work and its *contribution to the department's efforts*, which is the second factor. Finally, I find that every job has its *problems*, and while there's always a costly *solution*, there's usually an economical one as well, whether it's in terms of time or money." Give an example from your experience that illustrates those points.

"What is your energy level like? Describe a typical day."

You must demonstrate good use of your *time* and show that you believe in *planning* your day beforehand; you must also show that when your day is over, you *review* your own performance to make sure you are reaching the *desired goals*. No one wants a part-time employee, so you should sell your *energy* level. For example, your answer might end with, "At the end of the day when I'm ready to go home, I make a rule always to type one more letter [make one more call, etc.]. Then I clear my desk, *review* the day's *achievements*, and *plan* for the next day."

In many of the discussions about how to answer questions, you will learn valuable lessons that will help you be a more successful professional. For example, from the previous question you might pick up some useful, and successful, ideas about the "Plan, Do, Review" cycle that successful people apply every day to keep themselves organized and on track.

"Why do you want to work here?"

To answer this question, you must have researched the company and built a dossier. Your research and visits to the company Web site are now to be rewarded. Reply with the company's attributes as you see them. Cap your answer with reference to your belief that the company can provide you with a stable and happy work environment—the company has that reputation—and that such an atmosphere would encourage your best work: "I have a bachelor's degree in communications, and I've worked in pharmaceutical sales for three years. I am currently ranked fourth in the region. I have long competed against your company, and I know and respect your products [you'll add plenty of specific details to show you really know the company]. Your position in Macon will also help me get closer to family."

"What kind of experience do you have for this job?"

This is a golden opportunity to sell yourself, but before you do, be sure you know what is most critical to the interviewer. The interviewer is not just looking for a competent engineer, accountant, or what-have-you—he or she is looking for someone who can contribute quickly to the current projects. When interviewing, companies invariably give everyone a broad picture of the job, but the person they hire will be a *problem solver*, someone who can *contribute* to the specific projects in the first six months. Only by asking will you identify the areas of your interviewer's greatest urgency and therefore interest.

If you do not know the projects you will be involved with in the first six months, you must ask. Level-headedness and *analytical* ability are respected, and the information you get will naturally let you answer the question more appropriately. For example, a company experiencing shipping problems might appreciate this answer: "I have worked in the shipping and receiving area all my life in both durables and perishables. I understand *deadlines*, delivery schedules, and the *bottom-line* importance of getting the product shipped, and my awareness of *making money by saving money* has always kept rejects from careless handling to a bare minimum."

"What are the broad responsibilities of your job?"

This is becoming a very popular question with interviewers, and rightly so. There are three layers to it. First, it acknowledges that all employees nowadays are required to be more productivity-oriented and need to know how individual responsibilities fit into the big picture. Second, the answer provides some idea of how much you will have to be trained if and when you join the company. Third, it is a very effective knockout question—if you lack a comprehensive understanding of your job, that's it! You'll be knocked out then and there.

To answer effectively you need to understand the small role your job plays in the bigger picture of departmental responsibilities (including your responsibilities as a team player) and how the department's role in turn helps contribute to the bottom line. Whatever your job, you have customers, or end users, of your service; they are always front and center in your considerations. Explain your day-to-day responsibilities, whom you are serving with your presence, and how your function serves the profit motive of the organization.

"Describe how your job relates to the overall goals of your department and company."

This can be a standalone question or a follow-up to the last one (when your answer wasn't comprehensive). It examines your understanding of department and corporate missions and obliquely checks your ability to function as a team member. Consequently, whatever the specifics of your answer, include words to this effect: "The quality of my work directly affects the ability of others to do their work properly. As a team member, one has to be aware of the other players and our *common goals*."

"What aspects of your job do you consider most crucial?"

A wrong answer can knock you out of the running. The executive who describes expense reports as the job's most crucial aspect is a case in point. The question is designed to determine time management, prioritization skills, and any inclination for task avoidance. This question demands that you have a clear awareness of the role of your job in contributing to the overall success of the company.

"Are you willing to go where the company sends you?"

Unfortunately with this one, you are, as the saying goes, damned if you do and damned if you don't. What is the real question? Do they want you to relocate or just travel on business? If you simply answer "no," you will not get the job offer, but if you answer "yes," you could end up in Monkey's Eyebrow, Kentucky. So play for time and ask, "Are you talking about business travel, or is the company relocating?" In the final analysis, your answer should be "yes." You don't have to accept the job, but without the offer you have no decision to make. Your single goal at an interview is to sell yourself and win a job offer.

"What did you like/dislike about your last job?"

The interviewer is looking for incompatibilities. If a trial lawyer says he or she dislikes arguing a point with colleagues, the statement will weaken—if not immediately destroy—his or her candidacy.

Most interviews start with a preamble by the interviewer about the company. Pay attention: that information will help you answer the question. In fact, any statement the interviewer makes about the job or corporation can be used to your advantage.

So, in answer, you liked everything about your last job. You might even say your company taught you the importance of certain keys from the business, achievement, or professional profile. Criticizing a prior employer is a warning flag that you could be a problem employee. No one intentionally hires trouble, and that's what's behind the question. Keep your answer short and positive. You are allowed only one negative about past employers, and then only if your interviewer has a "hot button" about his or her department or company; if so, you will have written it down on your notepad. For example, the only thing your past employer could not offer might be something like "the ability to contribute more in different areas, as in the smaller environment you have here." You might continue with, "I really liked everything about the job. The reason I want to leave it is to find a position where I can make a greater contribution. You see, I work for a large company that encourages specialization of skills. The smaller environment you have here will, as I said, allow me to contribute far more in different areas." Tell them what they want to hear—replay the hot button.

Of course, if you interview with a large company, turn it around. "I work for a small company and don't get the time to specialize in one or two major areas." Then replay the hot button.

"What is the least relevant job you have held?"

If your least relevant job is not on your résumé, it shouldn't be mentioned. Some people skip over those six months between jobs when they worked as soda jerks just to pay the bills and would rather not talk about it, until they hear a question like this one. But a mention of a job that, according to all chronological records, you never had, will throw your integrity into question and your candidacy out the door.

Apart from that, no job in your profession has been a waste of time if it increases your knowledge about how the business works and makes money. Your answer will include: "Every job I've held has given me new insights into my profession, and the higher one climbs, the more important the understanding of the lower-level, more menial jobs. They all play a role in making the company profitable. And anyway, it's certainly easier to schedule and plan work when you have firsthand knowledge of what others will have to do to complete their tasks."

"What have you learned from jobs you have held?"

Tie your answer to your business and professional profile. The interviewer needs to understand that you seek and accept constructive advice, and that your business decisions are based on the ultimate good of the company, not your personal whim or preference. "More than anything, I have learned that what is good for the company is good for me. So I listen very carefully to directions and always keep my boss informed of my actions."

"How do you feel about your progress to date?"

This question is not geared solely to rate your progress; it also rates your self-esteem (personal profile keys). Be positive, yet do not give the impression you have already done your best work. Make the interviewer believe you see each day as an opportunity to learn and contribute, and that you see the environment at this company as conducive to your best efforts.

"Given the parameters of my job, my progress has been excellent. I know the work, and I am just reaching that point in my career where I can make significant contributions."

"Have you done the best work you are capable of doing?"

Say "yes," and the interviewer will think you're a has-been. As with all these questions, personalize your work history. For this particular question, include the essence of this reply: "I'm proud of my professional achievements to date, especially *[give an example]*. But I believe the best is yet to come. I am always motivated to give my best efforts, and in this job there are always opportunities to contribute when you stay alert."

"How long would you stay with the company?"

The interviewer might be thinking of offering you a job. So you must encourage him or her to sell you on the job. With a tricky question like this, end your answer with a question of your own that really puts the ball back in the interviewer's court. Your reply might be: "I would really like to settle down with this company. I take direction well and love to learn. As long as I am growing professionally, there is no reason for me to make a move. How long do you think I would be challenged here?"

"How long would it take you to make a contribution to our company?"

Again, be sure to qualify the question: In what area does the interviewer need rapid contributions? You are best advised to answer this with a question: "That is an excellent question. To help me answer, what do you anticipate my responsibilities will be for the first six or seven months?" or "What are your greatest areas of need right now?" You give yourself time to think while the interviewer concentrates on images of you working for the company. When your time comes to answer, start with: "Let's say I started on Monday the seventeenth. It will take me a few weeks to settle down and learn the ropes. I'll be earning my keep very quickly, but making a real contribution. . . . *[give a hesitant pause]* Do you have a special project in mind you will want me to get involved with?" That response could lead directly to a job offer, but if not, you already have the interviewer thinking of you as an employee.

"What would you like to be doing five years from now?"

The interviewer wants to know if you think of your career beyond it being a series of jobs. Do you intend to move up in the company hierarchy or do you hope to be doing the same job in five years without any interest in advancing? The danger here is that you don't know what the company wants or what the interviewer's personal agenda might be, so caution is advised, or perhaps a little further inquiry on your part first.

"From my research and what you have told me about the growth here, it seems that Organizational Development is where the heavy emphasis is going to be. It seems that's where you need the effort and where I could best contribute toward the company's goals. Are there opportunities for advancement within this area or are you looking for someone content with their level and professional expertise?"

Be guided by the interviewer's response; remember that at this point you don't have a job offer to evaluate so your main goal is to get a job offer on the table. You might continue along the lines of:

"Now five years out is farther than we can realistically see, so let me say this: I have always felt that professional skill development and delivering on current projects opens opportunities for the future. So if I can find a manager who is looking for someone with a desire to earn the respect of a reliable right hand, I'll be confident I'll get a shot at some exciting opportunities as needs develop."

"What are your qualifications?"

Be sure you don't answer the wrong question. Does the interviewer want job-related or academic job qualifications? Ask. If the question concerns job-related information, you need to know what problems must be tackled first before you can answer adequately. If you can determine this, you will also know what is causing the manager most concern. If you can show yourself as someone who can contribute to the solution of those projects or problems, you have taken a dramatic step ahead in the race for the job offer. Ask for clarification, then describe your appropriate professional behaviors tied in with relevant skills and achievements. You might say: "I can give you a general answer, but I feel my response might be more valuable if you could tell me about specific work assignments in the early months."

Or: "If the major task right now is to automate the filing system, I should tell you that in my last job I was responsible for creating a computerized database for a previously un-computerized firm."

"What are your biggest accomplishments?"

Keep your answers job related; from earlier exercises, a number of achievements should spring to mind. If you exaggerate contributions to major projects, you will be accused of suffering from "coffee-machine syndrome," the afflic-tion of a junior clerk who claimed success for an Apollo space mission based on his relationships with certain scientists, established at the coffee machine. You might begin your reply with: "Although I feel my biggest achievements are still ahead of me, I am proud of my involvement with . . . I made my contribution as part of that team and learned a lot in the process. We did it with hard work, con-centration, and an eye for the bottom line."

"How do you organize and plan for major projects?"

Effective planning requires both forward thinking ("Who and what am I going to need to get this job done?") and backward thinking ("If this job must be completed by the 20th, what steps must be made, and at what time, to achieve it?"). Effective planning also includes contingencies and budgets for time and cost overruns. Show that you cover all the bases.

"How many hours a week do you find it necessary to work to get your job done?"

No absolutely correct answer here. Some managers pride themselves on work-ing nights and weekends or on never taking their full vacation quota. Others pride themselves on their excellent planning and time management that allows them never to work more than regular office hours. You must pick the best of both worlds: "I try to plan my time effectively and usually can. Our business always has its rushes, though, so I put in whatever effort it takes to get the job finished." It is rare that the interviewer will then come back and ask for a specific number of hours. If that does happen, turn the question around: "It depends on the projects. What is typical in your department?" The answer will give you the right cue, of course.

"Tell me how you moved up through the organization."

A fast-track question, the answer to which says a lot about your personality, your goals, your past, your future, and whether you still have any steam left in you. The answer might be long, but try to avoid rambling. Include a fair sprin-kling of your professional behaviors in your stories and illustrations (because this is the perfect time to do it). As well as listing the promotions, demonstrate that they came as a result of dedicated, long-term effort, substantial contribu-tions, and flashes of genius.

"Can you work under pressure?"

You might be tempted to give a simple "yes" or "no" answer, but don't. It reveals nothing, and you lose the opportunity to sell your skills and value profiles.

Actually, this common question often comes from an unskilled interviewer, because it is closed-ended. (Ways to handle different types of interviewers are covered in Chapter 13, "The Other Side of the Desk.") As such, the question does not give you the chance to elaborate. Whenever you are asked a closed-ended question, mentally add: "Please give me a brief yet comprehensive answer." Do that, and you will give the information requested and seize an opportunity to sell yourself. For example, you could say: "Yes, I usually find it stimulating. However, I believe in planning and proper management of my time to reduce panic deadlines within my area of responsibility."

"What is your greatest strength?"

This is a chance to make some serious points about your candidacy; you want to make points in two distinct categories.

- First, you should talk about your job-specific skills. For example, an attorney might talk about her research skills, if possible giving an answer that shows that skill being put to good use on the job.
- Second, you will want to talk about some aspect of your behavioral profile. For example, that same attorney might talk about the roles that planning, organization, and time management play when carrying a heavy caseload.

The best answer is a balance between the job-specific skills and the behavioral profile of any serious professional.

"What are your outstanding qualities?"

This is essentially the same as an interviewer asking you what your greatest strengths are. While in the former question you might choose to pay attention to job-specific skills, this question asks you to talk about your personality profile. Now while you are fortunate enough to have a list of the business world's most desirable professional behaviors at the beginning of this chapter, try to do more than just list them. In fact, rather than offering a long "laundry list," you might consider picking out just two or three and giving an illustration of each.

"What interests you most about this job?"

Be straightforward, unless you haven't been given adequate information to determine an answer, in which case you should ask a question of your own to clarify. Perhaps you could say, "Before answering, could I ask you to tell me a little more about the role this job plays in the departmental goals?" or "Where is the biggest vacuum in your department at the moment?" or "Could you describe a typical day for me?" The additional information you gather with those questions provides the appropriate slant to your answer—that is, what is of greatest benefit to the department and to the company. Career-wise, that is obviously of the greatest benefit to you, too. Your answer then displays the personality traits that support the existing need. Your answer in part might include, "I'm looking for a challenge and an opportunity to make a contribution, so if you feel the biggest challenge in the department is _____, I'm the one for the job." Then include the professional behaviors and experience that support your statements. Perhaps: "I like a challenge, my background demonstrates excellent problem-solving abilities *[give some examples]*, and I always see a project through to the finish."

"What are you looking for in your next job?"

You want a company where your personal profile keys and professional profile keys will allow you to contribute to business value keys: "Ask not what your company can do for you, but what you can do for your company." The key word in the following example is "contribution": "My experience at the XYZ Corporation has shown me I have a talent for motivating people. That is demonstrated by my team's absenteeism dropping 20 percent, turnover steadying at 10 percent, and production increasing 12 percent. I am looking for an opportunity to continue that kind of contribution, and a company and supervisor who will help me develop in a professional manner."

"Why should I hire you?"

Your answer will be short and to the point. It will highlight areas from your background that relate to current needs and problems. Recap the interviewer's description of the job, meeting it point by point with your skills. Finish your answer with: "I have the qualifications you need *[itemize them]*, I'm a team player, I take direction, and I have the desire to make a thorough success."

"What can you do for us that someone else cannot do?"

This question will come only after a full explanation of the job has been given. If not, qualify the question with: "What voids are you trying to fill with this position?" Then recap the interviewer's job description, followed by: "I can bring to this job a determination to see projects through to a proper conclusion. I listen and take direction well. I am analytical and don't jump to conclusions. I understand we are in business to make a profit, so I keep an eye on cost and return." End with: "How do these qualifications fit your needs?" or "What else are you looking for?"

You finish with a question that asks for feedback or a powerful answer. If you haven't covered the interviewer's hot buttons, he or she will cover them now, and you can respond accordingly.

"Describe a difficult problem you've had to deal with."

This is a favorite tough question. It is not so much the difficult problem that's important—it's the approach you take to solving problems in general. It is designed to probe your professional profile; specifically, your analytical skills.

"Well, I always follow a five-step format with a difficult problem. One, I stand back and examine the problem. Two, I recognize the problem as the symptom of other, perhaps hidden, factors. Three, I make a list of possible solutions to the problem. Four, I weigh the consequences and cost of each solution, and decide on the best. And five, I go to my boss, outline the problem, make my recommendation, and ask for my superior's advice and approval."

Then give an example of a problem and your solution. Here is a thorough example: "When I joined my present company, I filled the shoes of a manager who had been fired. Turnover was very high. My job was to reduce turnover and increase performance. Sales of our new copier had slumped for the fourth quarter in a row, partly due to ineffective customer service. The new employer was very concerned, and he even gave me permission to clean house. The cause of the problem? The customer-service team never had any training. All my people needed was some intensive training. My boss gave me permission to join the American Society for Training and Development, which cost $120. With what I learned there, I turned the department around. Sales continued to slump in my first quarter. Then they skyrocketed. Management was pleased with the sales and felt my job in customer service had played a real part in the turnaround. My boss was pleased because the solution was effective and cheap. I only had to replace two customer-service people."

"What would your references say?"

You have nothing to lose by being positive. If you demonstrate how well you and your boss got along, the interviewer does not have to ask, "What do you dislike about your current manager?"

It is a good idea to ask past employers to give you a letter of recommendation. That way, you know what is being said. It reduces the chances of the company representative checking up on you, and if you are asked this question you can pull out a sheaf of rousing accolades and hand them over. If your references are checked by the company, it must by law have your written permission. That permission is usually included in the application form you sign. All that said, never offer references or written recommendations unless they are requested.

"Can we check your references?"

This question is frequently asked as a stress question to catch the too-smooth candidate off-guard. It is also one that is occasionally asked in the normal course of events. Comparatively few managers or companies ever check references—this astounds me, yet it's a fact of life. On the other hand, the higher up the corporate ladder you go, the more likely it is that your references will be checked. There is only one answer to this question if you ever expect to get an offer: "Yes."

Your answer may include: "Yes, of course you can check my references. However, at present, I would like to keep matters confidential, until we have established a serious mutual interest [i.e., an offer]. At such time I will be pleased to furnish you with whatever references you need from prior employers. I think you'll find they say I am professional, committed to making a difference with my presence, easy to be around and a team player."

You are under no obligation to give references of a current employer until you have a written offer in hand. You are also well within your rights to request that reference checks of current employers wait until you have started your new job.

Most people only ever talk to their references immediately before they are to be checked, if at all. I suggest you contact the people who you think will speak well of you at the beginning of your job search (or as soon as you read this). They might also be able to come up with job leads and introductions.

"What type of decisions did you make on your last job?"

If you have taken the time to deconstruct the target job in the way we discussed in Chapter 10, "The Five Secrets of the Hire," you will have a clear understanding of the job's expected deliverables and the decision-making events that typically accompany that job. You might expect the interviewer to follow with a question about "how you reached those decisions?" So this will often be a two-part question:

- The level and application of your decision-making
- The analytical processes applied.

This is an opportunity, however humble your position, to demonstrate your professional profile.

For example: "Being in charge of the mailroom, my job is to make sure people get information in a timely manner. The job is well defined, and my decisions aren't that difficult. I noticed a year or two ago that all activity in the company stopped in the middle of the morning when I took the mail around, because people were taking a break from work to read their mail. I had an idea and gave it to my boss. She got it cleared by the president, and ever since, we take any mail around just before lunch. Mr. Gray, the president, told me my idea improved productivity, saved time, and that he wished everyone was as conscientious."

"What was the last book you read (or movie you saw)? How did it affect you?"

It doesn't really matter what you say about the latest book or movie, just as long as you have read or seen it. Don't be like the interviewee who said the name of the first book that came to mind—*In Search of Excellence*—only to be caught by the follow-up, "To what extent do you agree with Peters's simultaneous loose/tight pronouncements?" Also, by naming such a well-known book, you have managed only to say that you are like millions of others, which doesn't make you stand out in the crowd. Better that you should name something less faddish—that helps to avoid nasty follow-up questions. You needn't mention the most recent book or movie you've seen; your answer should simply make a statement about you as a potential employee. Come up with a response that will set you apart and demonstrate your obvious superiority. Ideally you want to mention a work that in some way has helped you improve yourself; anything that has honed any of the admired professional behaviors will do this. For example there is a book on the Knock 'em Dead Web site that changed my life and could change yours: *How to Get Control of Your Time and Your Life* by Alan Lakein. Give this as an example, cite a time management tip, then make reference to the importance of time management for everyone.

"How do you handle pressure/tension?"

This question is different from "Can you handle pressure?"—it asks *how* you handle it. You could reply, "Tension is caused when you let things pile up. It is usually caused by letting other areas of responsibility slip by for an extended period. For instance, if you have a difficult presentation coming up, you may procrastinate in your preparations for it. I've seen lots of people do things like that—a task seems so overwhelming they don't know where to begin. I find that if you break those overwhelming tasks into little pieces, they aren't so overwhelming anymore (a useful time management tip from Lakein). So I suppose I don't so much handle tension as handle the causes of it, by not letting things slip in other areas that can give rise to it."

"How long have you been looking for another position?"

If you are employed, your answer isn't that important—a short or long time is irrelevant to you in any follow-up probes, because you are just looking for the right job, with the right people and outfit that offers you the right opportunities. If, on the other hand, you are unemployed at the time of the question, how you answer becomes more important. If you say, "Well, I've been looking for two years now," it isn't going to score you any points. The interviewer thinks, "Two years, huh? No one else wanted him in that time. I certainly don't." If you must talk of a period of several months or more be careful to add something like, "Well, I've been looking for about a year now. I've had offers in that time, but I have determined that as I spend most of my waking hours at work, the job I take, the company I join, and the people I work with have got to share values I can identify with. I don't want to work with clock-watchers; I want to work in a happy atmosphere where everyone is focused on productivity and really making a difference with their presence."

"Have you ever been fired?"

Say "no" if you can; if not, act on the advice given regarding the next question. Many people confuse getting laid off, being downsized, having their jobs automated out of existence or exported overseas with getting fired. So if you were laid off as part of general work force reduction, be straightforward, short, and then shut up. Do not over-talk; it makes you sound guilty.

"Why were you fired?"

If you have been terminated with cause, this can be a tough question to answer. Like it or not, termination with cause is usually justified, because managers loathe taking away someone's livelihood. Virtually no one fires an employee for the heck of it.

Having been fired creates questions in the mind of the interviewer. If you have been fired, the first thing to do is bite the bullet and take responsibility for the behaviors that led to the event, because ninety-nine times out of 100 the fault lies at your door. Remember the three fingers of blame: whenever we point the finger of blame at others for our problems we forget that three of our own fingers are pointing right back at us. If you cannot take responsibility for your actions you cannot change them, and the problems of that job will repeat themselves *ad infinitum* and destroy the true potential of your career.

If you can take real responsibility for your actions, you can clean up your act and clean up the past. Call the person who fired you; your aim is to clear the air, so whatever you do, don't be antagonistic. Reintroduce yourself, explain that you are looking (or, if you have been unemployed for a while, say you are "still looking") for a new job. Say that you appreciate that the manager had to do what was done and you learned from the experience. Then address specifically what you learned and ask, "If you were asked as part of a pre- or post-employment reference check, what would you say about me? How would you describe my leaving the company? Would you say that I was fired or that I simply resigned? You see, every time I tell someone about my termination, whoosh, there goes another chance of getting back to work!" Most managers will plump for the latter option (describing your departure as a resignation). Taking responsibility and cleaning up the past really works and is the first step on putting yourself back on a success track.

Back to answering the question. Whatever you do, don't advertise the fact you were fired. If you are asked, be honest, but make sure you have packaged the reason in the best possible light. Perhaps: "I'm sorry to say, I deserved it. I was having some personal problems at the time, and I let them affect my work. I was late to work and lost my motivation. My supervisor (whom, by the way, I still speak to) had directions to trim the work force anyway, and as I was hired only a couple of years ago, I was one of the first to go."

If you can find out the employee turnover figures, voluntary or otherwise, you might add: "Fifteen other people have left so far this year." A combination answer of this nature minimizes the stigma. You have even managed to demonstrate that you take responsibility for your actions, which shows your analytical and listening skills.

"Have you ever been asked to resign?"

When someone is asked to resign, it is a gesture on the part of the employer: "You can quit, or we will can you, so which do you want it to be?" Because you were given the option, though, that employer cannot later say, "I had to ask him to resign"—that is tantamount to firing and could lead to legal problems. In the final analysis, it is usually safe to answer "no."

"Were you ever dismissed from your job for a reason that seemed unjustified?"

Another sneaky way of asking, "Were you ever fired?" The sympathetic phrasing is geared toward getting you to reveal all the sordid details. The cold hard facts are that hardly anyone is ever fired without cause, and you're kidding yourself if you think otherwise. With that in mind, you can quite honestly say, "No," and move on to the next topic.

"In your last job, what were some of the things you spent most of your time on, and why?"

Employees come in two categories: goal-oriented (those who want to get the job done), and task-oriented (those who believe in "busy" work). You must demonstrate that you have good time-management skills, and that you are, therefore, goal-oriented, as that is what this question probes.

You might reply: "I work on the telephone like a lot of businesspeople; meetings also take up a great deal of time. What is important to me is effective time management and prioritization of activities based on the deliverables of my job. I find more gets achieved in a shorter time if a meeting is scheduled, say, immediately before lunch or at the close of business. I try to block my time in the morning and the afternoon for main thrust activities. At four o'clock, I review what I've achieved, what went right or wrong, and plan adjustments and my main thrust for tomorrow."

"In what ways has your job prepared you to take on greater responsibility?"

This is one of the most important questions you will have to answer. Only the context of the question can tell you if it is focused on your ability to do well in the new, more responsible, job, or whether it is to determine your potential for future growth; this determination will affect the particular slant of your answer. Again, your careful target job deconstruction will help you determine the kinds of specific information the employer is seeking. Regardless of context and other considerations, the interviewer is always hoping in part to see you take personal responsibility for your professional development, so your answer in part needs to demonstrate this. This simple example shows self-awareness, growth, planning and listening skills, and ethical behavior. Parts of it—perhaps the then-and-now aspect of the answer—can be adapted to your personal experience.

"When I started my job, my boss would brief me morning and evening. I made some mistakes, learned a lot, and got the work in on time. As time went by I took on greater responsibilities *[list some of them]*. Now, I meet with her every Friday to discuss the week and proposed directional changes, so that she can keep management informed. I think this demonstrates not only my growth but also the confidence management has in my judgment and ability to perform consistently above standard." The exact nature of your answer should reflect your ability to meet the deliverables of the target job.

"In what ways has your job changed since you originally joined the company?"

Very similar to the previous question, and you can use the same structural approach.

"What skills are most critical to this job?"

The question examines your practical understanding of the day-to-day responsibilities of the job, and the skills required to execute them (that target job deconstruction coming into play yet again). If your answer fails to demonstrate a clear grasp, you can kiss an offer goodbye. Even if you know your job well, always take a few minutes to deconstruct it into component parts and identify the skill sets necessary to execute each part of the job. As you identify each skill, try to come up with an illustration of your application of that skill, and work into it the professional behaviors that enable you to execute that skill. For example:

"With high-end marketing of product launches into new territories I think there are two overwhelming skills needed. First, there are strategic marketing skills: the identifying, prioritizing, and penetration of the new market—something I have done in the Atlanta area in both of my prior jobs. Second, I'd have to say negotiating skills. And here I'm not just talking about negotiation tactics, along with written and verbal communication skills—all of which are ongoing areas of study for me. But I'm also talking about skills in regulatory analysis, which have given me an edge in countless deals."

If, however, you are trying to break into a new profession, you need to do a little research to see if that profession is suitable for you. In the process, you will learn to answer the question in a convincing manner. Here are two sources that can supply the information you'll need:

- Talk to people already doing the job, through your personal contacts and through membership in a professional association.
- Look up the job in the *Dictionary of Occupational Titles* either in your local library or online at *www.occupationalinfo.org*.

Don't shy away from making this effort. The rewards can include job offers and a better understanding of what it takes to be successful in your chosen profession.

"What skills would you like to develop on this job?"

Behind the question is an interest in your motivation to do the work being offered. The interviewer is looking for a fit between your dreams and his reality. All worthwhile jobs require hard work and a desire to learn—a mindset often notable for its absence.

It is helpful to gather as much information about the job, the department, and their entwined futures as you can. The more information you have, the better you will be able to customize your answers to an employer's specific needs.

As most interviews start with a quick overview of the job and the department, try to turn this overview into an information-gathering conversation by showing an interest in the role of the department within the company and how this might affect the responsibilities of department members. These insights will help ensure the compatibility of your answers with the job's future. If this is not possible, fall back on the further development of core skills and professional behaviors that you know are pivotal to your profession. It's important to stress the "further" here; you don't want to give the impression of inadequacy in the basics.

"Why do you want to work in this industry?" or *"Why do you think you will shine in this profession?"*

These are both questions most likely to be asked either when you are at the entry level or perhaps an experienced professional in the midst of a strategic career shift. Your answer should speak both to your pragmatism and to your motivation. An answer along the following lines will work in both instances.

"At this point in my career I am looking at the profession/industry because I believe it offers stability and professional growth potential over the years [explain why]. *Also, I'll be using skills* [itemize strong skill sets that are relevant to the job] *that are areas of personal strength, from which I derive great personal satisfaction. So I think that my carefully considered choice of profession, the skills I can bring to the table, and my interest in* _____ *all lead to my confidence in being able to make a contribution."*

"How resourceful are you?"

This is a question about creativity and initiative; it is also asking you to talk about analytical skills, how you anticipate problems and how you approach them when they do arise. The problem you wrestled doesn't need to be of planetary proportions to show you in a positive light, because the question is really examining your professional behavior: it's not the problem so much as how you handle it. Talk about your analytical skills in discovering root causes, your resilience in the face of challenges, and your ability to stay with difficult tasks until completion, and you'll be thinking along the right lines.

Your answer can follow a simple sequence: the problem, your approach and solution, the result, and its value to the company . . . the PSRV process we discussed earlier.

As always, having an illustrative story ready enables the interviewer to "watch" you being resourceful. Besides, you never know when an interviewer will ask, "Can you give me an example of that?" as a follow-up question.

"How does this job compare with others you have applied for?"

This is a variation of more direct questions, such as "How many other jobs have you applied for?" and "Who else have you applied to?" but it is a slightly more intelligent question and therefore more dangerous. It asks you to compare. Answer the question and sidestep at the same time.

"No two jobs are the same, and this one is certainly unlike any other I have applied for." If you can highlight some of the interviewer's stated pluses about the job so much the better. Remember that first and foremost you are there to get a job offer. You have nothing to evaluate until then.

If you are pressed further, say, "Well, to give you a more detailed answer, I would need to ask you a number of questions about the job and the company." Ask about major projects: who succeeds at the job, and who fails, and why; how the company encourages professional growth; and so on. For more on good questions to ask, see Chapter 20, "Negotiating the Job Offer."

"What makes this job different from your current/last one?"

If you don't have enough information to answer the question, say so, and ask some of your own; "Well to help me answer this properly it would help if I knew a little more about . . ." Such questions might address responsibilities, deliverables of the job, extent of authority, and perceived role of the job within the company structure (see Chapter 20 on negotiation for many good questions to ask). Behind the question is the interviewer's desire to uncover the experience you are lacking. Focus on the positive: "From what I know of the job, I seem to have all the experience required to make a thorough success [itemize here, as it's a good opportunity to reinforce the match]. I would say that the major differences seem to be . . ." and here you play back the positive attributes of the department and company as the interviewer gave them to you, either in the course of the interview or in answer to your specific questions.

"Do you have any questions?"

A good question. Almost always, this is a sign that the interview is drawing to a close and that you have one more chance to make an impression. Remember the adage: People respect what you inspect, not what you expect.

Most people ask questions about money and benefits. These are nice-to-know questions that the interviewer is not really interested in discussing at this point. As your goal at the interview is to bring the interviewer to the point of offering you the job, these questions are really irrelevant at this point, and even detrimental. Better that you concentrate on gathering information that will help you further your candidacy. Create questions from any of the following:

- Find out why the job is open, who had it last, and what happened to him or her. Did he or she get promoted or fired? How many people have held this position in the last couple of years? What happened to them subsequently?
- Why did the interviewer join the company? How long has he or she been there? What is it about the company that keeps him or her there?
- To whom would you report? Will you get the opportunity to meet that person?
- Where is the job located? What are the travel requirements, if any?
- What type of training is required, and how long is it? What type of training is available?
- What would your first assignment be?
- What are the realistic chances for growth in the job? Where are the opportunities for greatest growth within the company?
- What are the skills and attributes most needed to get ahead in the company?
- Who will be the company's major competitor over the next few years? How does the interviewer feel the company stacks up against them?
- What has been the growth pattern of the company over the last five years? Is it profitable? How profitable? Is the company privately or publicly held?
- Is there a written job description? May you see it?

"What Kind of Person Are You Really, Mr. Jones?"

CHAPTER · CHAPTER · CHAPTER · CHAPTER · CHAPTER · CHAPTER · CHAPTER

12

LEARN THE TECHNIQUES an interviewer uses to find out whether you will fit into the company and department, and, most important, whether you are a good person to work with.

If you are offered the job and accept, you will be working together fifty weeks of the year, so the interviewer really wants to know if you are going to reduce his life expectancy. Every employer wants to know whether you will fit in with the rest of the staff, whether you are a team player, and most of all, whether you are manageable.

Here are questions the interviewer might use to examine this area. They will mainly be geared toward your behavior and attitudes in the past, because it is universally believed that your past actions predict your future behavior.

"How do you take direction?"

The interviewer wants to know whether you are open-minded and can be a team player. Can you follow directions or are you a difficult, high-maintenance employee? It is hoped that you are a low-maintenance professional who is motivated to ask clarifying questions about a project before beginning, and who then gets on with the job at hand, coming back with requests for direction as circumstances dictate.

This particular question can also be defined as "How do you accept criticism?" Your answer should cover both points: "I take direction well and recognize that it can come in two varieties, depending on the circumstances. There is carefully explained direction, when my boss has time to lay things out for me in detail; then there are those times when, as a result of deadlines and other pressures, the direction might be brief and to the point. While I have seen some people get upset with that, personally I've always understood that there are probably other considerations I am not aware of. As such, I take the direction and get on with the job without taking offense, so my boss can get on with her job."

"Would you like to have your boss's job?"

It is a rare boss who wants his or her livelihood taken away. On my own very first job interview, my future boss said, "Mr. Yate, it has been a pleasure to meet you. However, until you walked in my door, I wasn't out on the street looking for a new job." You see I had this case of wanting to start at the top rather than actually working my way up.

The interviewer wants to know if you are the type of person who will be confrontational or undermining. He also seeks to determine how goal-oriented and motivated you are in your work life—so you may also want to comment on your sense of direction. But while ambition is admired, it is admired most by those far enough above the fray not to be threatened. Be cautiously optimistic; perhaps, "Well, if my boss were promoted over the coming years, I would hope to have made a consistent enough contribution to warrant his consideration. It's not that I am looking to take anyone's job; rather, I am looking for a manager who will help me develop my capabilities.

"What do you think of your current/last boss?"

Be short, sweet, and shut up. People who complain about their employers are recognized as the people who cause the most disruption in a department. This question is the interviewer's way of finding out if you're going to cause trouble. "I liked her as a person, respected her professionally, and appreciated her guidance." The question is often followed by one that tries to validate your answer.

"Describe a situation where your work or an idea was criticized."

This is a doubly dangerous question as you are being asked to describe how you handle criticism and to detail possible faults. If you are asked this question, describe a poor idea that was criticized, not poor work. Poor work can cost money and is a warning sign to the interviewer.

One of the wonderful things about a new job is that you can leave the past entirely behind, so it does not matter how you handled criticism in the past. What does matter is how the interviewer would like you to handle criticism, if and when it becomes his unpleasant duty to dish it out; that's what the question is really about. So relate one of those it-seemed-like-a-good-idea-at-the-time ideas; you will want to put this situation in the past, address how you handled the criticism, and, just as important, what you learned from the experience. You might say something that captures the essence of this example: "*[after describing the situation]* . . . I listened carefully and asked a couple of questions for clarification. Then I fed back what I heard to make sure the facts were straight. I asked for advice, we bounced some ideas around, then I came back later and represented the idea in a more viable format. My supervisor's input was invaluable." Those are steps you go through to become maximally productive in these situations. Listen for understanding (not just waiting for your turn to speak), confirm the understanding, ask guidance for the desired solution, confirm the path/outcome expected, show that a satisfactory resolution was ultimately reached, recognize the positive impact of the manager, then demonstrate what you learned and how your thinking/approach has changed as a result.

"Tell me about yourself."

This is invariably on of the first questions we all face. It helps the interviewer get a picture of you, and it helps you get used to talking; it is not an invitation to ramble.

Your interviewers are meeting with you to see if you are the right person to fill a position that has been carefully defined by a job description. You will recall in Chapter 2 how I took you through that Target Job Deconstruction exercise, and the very clear picture it gave you of the issues an employer is likely to want to discuss. Taking the results of this exercise as your frame of reference, you have a clear idea of what the interviewer wants to hear about: how your professional life experiences have qualified you to be at this meeting, throwing your hat in the ring for this particular job. This question will frequently come up at the beginning of an interview, so it is worthwhile to spend a few minutes preparing a succinct statement that says who you are today and how you got here. For example:

I'm the Area Director of Marketing for the _____ metroplex area. I oversee all aspects of marketing to acquire and retain basic, digital, and online customers through tactics such as mass media and direct mail, as well as launch new products/services like VOD. I have a team of forty-six employees, which also includes twenty-six door-to-door sales reps.

I rose to this position year by year, climbing through the ranks based on my performance, achievement and an ever-growing frame of reference for my profession and our business. As we get into the nuts-and-bolts discussion of the job I hope to show you that I have a real understanding of the challenges faced by my direct reports and a steady hand with the managerial skills required for a motivated and productive department.

This isn't a question that you can answer effectively without thought and preparation. Take some time in advance to think about your career to date and how it has prepared you for the position at hand.

"How do you get along with different kinds of people?"

You don't have to talk about respect for others, the need for diversity, or how it took you ten years to realize Jane was a different sex and Charley a different color, because that is not what this question is about. If you respect others, you will demonstrate this by explaining to your interviewer how you work in a team environment (because this is, in reality, a "team player" question), and how you solicit and accept input, ideas, and viewpoints from a variety of sources. If you can give a quick, honest, illustration of learning from a coworker who is obviously different from you in some way, it won't hurt.

"Rate yourself on a scale of one to ten."

This question is meant to plumb the depths of your self-esteem and self-awareness. If you answer ten, you run the risk of portraying yourself as insufferable. On the other hand, if you say less than seven, you might as well get up and leave. You are probably best claiming to be an eight, saying that you always give of your best, which includes ongoing personal and professional development, so that in doing so you always increase your skills and therefore always see room for improvement. It helps to give an example, "I just read a great book on time management called *How to Get Control of Your Time and Your Life*, and found that a daily plan/do/review cycle to be a really useful tool for staying on top of and prioritizing multiple projects."

"What kinds of things do you worry about?"

Some questions, such as this one, can seem so off-the-wall that you might start treating the interviewer as a confessor in no time flat. Your private phobias have nothing to do with your job, and revealing them can get you labeled as unbalanced. It is best to confine your answer to the sensible worries of a conscientious professional. "I worry about deadlines, staff turnover, tardiness, back-up plans for when the computer crashes, or that one of my auditors burns out or defects to the competition—just the normal stuff. It goes with the territory, so I don't let it get me down." Whatever you identify as a worry might then be the subject of a follow-up question, so think through what you identify as worrying and in turn what you do to eradicate the worry.

"What is the most difficult situation you have faced?"

The question looks for information on two fronts: "How do you define difficult?" and "What was your handling of the situation?" You must have a story ready for this one in which the situation was tough and allowed you to show yourself in a good light. Avoid talking about problems with coworkers. As we have talked about the importance of problem solving throughout the book, and steps you can take to identify proper approaches and solutions, you should have numerous examples with which to illustrate your answer; just remember the sequence: *Problem, Solution, Result, Value.*

"What are some of the things that bother you?" "What are your pet peeves?" "Tell me about the last time you felt anger on the job."

These questions are so similar they can be treated as one. It is tremendously important that you show you can remain calm. Most of us have seen a colleague lose his or her cool on occasion—not a pretty sight and one every sensible employer wants to avoid. This question comes up more and more often the higher up the corporate ladder you climb, and the more frequent your contact with clients and the general public. To answer it, find something that angers conscientious workers. "I enjoy my work and believe in giving value to my employer. Dealing with clock-watchers and people who regularly get sick on Mondays and Fridays really bothers me, but it's not something that gets me angry." An answer of this nature will help you much more than the kind given by a California engineer, who went on for some minutes about how he hated the small-mindedness of people who don't like pet rabbits in the office.

"What have you done that shows initiative?"

The question probes whether you are a doer, someone who will look for ways to increase sales or save time or money—the kind of person who gives a manager a pleasant surprise once in a while, who makes life easier for coworkers. Be sure, however, that your example of initiative does not show a disregard for company policies and procedures.

"My boss has to organize a lot of meetings. That means developing agendas, letting employees around the country know the dates well in advance, getting materials printed, or, as is more often the case nowadays, organizing the Webinar and getting the PowerPoint graphics created and rehearsal times scheduled. Most people in my position would wait for the work to be given them. I don't. Every quarter, I sit down with my boss and find out the dates of all his meetings for the next six months. I immediately make the hotel and flight arrangements, and attend to all the Web-hosting details. I ask myself questions like, 'If the agenda for the July meeting is to reach the field at least six weeks before the meeting, when must it be finished by?' Then I come up with a deadline. I do that for all the major activities for all the meetings. I put the deadlines in his PDA; and mine two weeks earlier to ensure everything is done on time. My boss is the best organized, most relaxed manager in the company. None of his colleagues can understand how he does it."

"What are some of the things about which you and your supervisor disagreed?"

It is safest to state that you did not disagree.

"In what areas do you feel your supervisor could have done a better job?"

The same goes for this one. No one admires a Monday-morning quarterback.

You could reply, though: "I have always had the highest respect for my supervisor. I have always been so busy learning from Mr. Jones that I don't think he could have done a better job. He has really brought me to the point where I am ready for greater challenges. That's why I'm here."

"What are some of the things your supervisor did that you disliked?"

If you and the interviewer are both nonsmokers, for example, and your boss isn't, use it. Apart from that: "You know, I've never thought of our relationship in terms of like or dislike. I've always thought our role was to get along together and get the job done."

"How well do you feel your boss rated your job performance?"

This is one very sound reason to ask for written evaluations of your work before leaving a company. Some performance-review procedures include a written evaluation of your performance—perhaps your company employs it. If you work for a company that asks you to sign your formal review, you are quite entitled to request a copy of it. You should also ask for a letter of recommendation whenever you leave a job: you have nothing to lose. If you don't have written references, perhaps say: "My supervisor always rated my job performance well. In fact, I was always rated as being capable of accepting further responsibilities. The problem was there was nothing available in the company—that's why I'm here."

If your research has been done properly you can quote verbal appraisals of your performance from prior jobs. "In fact, my boss recently said that I was the most organized engineer in the work group, because. . . ."

"How did your boss get the best out of you?"

This is a manageability question, probing whether you are going to be a pain in the neck or not. Whatever you say, make it clear you don't appreciate being treated like a dishrag. You can give a short, general answer: "My last boss got superior effort and performance by giving me the same personal respect with which she liked to be treated herself." This book is full of answers that get you out of tight corners and make you shine, but this is one instance in which you really should tell it like it is. You don't want to work for someone who is going to make life miserable for you. Or you might add to it, going on to identify how your manager explained projects and their deliverables clearly to you at the outset along with their deadlines and kept you carefully appraised of any changes.

"How interested are you in sports?"

The interviewer is looking for your involvement in groups, as a signal that you know how to get along with others and pull together as a team.

"I really enjoy most team sports. I don't get a lot of time to indulge myself, but I am a regular member of my company's softball team." A recently completed survey of middle- and upper-management personnel found that the executives who listed group sports/activities among their extracurricular activities made an average of $3,000 per year more than their sedentary colleagues. Don't you just love baseball suddenly?

Apart from team sports, endurance sports are seen as a sign of determination: swimming, running, and cycling are all okay. Games of skill (bridge, chess, and the like) demonstrate analytical skills; given the recent popularity of poker and recognizing it as a game of analytical, math, or communication and negotiation skills I nevertheless feel that mentioning poker should be done carefully; you do not want to leave an image of yourself as a compulsive gambler.

"What personal characteristics are necessary for success in your field?"

You know the answer to this one: It's a brief recital of your learned professional behaviors.

You might say: "To be successful in my field? Drive, motivation, energy, confidence, determination, good communication, and analytical skills. Combined, of course, with the ability to work with others."

"Do you prefer working with others or alone?"

This question is usually used to determine whether you are a team player. Before answering, however, be sure you know whether the job requires you to work alone. Then answer appropriately. Perhaps: "I'm quite happy working alone when necessary. I don't need much constant reassurance. But I prefer to work in a group—so much more gets achieved when people pull together."

"Explain your role as a group/team member."

You are being asked to describe yourself as either a team player or a loner. Think for a moment about why the job exists in the first place: it is there to contribute to the bottom line in some way, and as such it has a specific role in the department to contribute toward that larger goal. Your department, in turn, has a similar, but larger, role in the company's bottom line. Your ability to link your small role to that of the department's larger responsibilities, and then to the overall success of the company, will demonstrate a developed professional awareness. Most departments depend on harmonious teamwork for their success, so describe yourself as a team player: "I perform my job in a way that helps others to do theirs in an efficient manner. Beyond the mechanics, we all have a responsibility to make the workplace a friendly and pleasant one to be in, and that means everyone working for the common good and making the necessary personal sacrifices toward it."

"How would you define a conducive work atmosphere?"

This is a tricky question, especially because you probably have no idea what kind of work atmosphere exists in that particular office. The longer your answer, the greater your chances of saying the wrong thing, so keep it short and sweet. "One where the team has a genuine interest in its work and desire to turn out a good product/deliver a good service."

"Do you make your opinions known when you disagree with the views of your supervisor?"

If you can, state that you come from an environment where input is encouraged when it helps the team's ability to get the job done efficiently. "If opinions are sought in a meeting, I will give mine, although I am careful to be aware of others' feelings. I will never criticize a coworker or a superior in an open forum;

besides, it is quite possible to disagree without being disagreeable. However, my past manager made it clear that she valued my opinion by asking for it. So, after a while, if there was something I felt strongly about, I would make an appointment to sit down and discuss it one-on-one."

"What would you say about a supervisor who was unfair or difficult to work with?"

"I would make an appointment to see the supervisor and diplomatically explain that I felt uncomfortable in our relationship, that I felt he or she was not treating me as a professional colleague, and therefore that I might not be performing up to standard in some way—that I wanted to right matters and ask for his or her input as to what I must do to create a professional relationship. I would enter into the discussion taking responsibility for any communication problems that might have existed, and that this wasn't just the manager's problem."

"Do you consider yourself a natural leader or a born follower?"

Ouch! The way you answer depends a lot on the job offer you are chasing. If you are a recent graduate, you are expected to have high aspirations, so go for it. If you are already on the corporate ladder with some practical experience in the school of hard knocks, you might want to be a little cagier. Assuming you are up for (and want) a leadership position, you might try something like this: "I would be reluctant to regard anyone as a natural leader. Hiring, motivating, and disciplining other adults and at the same time molding them into a cohesive team involves a number of delicately tuned skills that no honest person can say they were born with. Leadership requires first of all the desire; then it is a lifetime learning process. Anyone who reckons they have it all under control and have nothing more to learn isn't doing the employer any favors."

Of course, a little humility is also in order, because just about every leader in every company reports to someone, and there is a good chance that you are talking to such a someone right now. So you might consider including something like, "No matter how well developed any individual's leadership qualities, an integral part of leadership ability is to take direction from your immediate boss, and also to seek the input of the people being supervised. The wise leader will always follow good advice and sound business judgment wherever it comes from. I would say that given the desire to be a leader, the true leader in the modern business world must embrace both." How can anyone disagree with that kind of wisdom?

"Why do you feel you are a better [e.g.] manager/scientist/assistant than some of your coworkers?"

If you speak disparagingly of your coworkers, you will not put yourself in the best light. That is what the question asks you to do, so it poses some difficulties. The trick is to answer the question but not to accept the invitation to show yourself from anything but a flattering perspective. "I don't spend my time thinking about how superior I am, because that would be detrimental to our working together as a team. I believe, however, some of the qualities that make me an outstanding secretary are . . ." From here, go on to illustrate job-related skills and behavioral characteristics that make you a beacon of productivity.

"You have a doctor's appointment arranged for noon. You've waited two weeks to get in. An urgent meeting is scheduled at the last moment, though. What do you do?"

What a crazy question, you mutter. It's not. It is even more than a question—it is what I call a question shell. The question within the shell—in this instance, "Will you sacrifice the appointment or sacrifice your job?"—can be changed at will. This is a situational-interviewing technique, which poses an on-the-job problem to see how the prospective employee will respond. A Chicago company asks this question as part of its initial screening, and if you give the wrong answer, you never even get a face-to-face interview. So what is the right answer to this or any similar shell question?

Fortunately, once you understand the interviewing technique, it is quite easy to handle—all you have to do is turn the question around. "If I were the manager who had to schedule a really important meeting at the last moment, and someone on my staff chose to go to the doctor's instead, how would I feel?"

It is unlikely that you would be an understanding manager unless the visit were for a triple bypass. To answer, you start with an evaluation of the importance of the problem and the responsibility of everyone to make some sacrifices for the organization, and finish with: "The first thing I would do is reschedule the appointment and save the doctor's office inconvenience. Then I would immediately make sure I was properly prepared for the emergency meeting."

"How do you manage to interview while still employed?"

As long as you don't explain that you faked a dentist appointment to make the interview you should be all right. Beware of revealing anything that might make you appear at all underhanded. Best to make the answer short and sweet, and let the interviewer move on to richer areas of inquiry. Just explain that you had some vacation time due, or took a day off in lieu of overtime payments. "I had some vacation time, so I went to my boss and explained that I needed a couple of days off for some personal business and asked her what days would be most suitable. Although I plan to change jobs, I don't in any way want to hurt my current employer in the process by being absent during a crunch."

"How have your career motivations changed over the years?"

This question only crops up when you have enough years under your belt to be regarded as a tenured professional. The interviewer's agenda is to examine your emotional maturity and how realistic you are about future professional growth.

Your answer requires self-awareness. While the desire to rule the world can be seen as motivation in young professionals, it may not be interpreted so positively coming from a tenured corporate soldier, from whom more realism is expected.

Your answer should reflect a growing maturity as well as a desire to do a good job for its own reward, and for making a contribution as part of the greater whole. Here's an example you can use as a starting point in crafting your own:

"I guess in earlier years I was more ego-driven, with everything focused on becoming a star. Over the years I've come to realize that nothing happens with a team of one—we all have to function as part of a greater whole if we are to make meaningful contributions with our professional presence. Nowadays I take great pleasure in doing a job well, in seeing it come together as it should, and especially in seeing a group of professionals working together in their different roles to make it happen. Maybe the best way to say this is that I've discovered that the best way to stand out is to be a real team player and not worry about standing out."

"How do you regroup when things haven't gone as planned?"

In reality, we can all react to adversity in pretty much the same way we did as kids, but that isn't always productive. Here's a way you can deal with setbacks in your professional life and wow your interviewer in the process.

"I pause for breath and reflection for as long as the situation allows—this can be a couple of minutes or overnight. I do this to analyze what went wrong and why. I'm also careful to look for the things that went right, too. I'll examine alternate approaches and, time allowing, I'll get together with a peer or my boss and review the whole situation and my proposed new approaches to get a second opinion."

You can go on to explain that the next time you face the same kind of problem you'll know what to avoid, what to do more of, and what other new approaches you can try.

You might consider finishing your answer with a statement about the beneficial effects of experiencing problems. "Over the years I've learned just as much from life's problems as from its successes."

"What would your coworkers tell me about your attention to detail?"

Say that you are shoddy and never pay attention to the details, and you'll hear a whoosh as your job offer flies out the window.

Your answer obviously lies in the question. You pay attention to detail, your analytical approach to projects helps you identify all the component parts of a given job, and your time-management and organizational skills ensure that you get the job done in a timely manner without anything falling through the cracks.

"When do you expect a promotion?"

Tread warily, show you believe in yourself, and have both feet firmly planted on the ground. "That depends on a few criteria. Of course, I cannot expect promotions without the performance that marks me as deserving of promotion. I also need to join a company that has the growth necessary to provide the opportunity. I hope that my manager believes in promoting from within and will help me grow so that I will have the skills necessary to be considered for promotion when the opportunity comes along."

If you are the only one doing a particular job in the company, or you are in management, you need to build another factor into your answer. "As a manager, I realize that part of my job is to have done my succession planning and that I must have someone trained and ready to step into my shoes before I can expect to step up. That way I play my part in preserving the chain of command." To avoid being caught off-guard with queries about your having achieved that in your present job, you can finish with: "Just as I have done in my present job, where I have a couple of people capable of taking over the reins when I leave."

"Tell me a story."

Wow. What on earth does the interviewer mean by that question? You don't know until you get him or her to elaborate. Ask, "What would you like me to tell you a story about?" To make any other response is to risk making a fool of yourself. Very often the question is asked to see how analytical you are: people who answer the question without qualifying show they do not think things through carefully. The subsequent question will be about either your personal or professional life. If it is about your personal life, tell a story that shows you like people and are determined. Do not discuss your love life. If the subsequent question is about your professional life, tell a story that demonstrates your willingness and manageability.

"What have your other jobs taught you?"

Talk about the professional skills you have learned and the professional behaviors you have polished. Many interviewees have had success finishing their answer with: "There are two general things I have learned from past jobs. First, if you are confused, ask—it's better to ask a dumb question than make a dumb mistake. Second, it's better to promise less and produce more than to make unrealistic forecasts."

"Define cooperation."

The question asks you to explain how to function as a team player in the workplace. Your answer could be: "Cooperation is a person's ability to sacrifice personal wishes and beliefs whenever necessary to assure the department reaches its goals. It is also a person's desire to be part of a team, and by hard work and goodwill make the department greater than the sum of its parts."

"What difficulties do you have tolerating people with different backgrounds and interests from yours?"

Another "team player" question with the awkward implication that you do have problems. Say, "I don't have any," but don't leave it there.

"I don't have any problems working with people with different backgrounds than myself. In fact I find it energizing; different backgrounds mean different life experiences and different ways of coming at problems. The opportunity to work with people different from yourself is a golden opportunity."

"In hindsight, what have you done that was a little harebrained?"

You are never harebrained in your business dealings, and you haven't been harebrained in your personal life since graduation, right? The only safe examples to use are ones from your deep past that ultimately turned out well. One of the best, if it applies to you, is: "Well, I guess the time I bought my house. I had no idea what I was letting myself in for, and at the time, I really couldn't afford it. Still, I managed to make the payments, though I had to work like someone possessed. Yes, my first house—that was a real learning experience." Not only can most people relate to this example, but it also gives you the opportunity to sell one or two of your very positive and endearing professional behaviors.

◆ ◆ ◆

If you think the interview is only tough for the interviewee, it's time to take a look at the other side of the desk. Knowing what's going on there can really help you shine.

THE OTHER SIDE OF THE DESK

TWO TYPES OF interviewers can pose problems for the unprepared: the highly skilled and the unconscious incompetent. Find out how to recognize and respond to each one.

There are two terrible places to be during an interview—in front of the desk wondering what on earth is going to happen next and behind the desk asking the questions. The average interviewer dreads the meeting almost as much as the interviewee, yet for opposite reasons.

Business frequently yields to the mistaken belief that any person, on being promoted to the ranks of management, becomes mystically endowed with all necessary managerial skills. That is a fallacy; perhaps only half of all managers have been taught how to interview. Most just bumble along and pick up a certain proficiency over a period of time.

Two types of interviewers can spell disaster for the unprepared. One is the totally incompetent interviewer, who may even lack the ability to phrase a question adequately. The other is a highly skilled interviewer, who has been trained in systematic techniques for probing your past performance and future potential. Both are equally dangerous when it comes to winning the job offer.

The Skilled Interviewer

Skilled interviewers understand that a manager's first job is to get work done through others, so they recognize that making the right hires is a serious task. They know exactly what they want to discover, having taken the time to learn the strategies that will help them hire only the best for their company. They follow a set format for the interview process to ensure objectivity in the selection process, and a set sequence of questions to ensure the facts are gathered logically and in the right areas; all this in turn ensures productive hires.

There are many ways for a manager to build and conduct a structured interview, but all have similar goals.

- To ensure a systematic coverage of your work history and applicable job-related skills
- To determine ability, motivation, and manageability and team orientation, problem-solving skills, and your professional behavior profile
- To provide a technique for gathering all the relevant facts
- To provide a uniform strategy that objectively evaluates all job candidates

An interviewer using structured interview techniques will usually follow a standard format for each interview to help maintain objectivity. The interview will begin with small talk and a brief introduction to relax you. Following close on the heels of that chit-chat comes a statement designed to assure you that baring your faults is the best way to get the job. It's not—but neither is it necessary for you to lie. Your interviewer will then outline the steps in the interview. This will include you walking through a chronological description of your work history, then specific questions about different aspects of your experience. Finally, you will be given an opportunity to ask your own questions.

Sounds pretty simple, huh? Well, watch out! The skilled interviewer knows exactly what questions to ask, why they will be asked, in what order they will be asked, and what the desired responses are. He or she will interview and evaluate every applicant for the job in exactly the same fashion. You are up against a pro.

Like the hunter who learns to think like his or her prey, you will find the best way to win over the interviewer is to think like the interviewer, to understand what he or she is likely to ask and why. To do that, you must learn how the interviewer has prepared for you. By going through the same process, you will beat out your competitors for the job offer.

The dangerous part of this type of structured interview is called "skills evaluation." The interviewer has analyzed all the different skills it takes to do the job, and all the professional behaviors that complement those skills. Armed with this analysis, he or she has developed a series of carefully sequenced questions to draw out your relative merits and weaknesses.

Graphically, it looks like this:

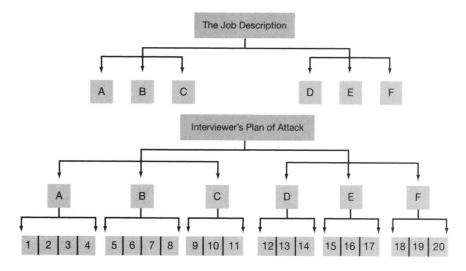

Letters A through F represent the separate skill sets (or deliverables, as they are often called) necessary to do the job; numbers 1 through 20 are questions asked to identify and verify each particular skill. This is where the tough questions will come, and the only way to prepare effectively is to take the interviewer's viewpoint and complete this exercise in its entirety. That effort requires a degree of objectivity but will generate multiple job offers. You have already done a little work in this area, when you were tweaking your résumé.

> ✎ Look at the position you seek. What role does it play in helping the company achieve its corporate mission and make a profit?
> ✎ What are the five most important duties of that job?
> ✎ From a management viewpoint, what are the skills and attributes necessary to perform each of these tasks?

Write it all down. Now, put yourself in the interviewer's shoes. What topics would you examine to find out whether a person can really do the job? If for some reason you get stuck in the process, use your past experience. You have worked with good and bad people, and their work habits and skills will lead you to develop the potential questions and thereby the essence of the correct answers. When you do this exercise, you will not only understand what it will take to get the job, but you will also know what you will have to do, and how you will have to behave to succeed, once in the saddle.

Each skill set or deliverable you identify is fertile ground for the interviewer's questions. Don't forget the intangible skills that are so important to many jobs—like self-confidence and creativity—because the interviewer won't. Develop a number of questions for each skill set you identify.

Looking back at coworkers (and still wearing the manager's hat), what are the professional behaviors that would make life easier for you as a manager? These dimensions are likely to be examined by the interviewer. Once you have identified the questions you would ask in the interviewer's position, you are in a position to build great answers.

If you are entering the world of work for the first time, or making a substantial career shift, you might not have the knowledge to analyze the job's deliverables. In this case go back to your networks and call people already in the profession to identify the skill sets and behaviors necessary to succeed in the initial target job of your new career.

This is how managers are trained to develop structured interviews. You now have the inside track; we'll develop answers over the coming pages.

These sharks have some juicy questions with which to probe your abilities, attitude, and professional behavior profile. Now we are going to lay out some of the most challenging questions they can ask, and show what is behind those questions and how you should approach building your answers. Notice these questions tend to present a problem for you to solve but in no way lead you toward the answer. They are often two- and three-part questions as well. The additional question that can be tagged onto them all is, "What did you learn from this experience?" Assume it is included whenever you get one of these questions—you'll be able to sell different aspects of your success profile.

"You have been given a project that requires you to interact with different levels within the company. How do you do this? What levels are you most comfortable with?"

This is a two-part question that probes communication and self-confidence skills. The first part asks how you interact with superiors and motivate those working with and for you on the project. The second part is saying, "Tell me whom you regard as your peer group—help me categorize you." To cover those bases, include the essence of this: "There are two types of people I would interact with on a project of this nature. First, there are those I report to, who bear the ultimate responsibility for its success. With them, I determine deadlines and a method for evaluating the success of the project. I outline my approach, breaking the project down into component parts, getting approval on both the approach and the costs. I would keep my supervisors updated on a regular basis and seek input whenever needed. My supervisors would expect three things from me: the facts, an analysis of potential problems, and that I not be intimidated, as this would jeopardize the project's success. I would comfortably satisfy those expectations.

"The other people to interact with on a project like this are those who work with and for me. With those people, I would outline the project and explain how a successful outcome will benefit the company. I would assign the component parts to those best suited to each, and arrange follow-up times to assure completion by deadline. My role here would be to facilitate, motivate, and bring the different personalities together to form a team.

"As for comfort level, I find this type of approach enables me to interact comfortably with all levels and types of people."

"Tell me about an event that really challenged you. How did you meet the challenge? In what way was your approach different from that of others?"

This is a straightforward, two-part question. The first part probes your problem-solving abilities. The second asks you to set yourself apart from the herd. Outline the problem. The clearer you make the situation, the better. Having done so, explain your solution, its value to your employer, and how it was different from other approaches:

"My company has offices all around the country; I am responsible for seventy of them. My job is to visit each office on a regular basis and build market-penetration strategies with management, and to train and motivate the sales and customer service forces. When the recession hit, the need to service those offices was more important than ever, yet the traveling costs were getting prohibitive.

"Morale was an especially important factor: you can't let outlying offices feel defeated. I reapportioned my budget and did the following: I dramatically increased telephone contact with the offices and instituted a monthly sales-technique letter—how to prospect for new clients, how to negotiate difficult sales, and so forth. I bought and rented sales training and motivational tapes and sent them to my managers with instructions on how to use them in a sales meeting. I stopped visiting all the offices. Instead, I scheduled weekend training meetings in central locations throughout my area: one day of sales training and one day of management training, concentrating on how to run sales meetings, early termination of low producers, and so forth.

"While my colleagues complained about the drop in sales, mine increased, albeit by a modest 6 percent. After two quarters, my approach was officially adopted by the company."

"Give me an example of a method of working you have used. How did you feel about it?"

You have a choice of giving an example of either good or bad work habits. Give a good example, one that demonstrates your understanding of corporate goals, your organizational skills, analytical ability, or time management skills.

You could say: "Maximum productivity requires focus and demands organization and time management. I do my paperwork at the end of each day, when I review the day's achievements; with this done, I plan for tomorrow. When I come to work in the morning, I'm ready to get going without wasting time. I try to schedule meetings right before lunch; people get to the point more quickly if it's on their time. I feel this is an efficient and organized method of working."

"When you joined your last company and met the group for the first time, how did you feel? How did you get along with them?"

Your answer should include: "I naturally felt a little nervous, but I was excited about the new job. I shared that excitement with my new friends, and told them that I was enthusiastic about learning new skills from them. I was open and friendly, and when given the opportunity to help someone myself, I jumped at it."

"In your last job, how did you plan to interview?"

That's an easy one. Just give a description of how the skilled interviewer prepares.

"How have you benefited from your disappointments?"

Disappointments are different from failures. It is an intelligent—probably trained—interviewer who asks this one. This question is also an opportunity for the astute interviewee to shine. The question itself is positive—it asks you to show how you benefited; also, it doesn't ask you to give specific details of specific disappointments, so you don't have to open your mouth and insert your foot. Instead, be general. Edison once explained his success as an inventor by claiming that he knew more ways not to do something than anyone else living: you can do worse than to quote him. In any event, sum up your answer with, "I treat disappointments as a learning experience; I look at what happened, why it happened, and how I would do things differently in each stage should the same set of circumstances appear again. That way, I put disappointment behind me and am ready with renewed vigor and understanding to face the new day's problems."

A side note: a person with strong religious beliefs may be tempted to answer a question like this in terms of religious values. If you benefit from disappointments in a spiritual way, remember that not everyone feels the same as you do. More important, the interviewer is, by law, prohibited from talking about religion with you, so you can unwittingly put the interviewer in an awkward position of not knowing how to respond. Making an interviewer feel awkward in any way is not the way to win a job offer.

"What would you do if you had a decision to make and no procedure existed?"

This question probes your analytical skills, integrity, and dedication. Most of all, the interviewer is testing your manageability and adherence to procedures—the "company way of doing things." You need to cover that with, "I would act without my manager's direction only if the situation was urgent and my manager was not available. Then, I would take command of the situation, make a decision based on the facts, and implement it. I would update my boss at the earliest opportunity." If possible, tell a story to illustrate.

"That is an excellent answer. Now to give me a balanced view, can you give me an example that didn't work out so well?"

There are two techniques that every skilled interviewer will use, especially if you are giving good answers. In this question, the interviewer looks for negative balance; in the follow-up, the person will look for negative confirmation. Here, you are required to give an example of an inadequacy. The trick is to pull something from the past, not the present, and to finish with what you learned from the experience. For example: "That's easy. When I first joined the work force, I didn't really understand the importance of systems and procedures. There was one time when I was too anxious to contribute and didn't have the full picture. There was a sales visit report everyone had to fill out after visiting a customer. I always put a lot of effort into it until I realized it was never read; it just went in the files. So I stopped doing it for a few days to see if it made any difference. I thought I was gaining time to make more sales for the company. I was so proud of my extra sales calls, I told the boss at the end of the week. My boss explained that the records were for the long term, so that should my job change, the next salesperson would have the benefit of a full client history. It was a long time ago, but I have never forgotten the lesson: there's always a reason for systems and procedures. I've had the best-kept records in the company ever since."

To look for negative confirmation, the interviewer may then say something like, "Thank you. Now can you give me another example?" He or she is trying to confirm a weakness. If you help, you could cost yourself the job. Here's your reaction: You sit deep in thought for a good ten seconds, then look up and say firmly, "No, that's the only occasion when anything like that happened." Shut up and refuse to be enticed further.

The Unconscious Incompetent

Now you should be ready for almost anything a professional interviewer could throw at you. Your foresight and strategic planning will generate multiple offers of employment for you in all circumstances except one, and that's when you face the unconsciously incompetent interviewer. He or she is probably more dangerous to your job-offer status than everything else combined.

The poor interviewer, consciously or otherwise, bases hiring decisions on "experience" and "knowledge of mankind" and "gut feeling." In any event, he or she is an unconscious incompetent. You have probably been interviewed by one in your time. Remember leaving an interview and, upon reflection, feeling the interviewer knew absolutely nothing about you or your skills? If so, you know how frustrating that can be. In the future, good managers who are poor interviewers will be offering jobs with far greater frequency than ever before. Understand that a poor interviewer can be a wonderful manager; interviewing skills are learned, not inherited or created as a result of a mystical corporate blessing.

The unconscious incompetents abound. Their heinous crime can only be exceeded by your inability to recognize and take advantage of the proffered opportunity. As in handling the skilled interviewer, it is necessary to imagine how the unconscious incompetent thinks and feels. There are many manifestations of the poor interviewer. Each of the next examples is followed by instructions for appropriate handling of the unique problems posed for you.

✎ **Example One:** The interviewer's desk is cluttered, and the résumé or application that was handed to him or her a few minutes before cannot be found.

Response: Sit quietly through the bumbling and searching. Check out the surroundings. Breathe deeply and slowly to calm any lingering interview nerves. As you bring your adrenaline under control, you produce a certain calming effect to the interviewer and the interview. (This example, by the way, is the most common sign of the unconscious incompetent.)

✎ **Example Two:** The interviewer experiences constant interruptions from the telephone or people walking into the office.

Response: This provides good opportunities for selling yourself. Make a note on your pad of where you were in the conversation and refresh the interviewer on the point when you start talking again. He or she will be impressed with your level head and good memory. The interruptions also give time, perhaps, to find something of common interest in the office, something you can compliment. You will also have time to compose the suitable value key follow-up to the point made in the conversation prior to the interruption.

✎ **Example Three:** The interviewer starts with an explanation of why you are both sitting there, and then allows the conversation to degenerate into a lengthy diatribe about the company.

Response: Show interest in the company and the conversation. Sit straight, look attentive, make appreciative murmurs, and nod at the appropriate times until there is a pause. When that occurs, comment that you appreciate the background on the company, because you can now see more clearly how the job fits into the general scheme of things and that you see, for example, how valuable communication skills would be for the job. Could the interviewer please tell you some of the other job requirements? Then, as the job's functions are described, you can interject appropriate information about your background with questions like, "Would it be of value, Mr. Smith, if I described my experience with. . . ?"

✎ **Example Four:** The interviewer begins with, or quickly breaks into, the drawbacks of the job. The job may even be described in totally negative terms. That is often done without giving a balanced view of the duties and expectations of the position.

Response: An initial negative description often means that the interviewer has had bad experiences hiring for the position. Your course is to make it known that you recognize the importance of (for example) reliability, especially in this particular type of job. (You will invariably find in these instances that what your interviewer has lacked in the past is someone with a serious understanding of value keys.) Illustrate your proficiency in that particular aspect of your profession with a short example from your work history. Finish your statements by asking the interviewer what some of the biggest problems to be handled in the job are. The questions demonstrate your understanding, and the interviewer's answers outline the areas from your background and skills to which you should draw attention.

✎ **Example Five:** The interviewer spends considerable time early in the interview describing "the type of people we are here at XYZ Corporation."

Response: You have always wanted to work for a company with that atmosphere. It creates the type of work environment that is conducive to a person really giving his or her best efforts.

✎**Example Six:** The interviewer asks closed-ended questions, ones that demand no more than a yes-or-no answer (e.g., "Do you pay attention to detail?"). Such questions are hardly adequate to establish your skills, yet you must handle them effectively to secure the job offer.

Response: A yes-or-no answer to a closed-ended question will not get you that offer. The trick is to treat each closed-ended question as if the interviewer has added, "Please give me a brief yet thorough answer." Closed-ended questions also are often mingled with statements followed by pauses. In those instances, agree with the statement in a way that demonstrates both a grasp of your job and the interviewer's statement. For example: "That's an excellent point, Mr. Smith. I couldn't agree more that the attention to detail you describe naturally affects cost containment. My track record in this area is. . . ."

✎**Example Seven:** The interviewer asks a stream of negative questions (as described in the next chapter, "The Stress Interview").

Response: Use the techniques and answers described earlier. Give your answers with a smile and do not take the questions as personal insults; they are not intended that way. The more stressful the situations the job is likely to place you in, the greater the likelihood of your having to field negative questions. The interviewer wants to know if you can take the heat.

✎**Example Eight:** The interviewer has difficulty looking at you while speaking.

Response: The interviewer is someone who finds it uncomfortable being in the spotlight. Try to help him or her by being a good audience. Ask specific questions about the job responsibilities and offer your skills in turn.

A hiring manager will often arrange for you to meet with two or three other people. Frequently, the other interviewers have been neither trained in appropriate interviewing skills nor told the details of the job for which you are interviewing. So you will take additional copies of your executive briefing with you to the interview to aid them in focusing on the appropriate job functions.

When you understand how to recognize and respond to these different types of interviewers, you will leave your interview having made a favorable first impression. No one forgets first impressions.

THE STRESS INTERVIEW

YOUR WORST NIGHTMARE can come true at a stress interview, but once you learn that these questions are just amplified versions of much simpler ones, you'll remain cool and calm. Also included in this chapter is a vital discussion on handling illegal interview questions.

For all intents and purposes, every interview is a stress interview. The interviewer's negative and trick questions can act as the catalyst for your own fear. The only way to combat that fear is to be prepared, to know what the interviewer is trying to do, and to anticipate the various directions he or she will take. Whenever you are ill-prepared for an interview, no one will be able to put more pressure on you than you do on yourself. Remember: A stress interview is just a regular interview with the volume turned all the way up—the music is the same, just louder. Only preparedness will keep you cool and collected.

You've heard the horror stories. An interviewer demands of a hapless applicant, "Sell me this pen," or asks, "How would you improve the design of a teddy bear?" Or the candidate is faced with a battery of interviewers, all demanding rapid-fire answers to questions like, "You're giving a dinner party. Which ten famous people would you invite and why?" When the interviewee offers evidence of foot-in-mouth disease by asking, "Living or dead?" he receives his just desserts: "Ten of each."

Such awful-sounding questions are thrown in to test your poise, to see how you react under pressure, and to plumb the depths of your confidence. Many people ruin their chances by reacting to them as personal insults rather than challenges and opportunities to shine.

Previously restricted to the executive suite for the selection of high-powered executives, stress interviews are now widespread throughout the professional world. They can come with all the intimidating and treacherous tricks your worst nightmare can devise. Yet a good performance at a stress interview can mean the difference between a job in the fast lane and a stalled career. The interviewers in a stress interview are invariably experienced and well organized, and have developed tightly structured procedures and advanced interviewing techniques. The questions and tension they generate have the cumulative effect of throwing you off balance and revealing the "real" you—rather than someone who can respond with last night's rehearsed answers to six or seven stock questions.

Stress questions can be turned to your advantage or merely avoided with nifty footwork. Whichever approach you choose, you will be among a select few who understand this line of questioning. As always, when addressing the questions in this chapter, remember to develop personalized answers that reflect your experience and profession. Practice your responses aloud—by doing that, your responses to these interview gambits will become more natural and will help you feel more confident during an interview. You might even consider making a recording of tough questions, spacing them at intervals of thirty seconds to two minutes. You can then play the tape back and answer the questions in real time.

As we will see in this chapter, reflexive questions can prove especially useful when the heat is on. Stress questions are designed to sort out the clutch players from those who freeze under pressure. Used with discretion, the reflexives ("... don't you think?") will demonstrate to the interviewer that you are able to function well under pressure. At the same time, of course, you put the ball back in the interviewer's court.

One common stress interview technique is to set you up for a fall: a pleasant conversation, one or a series of seemingly innocuous questions to relax your guard, then a dazzling series of jabs and body blows that can leave you gibbering. For instance, an interviewer might lull you into a false sense of security by asking some relatively stress-free questions: "What was your initial starting salary at your last job?" then, "What is your salary now?" then, "Do you receive bonuses?" etc. To put you on the ropes, he or she might then completely surprise you with, "Tell me what sort of troubles you have living within your means," or "Why aren't you earning more at your age?" Such interviewers are using stress in an intelligent fashion, to simulate the unexpected and sometimes tense events of everyday business life. Seeing how you handle unexpected stress gives a fair indication of how you will react to the real thing.

The sophisticated interviewer talks very little, perhaps only 20 percent of the time, and that time is spent asking questions. Few comments, and no editorializing on your answers, means that you get no hint, verbal or otherwise, about your performance.

The questions are planned, targeted, sequenced, and layered. The interviewer covers one subject thoroughly before moving on. Let's take the simple example of "Can you work under pressure?" As a reader of *Knock 'em Dead*, you know to answer that question with an example and thereby deflect the main thrust of the stress technique. The interviewer will be prepared for a simple yes-or-no answer; what follows will keep the unprepared applicant reeling.

"Can you work under pressure?"

A simple, closed-ended question that requires just a yes-or-no answer, but you won't get off so easy.

"Good, I'd be interested to hear about a time when you experienced pressure on your job."

An open-ended request to tell a story about a pressure situation. After this, you will be subjected to the layering technique—six layers in the following instance.

"Why do you think this situation arose?"

It's best if the situation you describe is not a peer's or manager's fault. Remember, you must be seen as a team player.

"When exactly did it happen?"

Asking when an event happened can often lead to further questions. This is why the process of self-discovery in earlier part of the book pays dividends throughout the entire interview cycle.

"How do you feel others involved could have acted more responsibly?"

An open invitation to criticize peers and superiors, which you should diplomatically decline.

"Who holds the responsibility for the situation?"

Another invitation to point the finger of blame, which should be avoided.

"Where in the chain of command could steps be taken to avoid that sort of thing happening again?"

This question probes your analytical skills and whether you are the type of person who always goes back to the scene of the crime to learn for the next time.

This is a reporter's technique of asking why, when, who, what, how, and where. The technique can be applied to any question you are asked and is frequently used to probe those success stories that sound too good to be true. You'll find them suddenly tagged on to the simple closed-ended questions as well as to the open-ended ones. Typically, they'll start with something like: "Share with me," "Tell me about a time when," or, "I'm interested in finding out about," followed by a request for specific examples from your work history.

After you've survived that barrage, a friendly tone may conceal another zinger: "What did you learn from the experience?" This question is geared to probe your judgment and emotional maturity. Your answer should emphasize whichever of the key professional behaviors your story was illustrating.

When an interviewer feels you were on the edge of revealing something unusual in an answer, you may well encounter "mirror statements." Here, the last key phrase of your answer will be repeated or paraphrased, and followed by a steady gaze and silence. For example, "So, you learned that organization is the key to management." The idea is that the silence and an expectant look will work together to keep you talking. It can be disconcerting to find yourself rambling on without quite knowing why. The trick is knowing when to stop. When the interviewer gives you an expectant look in this context, expand your answer (you have to), but by no more than a couple of sentences. Otherwise, you will get that creepy feeling that you're digging yourself into a hole.

There will be situations where you face more than one interviewer at a time. When these occur, remember the story of a female attorney who had five law partners all asking questions at the same time. As the poor interviewee got halfway through one answer, another question would be shot at her. Pausing for breath, she smiled and said, "Hold on, ladies and gentlemen. These are all excellent questions, and, given time, I'll answer them all. Now who's next?" In so doing, she showed the interviewers exactly what they wanted to see and what is behind every stress interview and every negatively phrased question—a desire to find the presence of poise and calm under fire, combined with a refusal to be intimidated.

You never know when a stress interview will raise its ugly head. Often it can be that rubber-stamp meeting with the senior vice president at the end of a series of grueling meetings. That is not surprising. While other interviewers are concerned with determining whether you are able, willing, and a good fit for the job in question, the senior executive who eventually throws you for a loop may be probing you for potential promotability.

The most intimidating stress interviews are recognizable before the interviewer speaks: no eye contact, no greeting, either silence or a noncommittal grunt, and no small talk. You may also recognize such an interviewer by his general air of boredom, lack of interest, or thinly veiled aggression.

"What is your greatest weakness?"

This is a direct invitation to put your head in a noose. Decline the invitation.

This is perhaps one instance where the need for ongoing education in the modern world of work can come to your rescue in a sticky situation. The changes in technology give everyone an ongoing challenge getting up to speed with new skills. Your answer can address these very issues, and in the process show yourself as someone capable of staying on top of a rapidly changing workplace.

"With all the legal and technological changes impacting finance these days, staying up to date is a real challenge. Then, of course, there's working out how this affects the job and developing new knowledge or skills the changes demand." You might well finish this with examples of how you are keeping up to speed with the technological changes that affect your competence and productivity.

This is an honest answer to which anyone can relate, and it's all the better if you complete it with a course of action such as: "I'm currently reading about. . . ."; "I just attended a weekend workshop where. . . ."; or "I'm signed up for classes at. . . ."

With this type of answer you identify your weakness as something that is only of concern to the most dedicated and forward-looking professionals in your field.

You can also consider the following effective alternatives.

If there is a minor part of the job at hand where you lack knowledge—but knowledge you will pick up quickly—use that. For instance: "I haven't worked with this type of spreadsheet program before, but given my experience with six other types, I don't think it should take me more than a couple of days to pick it up." Here you remove the emphasis from weakness and put it onto a developmental problem that is easily overcome. Be careful, however; this very effective ploy must be used with discretion.

Another good option is to give a generalized answer that takes advantage of value keys. Design the answer so that your weakness is ultimately a positive characteristic. For example: "I enjoy my work and always give each project my best shot. So when sometimes I don't feel others are pulling their weight, I find it a little frustrating. I am aware of that weakness, and in those situations I try to overcome it with a positive attitude that I hope will catch on."

Also consider the technique of putting a problem in the past. Here you take a weakness from way back when and show how you overcame it. It answers the question but ends on a positive note. An illustration: "When I first got into this field, I always had problems with my paperwork—leaving an adequate paper trail. To be honest, I let it slip once or twice. My manager sat me down and explained the potential troubles such behavior could cause. I really took it to heart, and I think you will find my records some of the best around today. You only have to tell me something once." With that kind of answer, you also get the added bonus of showing that you accept and act on criticism.

Congratulations! You have just turned a bear of a question into an opportunity to sell yourself. In deciding on the particular answer you will give, remember that the interviewer isn't really concerned about your general weaknesses—no one is a saint outside of the interview room. He or she is simply concerned about any red flags that might signal your inability to perform the job or work well under supervision.

"With hindsight, how could you have improved your progress?"

Here's a question that demands, "Tell me your mistakes and weaknesses." If you can mention ways of improving your performance without damaging your candidacy, do so. The end of your answer should contain something like: "Other than that, I don't know what to add. I have always given it my best shot." Then shut up.

"What kinds of decisions are most difficult for you?"

You are human—admit it, but be careful what you admit. If you have ever had to fire someone, you are in luck, because no one likes to do that. Emphasize that, having reached a logical conclusion, you act. If you are not in management, tie your answer to key profiles: "It's not that I have difficulty making decisions—some just require more consideration than others. A small example might be vacation time. Now, everyone is entitled to it, but I don't believe you should leave your boss in a bind at short notice. I think very carefully at the beginning of the year when I'd like to take my vacation, and then think of alternate dates. I go to my supervisor, tell him what I hope to do, and see whether there is any conflict. I wouldn't want to be out of the office for the two weeks prior to a project deadline, for instance. So by carefully considering things far enough in advance, I don't procrastinate, and I make sure my plans jibe with my boss and the department for the year."

Here you take a trick question and use it to demonstrate your consideration, analytical abilities, and concern for the department—and for the company's bottom line.

"Tell me about the problems you have living within your means."

This is a twister to catch you off guard. Your best defense is first of all to know that it exists, and second to give it short shrift. "I know few people who are satisfied with their current earnings. As a professional, I am continually striving to improve my skills and to improve my living standard. But my problems are no different from that of this company or any other—making sure all the bills get paid on time and recognizing that every month and year there are some things that are prudent to do and others that are best deferred."

"What area of your skills/professional development do you want to improve at this time?"

Another "tell me all your weaknesses" question. You should try to avoid damaging your candidacy by tossing around careless admissions. One effective answer to this is to say, "Well, from what you told me about the job, I seem to have all the necessary skills and background. What I would really find exciting is the opportunity to work on a job where . . ." At this point, you replay the interviewer's hot buttons about the job. You emphasize that you really have all the job-related skills and also tell the interviewer what you find exciting about the job. It works admirably.

You can reiterate one or two areas that combine personal strengths and the job's most crucial responsibilities, and finish with saying, "These areas are so important that I don't think anyone can be too good or should ever stop trying to polish their skills."

"Your application shows you have been with one company a long time without any appreciable increase in rank or salary. Tell me about this."

Ugh. A toughie. To start with, you should analyze why this state of affairs does exist (assuming the interviewer's assessment is accurate). When you have determined the cause, practice saying it out loud to yourself as you would say it during an actual interview. It may take a few tries. Chances are no matter how valid your explanation really is, it will come off sounding a little tinny or vindictive without some polishing. Avoid the sour-grapes syndrome at all costs.

Here are some tactics you can use. First of all, try to avoid putting your salary history on application forms. No one is going to deny you an interview for lack of a salary history if your skills match those the job requires. And of course, you should never put such unnecessary information on your résumé.

If the interviewer is intent, and asks you outright for this information, you'll find a great response in the section on salary histories in Chapter 20.

Now, we'll address the delicate matter of "Hey, wait a minute; why no promotions?" The interviewer has posed a truly negative inquiry. The more time either of you spend on it, the more time the interviewer gets to devote to concentrating on negative aspects of your candidacy. Make your answer short and sweet, then shut up. For instance, "My current employer is a stable company with a good working environment, but there's minimal growth there in my area—in fact, there hasn't been any promotion in my area since _____. Your question is the reason I am meeting here with you; I have the skills and ability to take on more responsibility, and I'm looking for a place to do that."

"If you had to stay in your current job, what would you spend more time on, and why?"

Without a little self-control you could easily blurt out what you consider to be your greatest weaknesses. Tricky question, but with a little foreknowledge your answer will shine.

Practically speaking, each of your job changes should occur within the context of an overall career-management strategy. While sensible career management blends personal fulfillment with ongoing solvency, an employer is only concerned with the latter. It's your continued employability that determines solvency, which is achieved by a growing competence in the profession-critical skills that make you desirable to employers.

Enlightened self-interest dictates that an ongoing career-management concern is to identify and develop the skills demanded in an ever-changing work environment. So your answer might begin in part, "In the modern world of work, existing skills always need to be improved and new skills learned, to handle the changing nature of our work. For instance, in this job [now give a job-specific example]. I think the organizational software now available can have a major impact on personal productivity, so. . . ."

With an answer along these lines you show foresight instead of a weakness.

"How do you stay current?"

The age of technological innovation in which we live means that the nature of every job is changing about as quickly as you turn these pages. Continual changes in the nature of your professional work mean you must look at ongoing professional education as the price of sustained employability. In your answer, talk about your appreciation of this and the importance of keeping abreast of changes in the profession, and then illustrate with the following:

- Courses you have taken and are planning to take
- Books you have read or book clubs you belong to
- Memberships in professional associations
- Subscriptions to professional journals

Such an answer will identify you as an aware, connected, and dedicated professional.

"Are you willing to take calculated risks when necessary?"

First, qualify the question: "How do you define calculated risks? What sort of risks? Give me an example of a risk you have in mind; what are the stakes involved?" That will show you exactly the right analytical approach to take in evaluating a calculated risk, and while the interviewer is rattling on, you have bought time to come up with an answer. Whatever your answer, you will include, "Naturally, I would never take any risk that would in any way jeopardize the safety or reputation of my company or colleagues. In fact, I don't think any employer would appreciate an employee at any level taking risks of any nature without first having a thorough briefing and chance to give input."

"See this pen I'm holding? Sell it to me."

This is not a request, as you might think, that would only be asked of a salesperson. In today's professional workplace, everyone is required to communicate effectively and sell appropriately—sometimes products, but more often ideas, approaches, and concepts. As such, you are being examined about your understanding of the features and benefits of selling, how quickly you think on your feet, and how effectively you use verbal communication. For example, the interviewer holds up a yellow highlighter. First you will want to establish the customer's needs with a few questions like, "What sort of pens do you currently use? Do you use a highlighter? Do you read reports and need to recall important points? Is comfort important to you?" Then you will proceed calmly, "Let me tell you about the special features of this pen and show you how they will satisfy your needs. First of all it is tailor-made for highlighting reports, and that will save you time in recalling the most important points. The case is wide for comfort and the base is flat so it will stand up and be visible on a cluttered work area. It's disposable—and affordable enough to have a handful for desk, briefcase, car, and home. And the bright yellow means you'll never lose it." Then close with a smile and a question of your own that will bring a smile to the interviewer's face: "How many gross shall we deliver?"

"How will you be able to cope with a change in environment after five years [for example] with your current company?"

Another chance to take an implied negative and turn it into a positive: "That's one of the reasons I want to make a change. After five years with my current employer, I felt I was about to get stale. Everyone needs a change of scene once in a while. It's just time for me to make some new friends, face some new challenges, and experience some new approaches. Hopefully, I'll have the chance to contribute from my experience."

"Why aren't you earning more at your age?"

Accept this as a compliment to your skills and accomplishments: "I have always felt that solid experience would stand me in good stead in the long run and that earnings would come in due course. Also, I am not the type of person to change jobs just for the money. At this point, I have a solid background that is worth something to a company." Now, to avoid the interviewer putting you on the spot again, finish with a question: "How much should I be earning now?" The figure could be your offer.

"What is the worst thing you have heard about our company?"

This question can come as something of a shock. As with all stress questions, your poise under stress is vital: if you can carry off a halfway decent answer as well, you are a winner. The best response to this question is simple. Just say with a smile and a laugh: "You're a tough company to get an interview with." It's true, it's flattering, and it shows that you are not intimidated.

"How would you define your profession?"

With questions that solicit your understanding of a topic, no matter how good your answer, you can expect to be interrupted in mid-reply with, "That has nothing to do with it," or "Whoever put that idea into your head?" Ninety-nine times out of a hundred these comments are not serious criticisms. Rather, they are tests to see how well you could defend your position in a no-holds-barred conversation with a client or the chairman of the board, people who usually say what they think. Defend yourself, without taking or showing offense.

First gain time and get the interviewer talking: "Why do you say that?" you ask, answering a question with a question. Turning the tables on your aggressor displays your poise, calm, and analytical skills better than any other response.

"Why should I hire an outsider when I could fill the job with someone inside the company?"

The question isn't as stupid as it sounds. Obviously, the interviewer has examined existing employees with an eye toward their promotion or reassignment. Just as obviously, the job cannot be filled from within the company. If it could be, it would be, and for two very good reasons: it is cheaper for the company to promote from within, and it is better for employee morale.

Hiding behind this intimidating question is a pleasant invitation: "Tell me why I should hire you." Your answer should include two steps. The first is a simple recitation of your skills and personality profile strengths, tailored to the specific requirements of the job.

For the second step, realize first that whenever a manager is filling a position, he or she is looking not only for someone who can do the job, but also for someone who can benefit the department in a larger sense. No department is as good as it could be—each has weaknesses that need strengthening. So in the second part of your answer, include a question of your own: "Those are my general attributes. However, if no one is promotable from inside the company, you must be looking to add strength to your team in a special way. How do you hope the final candidate will be able to benefit your department?" The answer to this is your cue to sell your applicable qualities.

"Have you ever had any financial difficulties?"

The potential employer wants to know whether you can control not only your own finances but also finances in general. If you are in the insurance field, for example—in claims, accounting, supervision, or management—you can expect to hear this one. The question, though, is not restricted to insurance: anyone, especially a person who handles money in day-to-day business, is fair game.

For someone to check your credit history, he or she must have your written consent. This is required under the 1972 Fair Credit and Reporting Act. Invariably, when you fill out a job application form, sign it, and date it, you've also signed a release permitting the employer to check your credit history. If you have already filled out the form, you might not hear this specific question during your interview, but your creditors might. I should note here that the reader who asked me about this question also described how she'd handled it during the interview: by describing her past problems with bankruptcy in every detail. However, in trying to be open and honest, she had actually done herself a disservice.

The interviewer does not want to hear sob stories. If your credit history is spotty, concentrate on the information that will damage your candidacy the least and enhance it the most. You might find it appropriate to bring the matter up yourself if you work in an area where your credit history is likely to be checked. If you choose to wait until the interviewer brings it up, you might say (if you had to file for bankruptcy, for instance), "I should tell you that some years ago, for reasons beyond my control, I was forced into personal bankruptcy. That has been behind me for some time. Today, I have a sound credit rating and no debts. Bankruptcy is not something I'm proud of, but I did learn from the experience, and I feel it has made me a more proficient account supervisor." The answer concentrates on today, not past history.

"How do you handle rejection?"

This question is common if you are applying for a job in sales, including face-to-face sales, telemarketing, public relations, and customer service. If you are after a job in one of these areas and you really don't like the heavy doses of rejection that are any salesperson's lot, consider a new field. The anguish you will experience will not lead to a successful career or a happy life.

With that in mind, let's look behind the question. The interviewer simply wants to know whether you take rejection as rejection of yourself or whether you simply accept it as a temporary rejection of a service or product. Here is a sample answer that you can tailor to your particular needs and background: "I accept rejection as an integral part of the sales process. If everyone said 'yes' to a product, there would be no need for the sales function. As it is, I see every rejection as bringing me closer to the customer who will say 'yes.' Sales is a profession of communication, determination, and resiliency, rejection is just part of the process; it's nothing personal. I always try to leave the potential customer with a good feeling as no sale today can well become a sale next month."

"Why were you out of work for so long?"

You must have a sound explanation for all gaps in your employment history. If not, you are unlikely to receive a job offer. Emphasize you were not just looking for another paycheck—you were looking for a company with which to settle and make a long-term contribution.

"I decided that I enjoy my work too much just to accept another paycheck. I determined that the next job I took would be one where I could do my best to make a solid contribution. From everything I have heard about this company, you are a group that expects people to pull their weight, because you've got a real job to do. I like that, and I would like to be part of the team. What do I have to do to get the job?"

You answer the question, compliment the interviewer, and shift the emphasis from your unemployment to how you can get the job offer.

"Why have you changed jobs so frequently?"

If you have jumped around, blame it on youth (even the interviewer was young once). Now you realize what a mistake your job-hopping was, and with your added domestic responsibilities you are now much more settled. Or you may wish to impress on the interviewer that your job-hopping was never as a result of poor performance and that you grew professionally as a result of each job change.

You could reply: "My first job had a long commute. I soon realized that, but I knew it would give me good experience in a very competitive field. Subsequently, I found a job much closer to home where the commute was only half an hour each way. I was very happy at my second job. However, I got an opportunity to really broaden my experience base with a new company that was just starting up. With the wisdom of hindsight, I realize that move was a mistake; it took me six months to realize I couldn't make a contribution there. I've been with my current company a reasonable length of time. So I have broad experience in different environments. I didn't just job-hop; I have been following a path to gain broad experience. So you see, I have more experience than the average person of my years, and a desire to settle down and make it pay off for me and my employer."

Or you can say: "Now I want to settle down and make my diverse background pay off in my contributions to my new employer. I have a strong desire to contribute and I am looking for an employer that will keep me challenged; I think this might be the company to do that. Am I right?"

"Tell me about a time when you put your foot in your mouth."

Answer this question with caution. The interviewer is examining your ability and willingness to interact pleasantly with others. The question is tricky because it asks you to show yourself in a poor light. Downplay the negative impact of your action and end with positive information about your candidacy. The best thing to do is to start with an example outside of the workplace and show how the experience improved your performance at work.

"About five years ago, I let the cat out of the bag about a surprise birthday party for a friend, a terrific faux pas. It was a mortifying experience, and I promised myself not to let anything like that happen again." Then, after this fairly innocuous statement, you can talk about communications in the workplace: "As far as work is concerned, I always regard employer-employee communications on any matter as confidential unless expressly stated otherwise. So, putting my foot in my mouth doesn't happen to me at work."

"Why do you want to leave your current job?" or "Why did you leave your last job?"

This is a common trick question. You should have an acceptable reason for leaving every job you have held, but if you don't, pick one of the six acceptable reasons from the employment industry formula, the acronym for which is CLAMPS:

- **C**hallenge: You weren't able to grow professionally in that position.
- **L**ocation: The commute was unreasonably long.
- **A**dvancement: There was nowhere for you to go. You had the talent, but there were too many people ahead of you.
- **M**oney: You were underpaid for your skills and contribution.
- **P**ride or prestige: You wanted to be with a better company.
- **S**ecurity: The company was not stable.

For example: "My last company was a family-owned affair. I had gone as far as I was able to go. It just seemed time for me to join a more prestigious company and accept greater challenges."

Under no circumstances should you badmouth a manager—even if she was a direct descendant of Attila the Hun. Doing so will only raise a red flag in the interviewer's mind: "Will he be complaining about me like this in a few months?"

"What interests you least about this job?"

This question is potentially explosive, but easily defused. Regardless of your occupation, there is at least one repetitive, mindless duty that everyone groans about and that goes with the territory. Use that as your example in a statement of this nature: "Filing is probably the least demanding part of the job. However, it is important to the overall success of my department, so I try to do it with a smile." This shows that you understand that it is necessary to take the rough with the smooth in any job.

"What was there about your last company that you didn't particularly like or agree with?"

You are being checked out as a potential fly in the ointment. If you have to answer, you might discuss the way the company policies or directives were sometimes consciously misunderstood by some employees who disregarded the bottom line—the profitability of the corporation.

Another option: "You know how it is sometimes with a big company. People lose awareness of the cost of things. There never seemed to be much concern about economy or efficiency. Everyone wanted his or her year-end bonus, but only worried about it in December. The rest of the year, nobody gave a hoot. I think that's the kind of thing we could be aware of almost every day, don't you agree?"

Or: "I didn't like the way some people gave lip service to 'the customer comes first,' but really didn't go out of their way to keep the customer satisfied. I don't think it was a fault of management, just a general malaise that seemed to affect a lot of people."

"What do you feel is a satisfactory attendance record?"

There are two answers to this question—one if you are in management, and one if you are not. As a manager: "I believe attendance is a matter of management, motivation, and psychology. Letting the employees know you expect their best efforts and won't accept half-baked excuses is one thing. The other is to keep your employees motivated by a congenial work environment and the challenge to stretch themselves. Giving people pride in their work and letting them know you respect them as individuals have a lot to do with it, too."

If you are not in management, the answer is even easier: "I've never really considered it. I work for a living, I enjoy my job, and I'm rarely sick."

"What is your general impression of your last company?"

Always answer positively. Keep your real feelings to yourself, whatever they might be. There is a strong belief among the management fraternity that people who complain about past employers will cause problems for their new ones. Your answer is, "Very good" or "Excellent." Then smile and wait for the next question.

"What are some of the problems you encounter in doing your job, and what do you do about them?"

Note well the old saying, "A poor workman blames his tools." Your awareness that careless mistakes cost the company good money means you are always on the lookout for potential problems. Give an example of a problem you recognized and solved.

For example: "My job is fairly repetitive, so it's easy to overlook problems. Lots of people do. However, I always look for them; it helps keep me alert and motivated, so I do a better job. To give you an example, we make computer-memory disks. Each one has to be machined by hand, and, once completed, the slightest abrasion will turn one into a reject. I have a steady staff and little turnover, and everyone wears cotton gloves to handle the disks. Yet about six months ago, the reject rate suddenly went through the roof. Is that the kind of problem you mean? Well, the cause was one that could have gone unnoticed for ages. Jill, the section head who inspects all the disks, had lost a lot of weight and her diamond engagement ring was slipping around her finger, scratching the disks as she passed them and stacked them to be shipped. Our main client was giving us a big problem over it, so my looking for problems and paying attention to detail really paid off."

The interviewer was trying to get you to reveal weak points; you avoided the trap.

"What are some of the things you find difficult to do? Why do you feel that way?"

This is a variation on a couple of earlier questions. Remember, anything that goes against the best interests of your employer is difficult to do. If you are pressed for a job function you find difficult, answer in the past tense. That way, you show that you recognize the difficulty, but that you obviously handle it well.

"That's a tough question. There are so many things that are difficult to learn in our business if you want to do the job right. I used to have forty clients to sell to every month, and I was so busy touching base with all of them that I never got a chance to sell to any of them. So I graded them into three groups. I called on the top 20 percent of my clients every three weeks. The balance of my clients I called on once a month, but with a difference—each month, I marked ten of them to spend time with and really get to know. I still have difficulty reaching all forty of my clients in a month, but my sales have tripled and are still climbing.

"Jobs have pluses and minuses. What were some of the minuses on your last job?"

A variation on the question, "What interests you least about this job?" which was handled earlier. Use the same type of answer. "Like any salesperson, I enjoy selling, not doing the paperwork. But as I cannot expect the customer to get the goods, and me my commission, without following through on this task, I grin and bear it. Besides, if I don't do the paperwork, that holds up other people in the company."

If you are not in sales, use the sales force as a scapegoat: "In accounts receivable, it's my job to get the money in to make payroll and good things like that. Half the time, the goods get shipped before I get the paperwork because sales says, 'It's a rush order.' That's a real minus to me. It was so bad at my last company that we tried a new approach. We met with sales and explained our problem. The result was that incremental commissions were based on cash in, not on bill date. They saw the connection, and things are much better now."

"What kinds of people do you like to work with?"

This is the easy part of a tricky three-part question. Obviously, you like to work with people who have pride, honesty, integrity, and dedication to their work. Now . . .

"What kinds of people do you find it difficult to work with?"

The second part of the same question. You could say: "People who don't follow procedures, or slackers—the occasional rotten apples who don't really care about the quality of their work. They're long on complaints, but short on solutions." Which brings us to the third part of the question . . .

"How have you successfully worked with this difficult type of person?"

This is the most difficult part to answer. You might reply: "I stick to my guns, stay enthusiastic, and hope some of it will rub off. I had a big problem with one guy—all he did was complain, and always in my area. Eventually, I told him how I felt. I said if I were a millionaire, I'd have clearly all the answers and wouldn't have to work, but as it was, I wasn't, and had to work for a living. I told him that I really enjoyed his company, but I didn't want to hear it anymore. Every time I saw him after that, I presented him with a work problem and asked his advice. In other words I challenged him to come up with positives, not negatives."

You can go on that sometimes you've noticed that such people simply lack enthusiasm and confidence, and that energetic and cheerful coworkers can often change that. If the interviewer follows up with an inquiry about what you would do if no amount of good effort on your part solved the problem, respond, "I would maintain cordial relations, but not go out of my way to seek more than a businesslike acquaintance. Life is too short to be de-motivated by people who always think their cup is half empty."

"How did you get your last job?"

The interviewer is looking for initiative. If you can, show it. At the least, show determination.

"I was turned down for my last job for having too little experience. I asked the manager to give me a trial before she offered it to anyone else. I went in and asked for a list of companies they'd never sold to, picked up the phone, and in that hour I arranged two appointments. How did I get the job? In a word, determination!"

"How would you evaluate me as an interviewer?"

The question is dangerous, maybe more so than the one asking you to criticize your boss. Whatever you do, of course, don't tell the truth if you think the interviewer is an incompetent. It may be true, but it won't get you a job offer. This is an instance where honesty is not the best policy. It is best to say, "This is one of the toughest interviews I have ever been through, and I don't relish the prospect of going through another. Yet I do realize what you are trying to achieve." Then go on to explain that you understand the interviewer wants to know whether you can think on your feet, that there is pressure on the job, and that he or she is trying to simulate some of that real-life pressure in the interview. You may choose to finish the answer with a question of your own: "How do you think I fit the profile of the person you need?"

"I'm not sure you're suitable for the job."

Don't worry about the tone of the statement—the interviewer's "I'm not sure" really means, "I'd like to hire you, so here's a wide-open opportunity to sell me on yourself." He or she is probing three areas from your personal profile: your confidence, determination, and listening profiles. Remain calm and put the ball straight back into the interviewer's court: "Why do you say that?" You need both the information and time to think up an appropriate reply, but it is important to show that you are not intimidated. Work out a program of action for this question; even if the interviewer's point regarding your skills is valid, come back with value keys and alternate compatible skills. Counter with other skills that show your competence and learning ability, and use them to show that you can pick up the new skills quickly. Tie the two together and demonstrate that with your other attributes you can bring many pluses to the job. Finish your answer with a reflexive question that encourages a "yes" answer.

"I admit my programming skills in that language are a little light. However, all languages have similarities, and my experience demonstrates that with a competence in four other languages, getting up to speed with this one will take only a short while. Plus, I can bring a depth of other experience to the job." Then, after you itemize your experience: "Wouldn't you agree?"

If the reason for the question is not a lack of technical skills, it must be a question about one of your key profile areas. Perhaps the interviewer will say, "You haven't convinced me of your determination." This is an invitation to sell yourself, so tell a story that demonstrates determination.

For example: "It's interesting you should say that. My present boss is convinced of my determination. About a year ago we were having some problems with a union organization in the plant. Management's problem was our 50 percent Spanish monolingual production work force. Despite the fact that our people had the best working conditions and benefits in the area, they were strongly pro-union. If they were successful, we would be the first unionized division in the company. No one in management spoke Spanish, so I took a crash Berlitz course—two hours at home every night for five weeks. I got one of the maintenance crew to help me with my grammar and diction. Then a number of other production workers started saying simple things to me in Spanish and helping me with the answers. I opened the first meeting with the work force to discuss the problems. My *'Buenos dias. Me llamo Brandon'* got a few cheers. We had demonstrated that we cared enough to try to communicate. Our division never did unionize, and my determination to take the extra step paid off and allowed my superiors to negotiate from a position of caring and strength. That led to English lessons for the Spanish-speaking, and Spanish lessons for the English-speaking. We are now a bilingual company, and I think that shows we care. Wouldn't you agree my work in that instance shows determination?"

"Wouldn't you feel better off in another firm?"

Relax, things aren't as bad as you might assume. This question is usually asked if you are really doing quite well or if the job involves a certain amount of stress. A lawyer, for example, might well be expected to face this one. The trick is not to be intimidated. Your first step is to qualify the question. Relax, take a breath, sit back, smile, and say, "You surprise me. Why do you say that?" The interviewer must then talk, giving you precious time to collect your wits and come back with a rebuttal.

Then answer "no," and explain why. All the interviewer wants to see is how much you know about the company and how determined you are to join its ranks. Your earlier research and knowledge of personal profile keys (determination) will pay off again. Overcome the objection with an example, show how that will help you contribute to the company, and end with a question of your own. In this instance, the question has a twofold purpose: first, to identify a critical area to sell yourself; and second, to encourage the interviewer to consider an image of you working at the company.

You could reply: "Not at all. My whole experience has been with small companies. I am good at my job and in time could become a big fish in a little pond. But that is not what I want. This corporation is a leader in its business. You have a strong reputation for encouraging skills development in your employees. This is the type of environment I want to work in. Coming from a small company, I have done a little bit of everything. That means that no matter what you throw at me, I will learn it quickly. For example, what would the first project I would be involved with be?"

You end with a question of your own that gets the interviewer focusing on those immediate problems. You can then explain how your background and experience can help.

"What would you say if I told you your presentation this afternoon was lousy?"

"If" is the key word here, with the accusation there only for the terminally neurotic. The question is designed to see how you react to criticism and so tests your manageability. No company can afford to employ the thin-skinned applicant today. You will come back and answer the question with a question of your own. An appropriate response would be: "First of all, I would ask which aspects of my presentation were lousy. My next step would be to find out where you felt the problem was. If there was miscommunication, I'd clear it up. If the problem was elsewhere, I would seek your advice and be sure that the problem did not recur." This would show that when it is a manager's duty to criticize performance, you are an employee who will respond in a businesslike and emotionally mature manner.

The Illegal Question

Of course, one of the most stressful—and negative—question is the illegal one, a question that delves into your private life or personal background. Such a question will make you uncomfortable if it is blatant, and could also make you angry.

Your aim, however, is to overcome your discomfort and to avoid getting angry: you want to get the job offer, and any self-righteousness or defensive reaction on your part will ensure you *don't* get it. You may feel angry enough to get up and walk out, or say things like, "These are unfair practices; you'll hear from my lawyer in the morning." But the result will be that you won't get the offer, and therefore won't have the leverage you need. Remember, no one is saying you can't refuse the job once it's offered to you.

So what is an illegal question? Title VII is a federal law that forbids employers from discriminating against any person on the basis of sex, age, race, national origin, or religion. More recently, the Americans with Disabilities Act was passed to protect this important minority.

✎ **An interviewer may not ask** about your religion, church, synagogue, or parish, the religious holidays you observe, or your political beliefs or affiliations. He or she may not ask, for instance, "Does your religion allow you to work on Saturdays?" But the interviewer may ask something like, "This job requires work on Saturdays. Is that a problem?"

✎ **An interviewer may not ask** about your ancestry, national origin, or parentage; in addition, you cannot be asked about the naturalization status of your parents, spouse, or children. The interviewer cannot ask about your birthplace. But the interviewer may ask (and probably will, considering the current immigration laws) whether you are a U.S. citizen or a resident alien with the right to work in the United States.

✎ **An interviewer may not ask** about your native language, the language you speak at home, or how you acquired the ability to read, write, or speak a foreign language. But he or she may ask about the languages in which you are fluent, if knowledge of those languages is pertinent to the job.

✎ **An interviewer may not ask** about your age, your date of birth, or the ages of your children. But he or she may ask you whether you are over eighteen years old.

✎ **An interviewer may not ask** about maiden names or whether you have changed your name; your marital status, number of children or dependents, or your spouse's occupation; or whether (if you are a woman) you wish to be addressed as Miss, Mrs., or Ms. But the interviewer may ask about how you like to be addressed (a common courtesy) and whether you have ever worked for the company before under a different name. (If you have worked for this company or other companies under a different name, you may want to mention that, in light of the fact that this prospective manager may check your references and additional background information.)

As you consider a question that seems to verge on illegality, take into account that the interviewer may be asking it innocently and may be unaware of the laws on the matter. Your best bet is to be polite and straightforward, just as you would be in any other social situation. You also want to move the conversation to an examination of your skills and abilities, not your status. Here are some sample illegal questions—and some possible responses. For questions about age discrimination, see Appendix B. Remember, your objective is to get job offers; if you later decide that this company is not for you, you are under no obligation to accept the position.

"What religion do you practice?"

If you do practice, you can say, "I attend my church/synagogue/mosque regularly, but I make it my practice not to involve my personal beliefs in my work. My work for the company and my career are too important for that."

If you do not practice a religion, you may want to say something like, "I have a set of personal beliefs that are important to me, but I do not attend any organized services. And I do not mix those beliefs with my work, if that's what you mean."

"Are you married?"

If you are, the company is concerned with the impact your family duties and future plans will have on your tenure there. Your answer could be, "Yes, I am. Of course, I make a separation between my work life and my family life that allows me to give my all to a job. I have no problem with travel or late hours; those things are part of this line of work. I'm sure my references will confirm this for you."

"Do you plan to have children?"

This isn't any of the interviewer's business, but he or she wants to know whether you will leave the company early to raise a family. You can answer "no," of course, since a no answer isn't binding (its only about your current plans). If you answer "yes," you might add, "but those plans are for the future, and they depend on the success of my career. Certainly, I want to do the best, most complete job for this company I can. I consider that my skills are right for the job and that I can make a long-range contribution. I certainly have no plans to leave the company just as I begin to make meaningful contributions."

If the questions become too pointed, you may want to ask—innocently— "Could you explain the relevance of that issue to the position? I'm trying to get a handle on it." That response, however, can seem confrontational; you should only use it if you are *extremely* uncomfortable, or are quite certain you can get away with it. Sometimes, the interviewer will drop the line of questioning.

Illegal questions tend to arise not out of brazen insensitivity, but rather out of an interest in you. The employer is familiar with your skills and background, feels you can do the job, and wants to get to know you as a person. Outright discrimination these days is really quite rare. With illegal questions, your response must be positive—that's the only way you're going to get the job offer, and getting a job offer allows you to leverage other jobs. You don't have to work for a discriminatory company, but you can certainly use the firm to get to something better.

Mock Meetings, Role-Playing, and In-Basket Tests

Some employers use even more elaborate versions of the stress interview when selecting personnel. Groups of candidates may be put in a room together and asked to stage a mock meeting or be asked to give an impromptu presentation. You may even be asked to demonstrate your organization and time-management skills by sorting out and acting on an in-basket full of an overwhelming amount of supposedly urgent data, all while being interrupted by telephone calls.

Collectively, these approaches are referred to as *assessment center techniques*. They are frequently run—on an employer's behalf—by a third-party operation that specializes in skill and aptitude tests. Some companies use this approach when hiring executives, some when choosing sales and customer service professionals, and others when identifying the best candidates for administrative positions. Unfortunately, assessment center techniques are so common today that anyone in the job market risks facing their myriad tortures. The good news is that I have one or two techniques that can help.

One of the reasons that assessment center techniques are growing in popularity is the corporate world's increasing focus on teamwork. Many employers figure they can hire the best workers for a team environment by using group interviews. (Forget the fact that assessment centers haven't proven themselves better or worse than other selection methods!) Since you may encounter this old-new approach during your job search, I want you to be ready for it.

Racks, Beds of Nails, and Iron Maidens

Assessment centers use a broad variety of techniques, including:

- Mock meetings
- In-basket tests
- Role-playing

With these selection techniques, forewarned is forearmed. With a little bit of time to prepare, and an understanding of how these situations work, you can survive anything they might throw at you. Besides, it's only pretend—so there's no need to break out in a cold sweat.

Mock Meetings: Taking Control, Taking Charge, and Being a Team Player

Some employers will want to see you take charge of, or perhaps take over, the leadership of the group. Others want to see your skills at interacting with people. Some employers will want to see both. Your first step in preparing for a mock meeting is to outline the challenges you would face in the daily routine of the job you've applied for. These challenges are likely to form the basis of the situations you'll be asked to respond to. For example, if your job will involve making sales presentations on big-ticket items to groups of people, you can expect the mock meeting to include all of the difficult questions, problems, and people you would be likely to meet in such a context. There are only two differences: first, the whole range of problems is going to appear in one meeting, and second, it's just pretend. If you are a competent professional and react to the situations you face in a professional manner, you'll do just fine.

Your assessors may set up a leaderless group discussion and watch what happens. These groups may include an assortment of applicants, existing employees, and selection center staff—some of them "planted" there to cause disruption or otherwise throw you off balance. Just knowing who is who and why they're there can be a big help. Now that overwhelmingly belligerent SOB can be treated as what he really is: a test of your assertiveness skills.

Anything you face in one of these situations will mirror the challenges you face in the real work world. If your appraisal of the job is that "taking control" and "demonstrating leadership" are likely to be the goals of the mock meeting, *how* you take control and demonstrate leadership will be crucial to your success. You need to set a standard of democratic leadership; you have to become the parent who sets firm limits, but gives support. Be sure to give everyone "air time," while keeping the group on-target and on-schedule.

Sometimes taking charge can be dangerous, however. If you come across as too tough, bossy, or autocratic, forget it! You can't just say, "okay, this is a test of my decision-making and leadership skills, so move over, rover, and let *me* take over." You should encourage a more team-oriented approach: "Let's take a moment to gather our thoughts, then each, in turn, address the issues from our unique perspective." You must keep the meeting moving if someone tries to dominate the discussion or move it away from the agenda. You can then demonstrate your leadership by thanking everyone for his or her contributions.

If someone else beats you to the punch and assumes the leadership role, don't try to show everyone how tough you are by fighting to regain control. Instead, act like the archetypal active team member. Use the time you have while the leader is busy managing the meeting to plan your strategy and develop your contributions to the idea or plan the group is working on. Position yourself as a team player and consensus builder, but show that you can take the initiative, too.

From this position, you can be ready to scoop the opposition at the end of the meeting. While the "leader" is busy making sure that every voice gets heard, you can prepare to help the group summarize its common ground, and establish possible next steps.

In-Basket: A Test of Organized Action

You're staring at a huge stack of reports, memos, and phone messages on your desk. The red light on the phone is flashing to let you know you've got voice mail messages. The computer screen glares at you, with a dozen as-yet-unread e-mail messages. Confronting applicants with a virtual day at the office is yet another way companies try to separate the wheat from the chaff. In this example, you're facing an in-basket test of your time-management and organization skills.

The in-basket test confronts the job candidate with overwhelming amounts of information, and often with conflicting priorities. Then the observers sit back, put their feet up, and watch you wither or shine before their eyes. There are many ways to tackle this kind of test, but the main thing is to make sure that you come prepared with a system to prioritize and organize the work.

Alan Lakein, the godfather of time management, introduced me to a wildly effective and widely accepted approach to time management. Take everything out of the in-basket and place it in one of three piles:

- The A pile is urgent, and you will act on it "today"—in other words, during the test.
- The B pile is important and needs attention. You'll start on it when and if you get through your A pile. If not, much of it will move into your A pile, as you plan for "tomorrow" at the end of "today."
- The C pile is to file or just put in a drawer. It is still important work, but not as urgent as your A and B work. If someone makes it urgent for you—via a telephone call or an urgent e-mail message—you'll know where to find it.

Working out these priorities is the first step in acing an in-basket test. Once established, you'll be able to prioritize those pesky interruptions that are always programmed into this particular type of test. When the calls come in, as they inevitably will, you must have a system in place that can help you decide how to respond. For example, you need to find out:

- Who's calling, and that person's title. You want to establish their name, department, and reporting relationship. If your "boss" of the day calls, he or she has the power to move something from your C pile directly to your A pile.
- What they're calling about. You can put the person on hold while you find the appropriate paperwork, consider the relative importance of the call, and decide how to handle it with efficiency and professionalism.

It is important, at the end of the test, to make sure that the assessor understands that you have been using an effective and logical system. *How to Get Control of Your Time and Your Life*, by Alan Lakein, can teach you world-class time management and organization skills.

Role-Playing

You may be asked to handle a sticky personnel problem, an employee calling in sick from the golf course, a malfunctioning team, an inventory problem, a broken machine, or cold calls to a series of prospective "clients." The goal of role-playing is invariably to see how you handle the people and situations that are likely to crop up in the day-to-day execution of your duties.

Are you a hard-nosed SOB, or do you cave in at the slightest pressure? Do you want the world to love and admire you, or are you out to settle a score? How do you handle a belligerent customer or salvage a tough sale when it turns sour at the last moment?

What's the best way to handle these situations? Consider the role you are playing: is it to land a job as a customer service representative, sales training specialist, vice president of finance, or union lawyer? You need to be clear about the job you're facing—and the challenges it typically generates. You will then understand exactly what the testers are looking for and the role you should play in their scenarios.

In each of these stressful interviewing situations the key is to determine which professional hat you should be wearing and to demonstrate the behaviors the testers will expect from someone wearing that hat. For more on getting in touch with the professional you, see Chapter 22, "How to Ace the Psychological Tests."

Interviewers may pull all kinds of tricks on you, but you will come through with flying colors once you realize they're trying to discover something extremely simple—whether or not you can take the heat. After all, those interviewers are only trying to sort out the good corporate warriors from the walking wounded. If you are asked and successfully handle these tricks and negatively phrased questions, the interviewer will look on you favorably. Stay calm, give as good as you get, and take it all in stride. Remember that no one can intimidate you without your permission.

STRANGE VENUES FOR JOB INTERVIEW

LEARN THE TIPS that will help you master interviews in noisy, distracting hotel lobbies, restaurants, at poolside, and in other unusual settings.

Why are some interviews conducted in strange places? Are meetings in noisy, distracting hotel lobbies designed as a form of torture? What are the real reasons that an interviewer invites you to eat at a fancy restaurant?

For the most part, these tough-on-the-nerves situations happen because the interviewer is a busy person, fitting you into a busy schedule. A woman I know had heard stories about tough interview situations but never expected to face one herself. It happened at a retail convention in Arizona, to which she had been asked for a final interview. The interview was conducted by the pool. The interviewer was there, taking a short break between meetings, in his bathing suit. The first thing the interviewer did was suggest that my friend slip into something comfortable.

That scenario may not lurk in your future, but the chances are you will face many tough interview situations in your career. They call for a clear head and a little gamesmanship if you want to stay ahead of the competition. The interviewee at the pool used both. She removed her jacket, folded it over the arm of the chair, and seated herself, saying pleasantly, "That's much better. Where shall we begin?"

It isn't easy to remain calm at such times. On top of interview nerves, you're worried about being overheard in a public place, or (worse) surprised by the appearance of your current boss. That last item isn't too far-fetched. It actually happened to a reader from San Francisco. He was being interviewed in the departure lounge at the airport when his boss walked through the arrivals door. Oops—he had asked for the day off "to go to the doctor."

Could he have avoided the situation? Certainly, if he had asked about privacy when the meeting was arranged. That would have reminded the interviewer of the need for discretion. The point is to do all you can in advance to make such a meeting as private as possible. Once that's done, you can ignore the rest of the world and concentrate on the interviewer's questions.

Hotel Lobbies and Other Strange Places

Strange interview situations provide other wonderful opportunities to embarrass yourself. You come to a hotel lobby in full corporate battle dress: coat, briefcase, perhaps an umbrella. You sit down to wait for the interviewer. "Aha," you think to yourself, opening your briefcase, "I'll show him my excellent work habits by delving into this computer printout."

That's not such a great idea. Have you ever tried rising with your lap covered with business papers, then juggling the briefcase from right hand to left to accommodate the ritual handshake? It's quite difficult. Besides, while you are sitting in nervous anticipation, pre-interview tension has no way of dissipating. Your mouth will become dry, and your "Good morning, I'm pleased to meet you" will come out sounding like a cat being strangled.

To avoid such catastrophes in places like hotel lobbies, first remove your coat on arrival. Instead of sitting, walk around a little while you wait. Even in a small lobby, a few steps back and forth will help you reduce tension to a manageable level. Keep your briefcase in your left hand (unless you are a leftie) at all times—it makes you look purposeful, and you won't trip over it when you meet the interviewer.

If, for any reason, you must sit, breathe deeply and slowly. This will help control the adrenaline that makes you feel jumpy.

A strange setting can actually put you on equal footing with the interviewer. Neither of you is on home turf, so in many cases the interviewer will feel just as awkward as you do. A little gamesmanship can turn the occasion to your advantage.

To gain the upper hand, get to the meeting site early to scout the territory. By knowing your surroundings, you will feel more relaxed. Early arrival also allows you to control the outcome of the meeting in other subtle ways. You will have time to stake out the most private spot in an otherwise public place. Corners are best. They tend to be quieter, and you can choose the seat that puts your back to the wall (in a physical sense, that is). In this position, you have a clear view of your surroundings and will feel more secure. The fear of being overheard will evaporate.

The situation is now somewhat in your favor. You know the locale, and the meeting place is as much yours as the interviewer's. You will have a clear view of your surroundings, and odds are that you will be more relaxed than the interviewer. When he or she arrives, say, "I arrived a little early to make sure we had some privacy. I think over here is the best spot." With that positive demonstration of your organizational abilities, you give yourself a head start over the competition.

The Meal Meeting

Breakfast, lunch, and dinner are the prime choices for interviewers who want to catch the seasoned professional off-guard. In fact, the meal is arguably the toughest of all tough interview situations. The setting offers the interviewer the chance to see you in a nonoffice (and therefore more natural) setting, to observe your social graces, and to consider you as a whole person. Here, topics that would be impossible to address in the traditional office setting will surface, often with virtually no effort on the part of the interviewer. The slightest slip in front of that wily old pirate—thinly disguised in a Brooks Brothers suit—could get your candidacy deep-sixed in a hurry.

Usually you will not be invited to a "meal meeting" until you have already demonstrated that you are capable of doing the job. An invitation to a meal means that you are under strong consideration, and therefore intense scrutiny.

This meeting is often the final hurdle and could lead directly to the job offer—assuming that you properly handle the occasional surprises that arise. The interviewer's concern is not whether you can do the job but whether you have the growth potential that will allow you to fill more senior slots as they become available.

But be careful. Many have fallen at the final hurdle in a close-run race. Being interviewed in front of others is bad enough; eating and drinking in front of them at the same time only makes it worse. If you knock over a glass or dribble spaghetti sauce down your chin, the interviewer will be so busy smirking that he or she won't hear what you have to say.

To be sure that they remain as attentive to the positive points of your candidacy as possible, let's discuss table manners.

Your social graces and general demeanor at the table can tell as much about you as your answer to a question. For instance, over-ordering food or drink can signal poor self-discipline. At the very least, it will call into question your judgment and maturity. Highhanded behavior toward waiters and busboys could reflect negatively on your ability to get along with subordinates and on your leadership skills. Those concerns are amplified when you return food or complain about the service, actions which, at the very least, find fault with the interviewer's choice of restaurant.

By the same token, you will want to observe how your potential employer behaves. After all, you are likely to become an employee, and the interviewer's behavior to servers in a restaurant can tell you a lot about what it will be like on the job.

Alcohol: Soon after being seated, you will be offered a drink—if not by your host, then by the waiter. There are many reasons to avoid alcohol at interview meals. The most important reason is that alcohol fuzzes your mind, and research proves that stress increases the intoxicating effect of alcohol. So, if you order something to drink, try to stick with something nonalcoholic, such as a club soda, Coke or Pepsi, or simply a glass of water.

If you do have a drink, never have more than one. If there is a bottle of wine on the table, and the waiter offers you another glass, place your hand over the top of your glass. It is a polite way of signifying no.

You may be offered alcohol at the end of the meal. The rule still holds true—turn it down. You need your wits about you even if the interview seems to be drawing to a close. Some interviewers will try to use those moments, when your defenses are at their lowest, to throw in a couple of zingers.

Smoking: Don't smoke unless encouraged. If both of you are smokers, and you are encouraged to smoke, never smoke between courses, only at the end of a meal. Even most confirmed nicotine addicts, like the rest of the population, hate smoke while they are eating.

Utensils: Keep all your cups and glasses at the top of your place setting and well away from you. Most glasses are knocked over at a cluttered table when one stretches for the condiments or gesticulates to make a point.

Here are some other helpful hints:

- Never speak with your mouth full.
- To be on the safe side order something that is easy to eat, as you are there for talking, not eating. Of course, while this rule makes sense in theory, you probably will be asked to order first, so ordering the same thing can become problematic. Solve the problem before you order by complimenting the restaurant during your small talk and then, when the menus arrive, asking, "What do you think you will have today?"
- Do not change your order once it is made, and never send the food back.
- Be polite to your waiters, even when they spill soup in your lap.
- Don't order expensive food. Naturally, in our heart of hearts, we all like to eat well, especially on someone else's tab. But don't be tempted. When you come right down to it, you are there to talk and be seen at your best, not to eat.
- Eat what you know. Stay away from awkward, messy, or exotic foods (e.g., artichokes, long pasta, and escargot, respectively). Ignore finger foods, such as lobster or spare ribs. In fact, you should avoid eating with your fingers altogether, unless you are in a sandwich joint, in which case you should make a point of avoiding the leaky, overstuffed menu items.
- Don't order salad. The dressing can often get messy. If a salad comes with the meal, request that the dressing be on the side. Then, before pouring it on, cut up the lettuce.
- Don't order anything with bones. Stick with fillets; there are few simple, gracious ways to deal with any type of bone.

✎Checks and Goodbyes: I know an interviewer whose favorite test of composure is to have the waiter, by arrangement, put the bill on the interviewee's side of the table. She then chats on, waiting for something interesting to happen. If you ever find yourself in a similar situation, never pick up the check, however long it is left by your plate. When ready, your host will pick it up, because that's the protocol of the occasion. By the same token, you should never offer to share payment.

When parting company, always thank the host for his or her hospitality and the wonderful meal. Of course, you should be sure to leave on a positive note by asking good-naturedly what you have to do to get the job.

◆ ◆ ◆

Strange interview situations can arise at any time during the interview cycle, and in any public place. Wherever you are asked to go, keep your guard up. Your table manners, listening skills, and overall social graces are being judged. The question on the interviewer's mind is: can you be trusted to represent the company gracefully and with professional demeanor?

WELCOME TO THE REAL WORLD

FOR THE RECENT graduate, here are some tough questions specifically tailored to discover your business potential.

Of all the steps a recent graduate will take up the ladder of success over the years, none is more important or more difficult than getting a foot on the first rung. The interviewing process designed for recent graduates is particularly rigorous, because management regards the hiring of entry-level professionals as one of its toughest jobs.

When a company hires experienced people, there is a track record to evaluate. With recent graduates, there is little or nothing. Often, the only solid things an interviewer has to go on are SAT scores and high school or college diplomas. That's not much on which to base a hiring decision—grades don't tell the interviewer whether you will fit in or make a reliable employee. Many recruiters liken the gamble of hiring recent graduates to storing wines for the future: they know some will develop into full-bodied, reliable vintages, but others will be disappointments. Recruiters have to find different ways to predict your potential accurately.

After relying, as best they can, on school performance to evaluate your ability, interviewers concentrate on questions that reveal how willing you are to learn and get the job done, and how manageable you are likely to be, both on average days and when the going gets rough.

Your goal is to stand out from all the other entry-level candidates as someone altogether different and better. Don't be like thousands of others who, in answer to questions about their greatest strength, reply lamely, "I'm good with people," or, "I like working with others." Such answers do not separate you from the herd. In fact, they brand you as average. To stand out, a recent graduate must recount a past situation that illustrates *how* he or she is good with people, or one that demonstrates an ability to be a team player.

Fortunately, the key professional behaviors discussed throughout the book are just as helpful for getting your foot on the ladder as they are for aiding your climb to the top. They will guide you in choosing the aspects of your personality and background that you should promote at the interview.

It isn't necessary to have snap answers ready for every question, because you never will. It is more important for you to pause after a question and collect your thoughts before answering; you must show that you think before you speak. That way, you will demonstrate your analytic abilities, which age feels youth has in short supply.

By the same token, occasionally asking for a question to be repeated is useful to gain time and is quite acceptable, as long as you don't do it with every question. And if a question stumps you, as sometimes happens, do not stutter incoherently. It is sometimes best to say, "I don't know" or, "I'd like to come back to that later." Odds are the interviewer will forget to ask again; if he or she doesn't, at least you've had some time to come up with an answer.

Knowing everything about a certain entry-level position is not necessary, because business feels it can teach you most things. But, as a vice president of Merrill Lynch once said, "You must bring to the table the ability to speak clearly." Knowing what is behind the questions that are designed especially for recent graduates will give you the time to build informative and understandable answers.

"How did you get your summer jobs?"

All employers look favorably on recent graduates who have any work experience, no matter what it is. "It is far easier to get a fix on someone who has worked while at school," says Dan O'Brien, head of employment at Grumman. "They manage their time better, are more realistic, and more mature. Any work experience gives us much more in common." So, as you make your answer, add that you learned business is about making a profit, doing things more efficiently, adhering to procedures, and putting out whatever effort it takes to get the job done. In short, treat your summer jobs, no matter how humble, as any other business experience.

In this particular question, the interviewer is looking for something that shows initiative, creativity, and flexibility. Here's an example: "In my town, summer jobs were hard to come by, but I applied to each local restaurant for a position waiting tables, called the manager at each one to arrange an interview, and finally landed a job at one of the most prestigious. I was assigned to the afternoon shift, but with my quick work, accurate billing, and ability to keep customers happy, they soon moved me to the evening shift. I worked there for three summers, and by the time I left, I was responsible for the training and management of the night-shift waiters, the allotment of tips, and the evening's final closing and accounting. All in all, my experience showed me the mechanics of a small business and of business in general."

"Which of the jobs you have held have you liked least?"

The interviewer is trying to trip you up. It is likely that your work experience contained a certain amount of repetition and drudgery, as all early jobs in the business world do. So beware of saying that you hated a particular job "because it was boring." Avoid the negative and say something along these lines: "All of my jobs had their good and bad points, but I've always found that if you want to learn, there's plenty to pick up every day. Each experience was valuable." Then describe a seemingly boring job, but show how it taught you valuable lessons or helped you hone different aspects of your personality profile.

"What are your future vocational plans?"

This is a fancy way of asking, "Where do you want to be five years from now?" The mistake all entry-level professionals make is to say, "In management," because they think that shows drive and ambition. It has become such a trite answer, though, that it immediately generates a string of questions most recent graduates can't answer: What is the definition of management? What is a manager's prime responsibility? A manager in what area? Your safest answer identifies you with the profession you are trying to break into and shows you have your feet on the ground: "I want to get ahead, and to do that I must be able to channel my energies and expertise into those areas that my industry and employer need. So in a couple of years I hope to have become a thorough professional with a clear understanding of the company, the industry, and where the biggest challenges and opportunities lie. By that time, my goals for the future should be sharply defined." An answer like that will set you far apart from your contemporaries.

"What college did you attend, and why did you choose it?"

The college you attended isn't as important as your reasons for choosing it—the question is trying to examine your reasoning processes. Emphasize that it was your choice, and you didn't go there as a result of your parents' desires or because generations of your family have always attended the Acme School of Welding. Focus on the practical: "I went to Greenbriar State—it was a choice based on practicality. I wanted a school that would give me a good education and prepare me for the real world. State has a good record for turning out students fully prepared to take on responsibilities in the real world. It is [or isn't] a big school, but/and it has certainly taught me some big lessons about the value of [whatever personality values apply] in the real world of business."

If the interviewer has a follow-up question about the role your parents played in the selection of your school, be wary—he or she is plumbing your maturity. It is best to reply that the choice of the school was yours, though you did seek the advice of your parents once you had made your selection, and they supported your decision.

"Are you looking for a permanent or temporary job?"

The interviewer wants reassurance that you are genuinely interested in the position and won't disappear in a few months to pursue postdoctoral studies in San Tropez. Try to go beyond saying, "Permanent." Explain why you want the job. You might say, "Of course, I am looking for a permanent job. I intend to make my career in this field, and I want the opportunity to learn the business, face new challenges, and learn from experienced professionals." You will also want to qualify the question with one of your own: "Is this a permanent or a temporary position you are trying to fill?" Don't be scared to ask. The occasional unscrupulous employer will hire someone fresh out of school for a short period of time—say, for one particular project—then lay him or her off.

"How did you pay for college?"

Avoid saying, "Oh, Daddy handled all of that," as it probably won't create the impression you'd like. Your parents may well have helped you out, but you should explain, if it's appropriate, that you worked part-time and took out loans (as most of us must during college).

"We have tried to hire people from your school/your major before, and they never seem to work out. What makes you different?"

Here's a stress question to test your poise and analytical skills. You can shout that, yes, of course you are different and can prove it. So far, though, all you know is that there was a problem, not what caused the problem. Respond this way: "First, may I ask you exactly what problems you've had with people from this background?" Once you know what the problem is (if one really exists at all—it may just be a curve ball to test your poise), you can illustrate how you are different—but only then. Otherwise, you run the risk of your answer being interrupted with, "Well, that's what everyone else said before I hired them. You haven't shown me you are different."

"I'd be interested to hear about some things you learned in school that could be used on the job."

While specific job-related courses could form part of your answer, they cannot be all of it. The interviewer wants to hear about "real-world" skills, so explain what the experience of college taught you rather than a specific course. In other words, explain how the experience honed your relevant personality profiles: "Within my major and minor I tried to pursue those courses that had most practical relevance, such as. . . . However, the greatest lessons I learned were the importance of. . . ." then list your personality profile strengths.

"Do you like routine tasks/regular hours?"

A trick question. The interviewer knows from bitter experience that most recent graduates hate routine and are hopeless as employees until they come to an acceptance of such facts of life. Explain that, yes, you appreciate the need for routine, you expect a fair amount of routine assignments before you are entrusted with the more responsible ones, and that that is why you are prepared to accept it as necessary. As far as regular hours go you could say, "No, there's no problem there. A company expects to make a profit, so the doors have to be open for business on a regular basis."

"What have you done that shows initiative and willingness to work?"

Again, tell a story about how you landed or created a job for yourself, or even got involved in some volunteer work. Your answer should show that you both handled unexpected problems calmly and anticipated others. Your willingness is demonstrated by the ways you overcame obstacles. For example: "I worked for a summer in a small warehouse. I found out that a large shipment was due in a couple of weeks, and I knew that room had to be made. The inventory system was outdated, and the rear of the warehouse was disorganized, so I came in on a Saturday, figured out how much room I needed, cleaned up the mess in the rear, and cataloged it all on the new inventory forms. When the shipment arrived, the truck just backed in. There was even room to spare."

Often after an effort above and beyond the call of duty, a manager might congratulate you, and if it happened to you in this instance, you might conclude your answer with the verbal endorsement: "The divisional manager happened along just when I was finishing the job, and he said he wished he had more people who took such pride in their work."

"Can you take instructions without feeling upset or hurt?"

This is a manageability question. If you take offense easily or bristle when your mistakes are pointed out, you won't last long with any company. Competition is fierce at the entry level, so take this as another chance to set yourself apart: "Yes, I can take instruction—and more important, I can take constructive criticism without feeling hurt. Even with the best intent, I will still make mistakes, and at times someone will have to put me back on the right track. I know that if I'm ever to rise in the company, I must first prove myself to be manageable."

"Have you ever had difficulties getting along with others?"

This is a combination question, probing willingness and manageability. Are you a team player or are you going to disrupt the department and make the interviewer's life miserable? This is a closed-ended question that requires only a yes-or-no answer, so give one and shut up.

"What type of position are you interested in?"

This is another of those questions that tempts you to mention management. Tell the interviewer you are interested in an entry-level job, which is what you will be offered anyway: "I am interested in an entry-level position that will enable me to learn this business inside and out and will give me the opportunity to grow when I prove myself, either on a professional or on the managerial ladder."

"What qualifications do you have that will make you successful in this field?"

There is more to answering this question than reeling off your academic qualifications. In addition you will want to stress relevant work experience and illustrate your strong points as they match the key professional behaviors required in the position you seek. It's a wide-open question that says, "Hey, we're looking for an excuse to hire you. Give us some help."

"Why do you think you would like this type of work?"

This is a deceptively simple question because there is no pat answer. It is usually asked to see whether you really understand what the specific job and profession entails on a day-to-day basis. To answer it requires you to have researched the company and job functions as carefully as possible. Call another company in the field and request to speak to someone doing the job you hope to get. Ask what the job is like and what that person does day-to-day. How does the job fit into the department? What contribution does it make to the overall efforts of the company? Why does he or she like that type of work? Armed with that information, you will show that you understand what you are getting into; most recent graduates do not.

"What's your idea of how industry works?"

The interviewer does not want a dissertation, just the reassurance that you don't think it works along the same lines as a registered charity. Your understanding should be something like this: "The role of any company is to make as much money as possible, as quickly and efficiently as possible, and in a manner that will encourage repeat business from the existing client base and new business from word of mouth and reputation." Finish with the observation that it is every employee's role to play as a team member in order to achieve those goals.

"Why do you think this industry will sustain your interest over the long haul?" or "Why do you think you will shine in this profession?"

Your answer should speak both to your pragmatism and to your motivation. "At this point in my career, I am looking at the industry because I believe it offers stability and professional growth potential over the years [explain why]. Also, I'll be using skills [itemize strong skill sets that are relevant to the job] that are areas of strength, from which I derive great personal satisfaction."

"What do you know about our company?"

This can be a simple conversation gambit, helping the interviewer know where to start in explaining the company activities, or it can be a more loaded question. In the tight job race we have today, the offer always goes to the person who is most knowledgeable and enthusiastic about the company. It makes sense when you think about it, because that knowledge and enthusiasm are endorsements of both the work and the place that the interviewer is a part of for the majority of his waking hours.

Enthusiasm for your profession and the job is a matter of your attitude. Learning something about the company is as simple as doing a little Internet research and personal networking.

For the Internet research aspect, browse the company Web site, and enter the company name or their products and services into a couple of search engines and absorb as much as time allows. Print out as much as you can and use it as bedtime reading the night before the interview. It's probably better than Sominex as a sleep aid, and it's good psychological preparation, too. For the networking aspect, talk to acquaintances who have knowledge of the company. Membership in the local chapter of a professional association is the best bet for learning about any company in your town.

You can't answer this question unless you have enough interest to research the company thoroughly. If you don't have that interest, you should expect someone who does will get the job.

"What do you think determines progress in a good company?"

Your answer will include all the positive professional behaviors you have been illustrating throughout the interview. Include allusions to the listening profile, determination, ability to take the rough with the smooth, adherence to systems and procedures, and the good fortune to have a manager who wants you to grow.

"Do you think grades should be considered by first employers?"

If your grades were good, the answer is obviously "yes." If they weren't, your answer needs a little more thought. "Of course, an employer should take everything into consideration. Along with grades will be an evaluation of willingness and manageability, an understanding of how business works, and actual work experience. Combined, such experience and professional skills can be more valuable than grades alone."

Many virtuous candidates are called for entry-level interviews, but only those who prepare themselves to answer the tough questions will be chosen. Interviews for recent graduates are partly sales presentations. The more you interview, the better you get, so don't leave preparing for them until the last minute. Start now and hone your skills to get a head start on your peers. A professor from a top-notch business school once told me: "You are taking a new product to market. Accordingly, you've got to analyze what it can do, who is likely to be interested, and how you are going to sell it to them." Take some time to get to know yourself and your particular values as they will be perceived in the world of business.

THE GRACEFUL EXIT

IS PARTING SUCH sweet sorrow? The end of an interview will more likely mean relief, but here are some dos and don'ts to bear in mind as your meeting comes to a close.

To paraphrase Shakespeare, all the working world's a stage, curtains rise and fall, and your powerful performance must be capped with a professional and memorable exit. To ensure you leave the right impression, this chapter will review the dos and don'ts of leaving an interview.

A signal that the interview is drawing to a close comes when you are asked whether you have any questions. Ask questions, and by doing so, highlight your strengths and show your enthusiasm. Remember, your goal at the interview is to generate a job offer. Make sure your exit is as graceful as your entrance.

Dos:

1. *Ask appropriate job-related questions.* When the opportunity comes to ask any final questions, review your notes. Bring up any relevant strengths that haven't been addressed.

2. *Show decisiveness.* If you are offered the job, react with enthusiasm. Then sleep on it. If it's possible to do so without making a formal acceptance, lock the job up now and put yourself in control; you can always change your mind later. Before making any commitment with regard to compensation, see Chapter 20, "Negotiating the Job Offer."

3. *When more than one person interviews you, be sure you have the correct spellings of their names.* "I enjoyed meeting your colleagues, Ms. Smith. Could you give me the correct spellings of their names, please?" This question will give you the names you forgot in the heat of battle and will demonstrate your consideration.

4. *Review the job's requirements with the interviewer.* Match them point-by-point with your skills and attributes.

5. *Find out whether this is the only interview.* If so, you must ask for the job in a positive and enthusiastic manner. Find out the time frame for a decision and finish with, "I am very enthusiastic about the job and the contributions I can make. If your decision will be made by the fifteenth, what must I do in the meantime to assure I get the job?"

6. *Ask for the next interview.* When there are subsequent interviews in the hiring procedure, ask for the next interview in the same honest and forthright manner: "Is now a good time to schedule our next meeting?"

7. *Keep yourself in contention.* A good leading question to ask is, "Until I hear from you again, what particular aspects of the job and this interview should I be considering?"

8. *Always depart in the same polite and assured manner in which you entered.* Look the interviewer in the eye, put on a smile (there's no need to grin), give a firm handshake, and say, "This has been an exciting meeting for me. This is a job I can do, and I feel I can contribute to your goals, because the atmosphere here seems conducive to doing my very best work. When will we speak again?"

Don'ts:

1. *Don't discuss salary, vacation, or benefits.* It is not that the questions are invalid, just that the timing is wrong. Bringing up such topics before you have an offer is asking what the company can do for you—instead, you should be saying what you can do for the company. Those topics are part of the negotiation (handled in Chapter 20, "Negotiating the Job Offer"); remember, without an offer you have nothing to negotiate.

2. *Don't press for an early decision.* Of course, you should ask, "When will I know your decision?" But don't press it. Don't try to use the "other opportunities I have to consider" gambit as leverage when no such offers exist—that annoys the interviewer, makes you look foolish, and may even force you to negotiate from a position of weakness. Timing is everything; the issue of how to handle other opportunities as leverage is explored in detail later.

3. *Don't show discouragement.* Sometimes a job offer can occur on the spot. Usually it does not. So don't show discouragement if you are not offered the job at the interview, because discouragement shows a lack of self-esteem and determination. Avoiding a bad impression is the foundation of leaving a good one, and the right image to leave is one of enthusiasm, guts, and openness—just the professional behaviors you have been projecting throughout the interview.

4. *Don't ask for an evaluation of your interview performance.* That forces the issue and puts the interviewer in an awkward position. You can say that you want the job, and ask what you have to do to get it.

FINISHING
TOUCHES

STATISTICS SHOW THAT the last person to get interviewed usually gets the job. Here are some steps you can take that will keep your impression strong.

THE SUCCESSFUL COMPLETION OF EVERY INTERVIEW is a big stride toward getting job offers, yet it is not the end of your job search.

A company rarely hires the first competent person it sees. A hiring manager will sometimes interview as many as fifteen people for a particular job, but the strain and pace of conducting interviews naturally dim the memory of each applicant. Unless you are the last person to be interviewed, the impression you make will fade with each subsequent interview the interviewer undertakes. And if you are not remembered, you will not be offered the job. You must develop a strategy to keep your name and skills constantly in the forefront of the interviewer's mind. These finishing touches often make all the difference.

Some of the suggestions here may not seem earth-shattering: just simple, sensible demonstrations of your manners, enthusiasm, and determination. But remember that today all employers are looking for people with that extra little something. You can avoid a negative or merely indifferent impression, and be certain of creating a positive one, by following these guidelines.

OUT OF SIGHT, OUT OF MIND

DON'T LET THE interviewer forget you! A good follow-up is simple. Here are eight steps that guarantee the continuation of your candidacy.

The first thing you do on leaving the interview is to breathe a sigh of relief. The second is to make sure that "out of sight, out of mind" will not apply to you. You do this by starting a follow-up procedure immediately after the interview.

Sitting in your car, on the bus, train, or plane, do a written recap of the interview while it's still fresh in your mind. Answer these questions:

- Whom did you meet? (names and titles)
- What does the job entail?
- What are the first projects, the biggest challenges?
- Why can you do the job?
- What aspects of the interview went well? Why?
- What aspects of the interview went poorly? Why?
- What is the agreed-upon next step?
- Where is the employer in the hiring cycle, when will a decision be made?
- What was said during the last few minutes of the interview?

Probably the most difficult—and most important—thing to do is to objectively analyze what aspects of the interview went poorly. A person does not get offered a job based solely on strengths, and those questions will be easy enough for you to answer; on the contrary, you may in part get that new job based on your lack of negatives as compared with the other candidates. It is therefore mandatory that you look for and recognize any negatives from your performance. This self-awareness is the only way to package and overcome those negatives as you progress in your follow-up procedure and during subsequent interviews.

After your analysis of the interview, your next step is to send the follow-up e-mail or letter to the interviewer. Sending a follow-up letter shows that you are organized and enthusiastic and motivated by the opportunity. In a tightly run job race, when there is nothing to choose between the ability and suitability of two candidates, the job offer always goes to the candidate who is most enthusiastic about the opportunity. It's common sense when you think about it from the employer's viewpoint: the enthusiastic person is going to put more effort into the job; additionally, your enthusiasm is flattering to the hiring manager.

1. Write a follow-up letter to be sent as an e-mail or as a traditional letter. It should make four points clear to the interviewer:
   - You understand the job and can do it
   - You paid attention to what was being said.
   - You are excited about the job, and want it.
   - You have the experience to contribute to those first major projects.
2. Here are some phrases you might find useful in expressing yourself:
   - "Upon reflection," or "Having thought about our meeting. . . ."
   - Recognize—"I recognize the importance of. . . ."
   - Listen—"Listening to the points you made. . . ."
   - Motivation—Let the interviewer catch your enthusiasm and see that you are motivated by the opportunity. It is very effective, especially as

your e-mail or letter may arrive while other applicants are stumbling their way through the interview.

- Impressed—Let the interviewer know you were impressed with the people/product/service/facility/market/position, but *do not overdo it*.
- Challenge—Show that you feel you would be challenged to do your best work in this environment.
- Confidence—There is a job to be done and a challenge to be met. Let the interviewer know you are confident of doing both well.
- Interest—If you want the job (or next interview), say so. At this stage, the company is buying and you are selling. Ask for the job in a positive and enthusiastic manner.
- Appreciation—As a courtesy and mark of professional manners, you must express appreciation for the time the interviewer took out of his or her busy schedule.

3. Whenever possible and appropriate, mention the names of the people you met at the interview. Draw attention to one of the topics that was of general interest to the interviewers.

4. Address the follow-up e-mail/letter to the main interviewer. You can send separate e-mails/letters to others in the selection cycle. Each makes a positive impression and shows extra effort and attention to detail.

5. Don't write too much. Keep it short—less than one page—and don't make any wild claims that might not withstand close scrutiny.

6. Send the letter within twenty-four hours of the interview. If the decision is going to be made in the next couple of days, e-mail the letter or hand-deliver it. The follow-up letter will help to set you apart from other applicants and will refresh your image in the mind of the interviewer just when it would normally be starting to dim.

7. If a hiring decision is imminent, follow up with an e-mail, then a telephone call, within twenty-four to forty-eight hours, as time constraints dictate; your follow-up is dictated by the time constraints of the employer. "Mr. Massie? Martin Yate. We met for an interview on Wednesday afternoon. I know you are making a decision by close of business tomorrow and I wanted to catch up with you personally to say":
- Thanks for your time
- I can do the job and this is why
- I am excited about the job and this is why
- I will make a good hire and this is why

8. If you are in an extended interview cycle, you will need to pace yourself a little differently. If you do not hear anything after five days (which is

quite normal), put in a telephone call to the interviewer; I have always thought it a good idea to make sure that the interviewer is reminded of your candidacy right before the weekend begins. Cover the same points as addressed in the last item, asking for either the job or the next interview in the cycle, whichever is appropriate.

Sometimes interview cycles can stretch into weeks and occasionally months, so there are a couple of considerations here. You can't e-mail and call every week, but you can touch base every couple of weeks. Google has a nice feature that allows you to track news on any topic you choose. Taking advantage of this allows you to keep up to speed on your profession and factors affecting it, and this knowledge-gathering can be put to additional good use.

E-mail a quick note with a link: "Mr. Massie, I just came across this article about the impact of _____ on productivity in our profession and thought you might like to see it. By the way, I am still determined to be your next [title]. Regards, Martin Yate."

Even better, print it out and, with a neatly handwritten note, for special effect and impact, you might send it via regular mail. You think I'm crazy? Think again. Everyone gets a ton of e-mail every day, but regular mail has diminished to a similar degree, so sending useful information through a less trammeled medium will help you stand out.

Now while you will follow up enthusiastically on all your interviews, you should recognize a difficult fact of life: the longer an interview cycle drags out, the less likely it is to result in an offer. So while you will follow up conscientiously with all your interviews, you will not place your professional future on the wings of a prayer. Instead you will continue to work your plan, making new contacts and generating new interviews on a consistent basis.

This is simply the sensible approach. Just as every job is not right for you, you will not be right for every job, so occasionally you may be told you are no longer in the running. In most instances this will be a signal to shrug your shoulders and move on, but once in a while it will happen with a job that you really want. The next chapter will show you practical ways to snatch victory from the jaws of defeat.

19

SNATCHING VICTORY FROM THE JAWS OF DEFEAT

REJECTION? IMPOSSIBLE! THEN again, you won't be right for every job. Here are some techniques that help you to create opportunities in the face of rejection.

During the interviewing process, there are bound to be interviewers who come to the erroneous conclusion that you are not the right person for the job they need to fill. When that happens, you will be turned down. Such an absurd travesty of justice can occur in different ways:

- At the interview
- In a letter of rejection
- During your follow-up telephone call

Whenever the turndown comes, you must be emotionally and intellectually prepared to take advantage of the opportunity being offered to you.

When you get turned down for the only prospect you have going, the rejection can be devastating to your ego. That is why I have stressed the wisdom of having at least a few interviews in process at the same time.

You will get turned down. No one can be right for every job. The right person for a job doesn't always get it, however—the best prepared and most determined often does. While you may be responsible in part for the initial rejection, you still have the power to correct the situation and win the job offer. What you do with the claimed victory is a different matter—you will then be in a seller's market with choice and control of your situation.

Almost every job you desire is obtainable once you understand the hiring process from the interviewer's side of the desk. Your initial—and temporary—rejection is attributable to one of these reasons:

- The interviewer does not feel you can do the job.
- The interviewer feels you lack a successful profile.
- The interviewer did not feel your personality would contribute to the smooth functioning of the department—perhaps you didn't portray yourself as either a team player or as someone willing to take the extra step.

With belief in yourself, you can still succeed. Repeat to yourself constantly through the interview cycle: "I will get this job, because no one else can give as much to this company as I can!" Do that and implement the following plan immediately when you hear of rejection, whether in person, via mail, or over the telephone.

✎**Step One:** Thank the interviewer for the time and consideration. Then ask politely: "To help my future job search, why wasn't I chosen for the position?" Assure the interviewer that you would truly appreciate an honest, objective analysis. Listen to the reply and do not interrupt. Use your time constructively and take notes. When the company representative finishes speaking, show that you understood the comments. (Remember, understanding and agreeing are different animals.)

"Thank you, Mr. Smith, now I can understand the way you feel. Because I don't interview that often I'm afraid my nerves got in the way. I'm very interested in working for your company [use an enthusiastic tone] and am determined to get the job. Let me meet with you once again. This time, when I'm not so nervous, I am confident you will see I really do have the skills you require" [then provide an example of a skill you have in the questionable area]. "You name the time and the place, and I will be there. What's best for you, Mr. Smith?"

End with a question, of course and note here that you're asking *when* you can meet again, and not *if*. An enthusiastic request like that is very difficult to refuse and will usually get you another interview—an interview, of course, at which you must shine.

Step Two: Check your notes and accept the company representative's concerns. Their validity is irrelevant; the important point is that the negative points represent the problem areas in the interviewer's perception of you. List the negative perceptions, and using the techniques, exercises, and value keys discussed throughout the book, develop different ways to overcome or compensate for every negative perception.

Step Three: Reread Part 3 of this book.

Step Four: Practice aloud the statements and responses you will use at the interview. If you can practice with someone who plays the part of the interviewer, that's even better. This will create a real interview atmosphere and increase your chances of success. Lacking a role-play partner, you can create that live answer by putting the anticipated objections and questions on a tape and responding to them.

Step Five: Study all available information on the company.

Step Six: Congratulate yourself continually for getting another interview after initial rejection. This is proof of your self-worth, ability, and tenacity. You have nothing to lose and everything to gain, having already risen phoenix-like from the ashes of defeat.

Step Seven: During the interview, ask for the job in a positive and enthusiastic manner. Your drive and staying power will impress the interviewer. All you must do to win the job is overcome the perceived negatives, and you have been given the time and information to prepare. Go for it.

Step Eight: Even when all has failed at the subsequent interview, do not leave without a final request for the job. Play your trump card: "Mr. Smith, I respect the fact that you allowed me the opportunity to prove myself here today. I am convinced I am the best person for the job. I want you to give me a trial, and I will prove on the job that I am the best hiring decision you have made this year. Will you give us both the opportunity?"

A reader once wrote to me as I was revising *Knock 'em Dead*, "I read the chapter entitled 'Snatching Victory from the Jaws of Defeat' and did everything you said to salvage what appeared to be a losing interview. My efforts did make a very good impression on the interviewer, but as it was finally explained to me, I really did not have equal qualifications for the job, and finally came in a close second. I really want to work for this growing company, and they say they have another position coming up in six months. What should I do?"

I know of someone who wanted a job working for a major airline. He had been recently laid off and had high hopes for a successful interview. As it happened, he came in second for the position. He was told that the firm would speak to him again in the near future. So he waited—for eight months. Finally, he realized that waiting for the job could only leave him unemployed. The moral of the story is that you must be brutally objective when you come out second-best, and, whatever the interviewer says, you must sometimes assume that you are getting the polite brush-off.

With that in mind, let's see what can be done on the positive side. First of all, send a thank-you note to the interviewer, acknowledging your understanding of the state of affairs and reaffirming your desire to work for the company. Conclude with a polite request to bear you in mind for the future.

Keep an eye out for any news item about the company in the press. Whenever you see something, cut it out and mail it to the interviewer with a very brief note that says something like: "I came across this in *Forbes* and thought you might find it interesting. I am still determined to be your next account manager, so please keep me in mind when the next opening occurs."

You can also call the interviewer once every couple of months, just to check in. Remember, of course, to keep the phone call brief and polite—you simply want to keep your name at the top of the interviewer's mind.

And maybe something will come of it. Ultimately, however, your only choice is to move on. There is nothing to gain by waiting on an interviewer's word. Go out and keep looking, because chances are that you will come up with an even better job. Then, if you still want to work for that company that gave you the brush-off, you will have some leverage.

Most people fail in their endeavors by quitting just before the dawn of success. Follow these directions and you can win the job. You have proven yourself to be a fighter, and that is universally admired. The company representative will want you to succeed because you are made of stuff that is rarely seen today. You are a person of guts, drive, and endurance—the hallmarks of a winner. Job turn-downs are opportunities to exercise and build on your strengths, and, by persisting, you may well add to your growing number of job offers, now and in the future.

NEGOTIATING THE JOB OFFER

THEY WANT YOU! Before you sign on the dotted line, however, you should be well schooled in the essentials of good salary and benefits negotiations. After all, you're never going to have this much leverage again unless you start over from square one, right?

The crucial period after you have received a formal offer and before you accept is probably the one point in your relationship with an employer at which you can say that you have the whip hand. The advantage, for now, is yours. They want you but don't have you; and their wanting something they don't have gives you a negotiating edge. An employer is also more inclined to respect and honor a person who has a clear understanding of his or her worth in the marketplace—they want a savvy and businesslike person.

You don't have to accept or reject the first offer, whatever it is. In most instances you can improve the initial offer in a number of ways, but you have to know something about the existing market conditions for those employed in your area of endeavor. If you are female, bear in mind that simply settling for a few points above your current rate of pay is bad advice for anyone and downright crazy for you.

The Women's Bureau of the U.S. Department of Labor tells us that men outearn women in nearly every field. (For what it's worth, my research could not turn up a single industry in which this was not the case.) Even if a woman's responsibilities, background, and accomplishments are exactly the same as those of her male colleague, she is statistically unlikely to take home a paycheck equal to his. According to the Women's Bureau, male engineers make 14.3 percent more than their female counterparts. Male mathematicians make 16.3 percent more. Male advertising and public relations professionals make 28 percent more. Male lawyers and judges make 28 percent more. And male editors and reporters make a whopping 43 percent more than women performing the same or comparable work. My belief is that much of the gap can be attributed to a simple lack of knowledge of professional negotiating skills, and that women in the workplace are picking these skills up fast.

Man or woman, there is no guarantee you are being paid what you are worth. The simple facts are these: if you don't get it while they want you and don't have you, you sure can't count on getting it once they do have you. When a thirty-year-old under-negotiates his or her salary by just $4,000 on a new job, it will cost that person a minimum of $140,000 over the course of a career. Remember, every subsequent raise will come from a proportionately lower base; due to inflation real dollars lost over an entire career span could actually be double this figure.

Online Resource

Bureau of Labor Statistics

www.bls.gov
This Web site contains a wealth of job-related and economic information (though dated) from around the nation. You'll find information on state unemployment rates, salary information, anticipated job growth-rates for particular industries, growing fields, and publications and research papers on prices, living conditions, and technology. You will also find *www.salary.com* a good resource for salary comparison; most Web sites have a salary calculator tool (often powered by Salary.com).

To get what you have coming at the negotiating table, take the time to understand what you have achieved, what you have to offer, and what you are worth to the employer. You should be able to get a better handle on that final item by doing good research, but remember that regional business conditions can affect pay levels.

Everything in this book has been written toward maximizing your professional worth, and salary negotiation is certainly no exception. There are no shortcuts. The ideas presented in this chapter will be helpful to you if they represent the culmination of your successful campaign to set yourself apart from the competition, but you cannot negotiate a terrific salary package if an employer is not convinced that you are in the top tier of applicants.

Follow this three-step procedure in planning your salary discussions with employers.

Step One: Before getting into negotiation with any employer, work out your minimum cash requirements for any job. What is it going to take to keep a roof over your head and bread on the table? It's necessary to know this figure, but you need never discuss it with anyone—knowing it is the foundation of getting what you need, what you are worth, and what you want.

Step Two: Get a grip on what your skills are worth in the current market. There are a number of ways to do that. Consider the resources and methods outlined below:

- You can find salary surveys on online employment sites.
- You may be able to find out the salary range for the level above you and the level beneath you at the company in question.
- Ask headhunters—they know better than anyone what the market will bear. You should, as a matter of career prudence, establish an ongoing relationship with a reputable headhunter, because you never know when his or her services will come in handy.
- Many professional journals publish annual salary surveys that you can consult.

Step Three: This is the fun part. Come up with the figure that would make you smile, drop dead, and go to heaven on the spot. (But try to keep it somewhere within the bounds of reality—multimillion-dollar offers being in relatively short supply for most of us.)

You now have three figures: a minimum, a realistic midpoint desired salary, and a dream salary.

Your minimum is for personal consumption—never discuss it with anyone. Put it aside, and what do you have left? A salary range, just like the one every employer has for every interview you attend. Yours extends from your midpoint to your dream salary. Yes, that range represents the "top half" of what you want or, more accurately, could conceivably accept—but there's a reason for that. In the event, you will find it is far easier to negotiate down than to negotiate up, and you must find a starting point that gives you every possible advantage.

Negotiate When You Can

I have said throughout *Knock 'em Dead* that your sole aim at the interview is to get the job offer, because without it you have nothing to negotiate. Once the offer is extended, the time to negotiate has arrived, and there will never be a more opportune time.

Although questions of salary are usually brought up after you are under serious consideration, you must be careful to avoid painting yourself into a corner when you fill out the initial company application form that contains a request for expected salary. Usually you can get away with "open" as a response; sometimes the form will instruct you not to write "open," in which case you can write "negotiable" or "competitive."

Online Resource

The crucial period after you have received a formal offer is when the issue of money is raised. You have an advantage—they want you but don't have you; you want to get as much as possible, as competitively as possible, while the company wants you. Getting what is best for you can require research into who gets paid what in your profession. Here are some resources for establishing salary norms:

> *www.wsj.com*   *www.homefair.com*
> *www.jobs.com*   *www.salary.com*

So much for basic considerations. Let's move on to the money questions that are likely to be flying around the room. The negotiation begins in earnest in two ways. The interviewer can bring up the topic with statements like:

- "How do you think you would like working here?"

- "People with your background always fit in well with us."
- "You could make a real contribution here."
- "Well, you certainly seem to have what it takes."

Or, if it is clearly appropriate to do so, you can bring on the negotiating stage. In that case, you can make mirror images of the above, which make the interviewer face the fact that you certainly are able to do the job, and that the time has therefore come to talk turkey:

- "How do you think I would fit in with the group?"
- "I feel my background and experience would definitely complement the work group, don't you?"
- "I think I could make a real contribution here. What do you think?"
- "I have what it takes to do this job. What questions are lingering in your mind?"

Now then. What do you do when the question of money is brought up before you have enough details about the job to negotiate from a position of knowledge and strength? Postpone money talk until you have the facts in hand. Do that by asking something like: "I still have one or two questions about my responsibilities, and it will be easier for me to talk about money when I have cleared them up. Could I first ask you a few questions about . . . ?"

Proceed to clarify duties and responsibilities, being careful to weigh the relative importance of the position and the individual duties to the success of the department you may join. The employer is duty-bound to get your services as reasonably as possible, while you have an equal responsibility to do the best you can for yourself. Your goal is not to settle for less than will enable you to be happy on the job—unhappiness at work can taint the rest of your life. The rest of the chapter is going to address the many questions that might be asked, or that you might ask, to bring matters to a successful conclusion.

"What is an adequate reward for your efforts?"

A glaring manageability question and money probe all in one. The interviewer probably already has a typist on staff who expects a Nobel Prize each time he or she gets out a faultless letter. Your answer should be honest and cover all bases. "My primary satisfaction and reward comes from a job well done and completed on time. The occasional good word from my boss is always welcome. Last but not least, I think everyone looks forward to a salary review."

"What is your salary history?" or "What was your salary progress on your last job?"

The interviewer is looking for a couple of things. First, he or she is looking for the frequency, percentage, and dollar value of your raises, which in turn tell him or her about your performance and the relative value of the offer that is about to be made. What you want to avoid is tying the potential offer to your salary history—the offer you negotiate should be based solely on the value of the job in hand. Again, this is even more important if you are a woman.

Your answer needs to be specifically vague. Perhaps: "My salary history has followed a steady upward path, and I have never failed to receive merit increases. I would be glad to give you the specific numbers if needed, but I shall have to sit down and give it some thought with a pencil and paper." The odds are that the interviewer will not ask you to do that; if he or she does, nod in agreement and say you'll get right to it when you get home. Don't begin the task until you are requested a second time, which is unlikely.

If for any reason you do get your back against the wall with this one, be sure to include in the specifics of your answer that "one of the reasons I am leaving my current job is that raises were standard for all levels of employees, so that despite my superior contributions, I got the same percentage raise as the tardy employee. I want to work in an environment where I will be recognized and rewarded for my contributions." Then end with a question: "Is this the sort of company where I can expect that?"

"What were you making on your last job?"

A similar but not identical question. It could also be phrased, "What are you making now?" or "What is your current salary?"

While I have said your current earnings should bear no relation to your starting salary on the new job, it can be difficult to make that statement clear to the interviewer without appearing objectionable. A short answer might include: "I am earning $X, although I do want you to know that a major reason for making a job change right now is to significantly increase my remuneration as currently I am underpaid for my skills and experience."

It is important to understand the "areas of allowable fudge." For instance, if you are considerably underpaid, you may want to weigh the dollar-value of such perks as medical and dental plans, pay in lieu of vacation, profit-sharing and pension plans, bonuses, stock options, and other incentives. For many people, those can add between 20 to 35 percent to their base salary—you might honestly be able to mention a higher figure than you at first thought possible. Also, if you are due for a raise imminently, you are justified in adding it in.

It isn't common for current or previous salaries to be verified by employers, although certain industries, because of legal requirements, check more than others do (for instance, the stock market or the liquor business). Before your "current salary" disappears through the roof, however, you should know that the interviewer can ask to see a payroll stub or W2 form at the time you start work or could make the offer dependent on verification of salary. After you are hired, the new employer may request verbal or written confirmation from previous employers, or might use an outside verification agency. In any instance where the employer contacts someone verbally or in writing, the employer must by law have your written permission to do so. That small print on the bottom of the job application form followed by a request for your signature usually authorizes the employer to do just that.

"Have you ever been refused a salary increase?"

This implies that you asked. An example of your justifiable request might parallel the following true story. An accountant in a tire distributorship made changes to an accounting system that saved $65,000 a year, plus thirty staff hours a week. Six months after the methods were obviously working smoothly, he requested a salary review, was refused, but was told he would receive a year-end bonus. He did: $75. If you can tell a story like that, by all means tell how you were turned down for a raise. If not, it is best to explain that your work and salary history showed a steady and marked improvement over the years.

"How much do you need to support your family?"

This question is sometimes asked of people who will be working in a sales job, where remuneration is based upon a draw against forthcoming commissions. If this scenario describes your income patterns, be sure you have a firm handle on your basic needs before you accept the position.

For salaried positions, this question is of dubious relevance. It implies the employer will try to get you at a subsistence salary, which is not why you are there. In this instance, give a range from your desired high-end salary down to your desired midpoint salary.

"How much will it take to get you?" "How much are you looking for?" "What are your salary expectations?" "What are your salary requirements?"

You are being asked to name a figure here. Give the wrong answer and you can get eliminated. It is always a temptation to ask for the moon, knowing you can come down later, but there are better approaches. It is wise to confirm your understanding of the job and its importance before you start throwing numbers around, because you will have to live with the consequences. You need the best possible offer without pricing yourself out of the market, so it's time to dance with one of the following responses.

"Well, let's see if I understand the responsibilities fully. . . ." You then proceed to itemize exactly what you will be doing on a daily basis and the parameters of your responsibilities and authority. Once that is done you will seek agreement: "Is this the job as you see it or have I missed anything?" Remember to describe the job in its most flattering and challenging light, paying special attention to the way you see it fitting into the overall picture and contributing to the success of the department, work group, and company. You can then finish your response with a question of your own: "What figure did you have in mind for someone with my track record?" or "What range has been authorized for this position?" Your answer will include, in part, something along the lines of, "I believe my skills and experience will warrant a starting salary between _____ and _____."

You also could ask, "What would be the salary range for someone with my experience and skills?" or "I naturally want to make as much as my background and skills will allow. If I am right for the job, and I think my credentials demonstrate that I am, I am sure you will make me a fair offer. What figure do you have in mind?"

Another good response is: "I would expect a salary appropriate to my experience and ability to do the job successfully. What range do you have in mind?"

Such questions will get the interviewer to reveal the salary range and concentrate his or her attention on the challenges of the job and your ability to accept and work with those challenges.

When you are given a range, you can adjust your money requirements appropriately, latching on to the upper part of the range. For example, if the range is $40,000 to $50,000 a year, you can come back with a range of $45,000 to $55,000.

Consequently, your response will include: "That certainly means we have something to talk about. While your range is $40,000 to $50,000, I am looking for a minimum of $45,000 with an ideal of $55,000. Tell me, what flexibility is there at the top of your salary range?" You need to know this to put yourself in the strongest negotiating position, and this is the perfect time and opportunity to gain the information and the advantage.

All this fencing is aimed at getting the interviewer to show his or her hand first. Ask for too much, and it's "Oh dear, I'm afraid you're overqualified"—to which you can reply, "So overpay me." (Actually, that works when you can carry it off with an ingratiating smile.)

When you have tried to get the interviewer to name a range and failed, you must come up with specific dollars and cents. The key is to understand that all jobs have salary ranges attached to them. Consequently, the last thing you will ever do is come back with a specific dollar figure—that traps you. Instead, you will mention your own range, which will be from your midpoint to your maximum. Remember, you can always negotiate down but can rarely negotiate up.

"What do you hope to be earning two to five years from now?"

A difficult question. The interviewer is probing your desired career and earning path and is trying to see whether you have your sights set high enough—or too high. Perhaps a jocular tone doesn't hurt here: "I'd like to be earning just about as much as I can work out with my boss!" Then, throw the ball back with your own question: "How much is it possible to make here?"

If you give a specific figure, the interviewer is going to want justification. If you come up with a salary range, you are advised also to have a justified career path to go along with it.

You could also say, "In two years, I will have finished my CPA requirements, so with that plus my additional experience, industry norms say I should be earning between $X and $Y. I would hope to be earning at least within that range, but hopefully with a proven track record of contributions, I would be making above the norm." The trick is to use industry statistics as the backbone of your argument, express confidence in doing better than the norm, and, whenever possible, stay away from specific job titles unless pressed. Web sites such as Salary.com allow you to identify salary norms for many jobs.

"Do you think people in your occupation should be paid more?"

This one can be used prior to serious salary negotiation to probe your awareness of how your job really contributes to the bottom line. Or it can occur in the middle of salary negotiations to throw you off balance. The safe and correct answer is to straddle the fence. "Most jobs have salary ranges that reflect the job's relative importance and contribution to a company. Those salary ranges reflect the norm for the great majority of people within that profession. That does not mean, however, that the extraordinary people in such a group are not recognized for the extra performance and skills. There are always exceptions to the rule."

Good Offers, Poor Offers

After a period of bantering back and forth like this, the interviewer names a figure, hopefully meant as a legitimate offer. If you aren't sure, qualify it: "Let me see if I understand you correctly: are you formally offering me the position at $X a year?"

The formal offer can fall into one of two categories.

✎**It sounds fair and equitable:** In that case, you still want to negotiate for a little more—employers almost expect it of you, so don't disappoint them. Mention a salary range again, the low end of which comes at about the level of their offer and the high end somewhat above it. You can say, "Well it certainly seems that we are close. I was hoping for something more in the range of $X to $Y. How much room do we have for negotiation here?"

No one will withdraw an offer because you say you feel you are worth more. After all, the interviewer thinks you are the best person for the job and has extended a formal offer, and the last thing he or she needs now is to start from square one again. The employer has a vested interest in bringing the negotiation to a satisfactory conclusion. At worst, the interviewer can stick to the original offer.

✎**It isn't quite what you expected:** Even if the offer isn't what you thought it would be, you still have options other than accepting or rejecting the offer as it stands. Your strategy for now is to run the money topic as far as you can in a calm and businesslike way. Once you have gone that far, you can back off and examine the other potential benefits of the job. That way you will leave yourself with an opening, if you need it, to hit the money topic once more at the close of negotiations.

If you feel the salary could do with a boost, say so. "I like the job, and I know I have what it takes to be successful in it. I would also be prepared to give you a start date of [e.g.] March 1 to show my sincerity. But quite honestly, I couldn't justify it with your initial salary offer. I hope that we have some room for negotiation here."

Or you can say, "I could start on March 1, and I do feel I could make a contribution here and become an integral part of the team. The only thing standing in the way is my inability to make ends meet based on your initial offer. I am very interested in the opportunity and flattered by your interest in me. If we could just solve this money problem, I'm sure we could come to terms. What do you think can be done about it?"

The interviewer will probably come back with a question asking how much you want. "What is the minimum you would be prepared to work for?" he or she might ask. You can reply, "I'd really like to make at least [now respond with your midpoint]. Is something in this range going to be a stumbling block?"

Depending on the interviewer's response, this is the time to be noncommittal but encouraging and to move on to the benefits included with the position: "Well, yes, that is a little better. Perhaps we should talk about the benefits."

Alternatively, the interviewer may come back with another question: "That's beyond our salary range for this job title. How far can you reduce your salary needs to fit our range?"

This question shows good faith and a desire to close the deal, but don't give in too easily—the interviewer is never going to want you as much as he or she does now. Your first response might be: "I appreciate that, but if it is the job title and its accompanying range that is causing the problem, couldn't we upgrade the title, thereby putting me near the bottom of the next range?" Try it—it often works. If it doesn't, it is probably time to move to other negotiable aspects of the job offer.

But not before one last try. You can take that final stab by asking, "Is that the best you can do?" With this question, you must look the interviewer directly in the eye, ask the question, and maintain eye contact. It works surprisingly well. Remember that the *tone* in which such a question is delivered is critically important: with the wrong intonation this can be interpreted as statement of contempt.

Negotiating Your Future Salary

At this point, you have probably ridden present salary as hard as you reasonably can (for a while, anyway)—so the time has come to shift the conversation to future remuneration.

"Even though the offer isn't quite what I'd hoped for to start the job, I am still interested. Can we talk about the future for a while?" Then you move the conversation to an on-the-job focus. Here are a few arrangements corporate headhunters frequently negotiate for their recruits.

A single, lump-sum signing bonus—nice to have, but it is money here today and gone tomorrow. Don't make the mistake of adding it onto the base. If you get a $2,500 signing bonus, that money won't be figured in for your year-end review—your raise will be based on your actual salary, so the bonus is less meaningful than it appears.

✎**A 60-, 90-, or 120-day performance review** with raise attached. You can frequently negotiate a minimum percentage increase here, if you have confidence in your abilities.

✎**A title promotion and raise** after two, three, or four months.

✎**A year-end bonus.** When you hear talk about a year-end bonus, don't rely on "what it's going to be this year" or "what it was last year," because the actual bonus will never bear any resemblance to either figure. Base your estimate of any bonus on a five-year performance history.

✎**Things other than cash.** Also in the realm of real disposable income are things like a company car, gas, maintenance, and insurance. They represent hard dollars you would not have to spend. It's not unusual to hear of employers paying car or insurance allowances, picking up servicing bills for your personal automobile, or paying gas up to a certain amount each month. But if you don't ask, you can never expect an employer to offer. What have you got to lose? The worst that can happen is that the employer declines. Remember to get any of those unusual goodies in writing—even respectable managers in respected companies can suffer amnesia.

Leverage and Evaluate the Offer

No two negotiations are alike, so there is no absolute model you can follow. Nevertheless, when you have addressed present and future remuneration, this might be the time to get some more information on the company and the job itself.

Even if you haven't agreed on a figure, you are probably beginning to get a feeling as to whether or not you can put the deal together; you know the employer wants to. Many of the following questions will be appropriate here, and some might even be appropriate at other times during the interview cycle.

Full knowledge of all the relevant facts is critical to your successful final negotiation of money and benefits. Your prudent selection of questions from this list will help you negotiate the best offers and choose the right job for you. (At this point, asking some pertinent questions from the following list also serves as a decompression device of sorts for both parties.) The questions come in these categories: nuts-and-bolts job clarification, job and department growth, corporate culture, and company growth and direction. The following section is also worth reading between first and second interviews.

Nuts and Bolts

First, if you have career aspirations, you want to land in an outfit that believes in promoting from within. To find out, ask a few of these questions: How long has the job been open? Why is it open? Who held the job last? What is he doing now? Promoted, fired, or quit? How long was he in that job? How many people have held this job in the last three years? Where are they now? How often have people been promoted from this position—and how many, and to where? Other questions that might follow include:

- "What is the timetable for filling the position?"

The longer the job has been open and the tighter the time frame for filling it, the better your leverage. This can also be determined by asking:

- "When do you need me to start? Why on that date particularly?"
- "What are the first projects to be addressed?" *or* "What are the major problems to be tackled and conquered?"
- "What do you consider the five most important day-to-day responsibilities of this job?"
- "What personality traits do you consider critical to success in this job?"
- "How do you see me complementing the existing group?"
- "Will I be working with a team, or on my own? What will be my responsibilities as a team member? What will be my leadership responsibilities?"
- "How much overtime is involved?"
- "How much travel is involved?" *and* "How much overnight travel?"

With overnight travel you need to find out the number of days per week and month, and, more important, whether you will be paid for weekend days or given comp time. I have known companies that regularly expect you to get home from a long weekend trip at one o'clock in the morning and be at work at 8:30 A.M. on Monday—all without extra pay or comp time.

- "How frequent are performance and salary reviews? And what are they based on—standard raises for all, or are they weighted toward merit and performance?"
- "How does the performance appraisal and reward system work? Exactly how are outstanding employees recognized, judged, and rewarded?"
- "What is the complete financial package for someone at my level?"

Job and Department Growth

Gauging the potential for professional growth in a job is very important for some, while for others it comes slightly lower down the list. Even if you aren't striving to head the corporation in the next few years, you will still want to know what the promotional and growth expectations are.

> • "To what extent are the functions of the department recognized as important and worthy of review by upper management?"

If upper management takes an interest in the doings of your work group, rest assured you are in a visible position for recognition and reward.

- "Where and how does my department fit into the company pecking order?"
- "What does the department hope to achieve in the next two to three years? How will that help the company? How will it be recognized by the company?"
- "What do you see as the strengths of the department? What do you see as weaknesses that you are looking to turn into strengths?"
- "What role would you hope I would play in these goals?"
- "What informal and formal benchmarks will you use to measure my effectiveness and contributions?"
- "Based on my effectiveness, how long would you anticipate me holding this position? When my position and responsibilities change, what are the possible titles and responsibilities I might grow into?"
- "What is the official corporate policy on internal promotion? How many people in this department have been promoted from their original positions since joining the company?"
- "How do you determine when a person is ready for promotion?"
- "What training and professional development programs are available to help me grow professionally?"
- "Does the company encourage outside professional development training? Does the company sponsor all or part of any costs?"
- "What are my potential career paths within the company?"
- "To what jobs have people with my title risen in the company?"
- "Who in the company was in this position the shortest length of time? Why? Who has remained in this position the longest? Why?"

Corporate Culture

All companies have their own way of doing things—that's corporate culture. Not every corporate culture is for you.

- "What is the company's mission? What are the company's goals?"
- "What approach does this company take to its marketplace?"
- "What is unique about the way this company operates?"
- "What is the best thing you know about this company? What is the worst thing you know about this company?"
- "How does the reporting structure work? What are the accepted channels of communication and how do they work?"
- "What kinds of checks and balances, reports, or other work-measurement tools are used in the department and company?"
- "What advice would you give me about fitting into the corporate culture—about understanding the way you do things here?"
- "Will I be encouraged or discouraged from learning about the company beyond my own department?"

Company Growth and Direction

For those concerned about employment stability and career growth, a healthy company is mandatory.

- "What expansion is planned for this department, division, or facility?"
- "What markets does the company anticipate developing?"
- "Does the company have plans for mergers or acquisitions?"
- "Currently, what new endeavors is the company actively pursuing?"
- "How do market trends affect company growth and progress? What is being done about them?"
- "What production and employee layoffs and cutbacks have you experienced in the last three years?"
- "What production and employee layoffs and cutbacks do you anticipate? How are they likely to affect this department, division, or facility?"
- "When was the last corporate reorganization? How did it affect this department? When will the next corporate reorganization occur? How will it affect this department?"
- "Is this department a profit center? How does that affect remuneration

The Package

Take-home pay is the most important part of your package. That means you must carefully negotiate any possible benefits accruing to the job that have a monetary value but are nontaxable and add to your physical and mental happiness. Below is a listing of commonly available benefits. Although many of these benefits are available to all employees at some companies, you should know that, as a rule of thumb, the higher up the ladder you climb, the more benefits you can expect. Because the corporate world and its methods of creating a motivated and committed work force are constantly in flux, never assume that a particular benefit will not be available to you.

The basic rule is to ask—if you don't ask, there is no way you will get something. A few years ago, it would have been unthinkable that anyone but an executive could expect something as glamorous as an athletic club membership in a benefits package. Today, however, more companies have a membership as a standard benefit, and an increasing number are even building their own health club facilities. What's this benefit worth in your area? Call a club and find out. Benefits in your package may include:

- 401K and other investment matching programs
- "Cafeteria" insurance plans—you pick the insurance benefits you want
- Car or car allowance
- Car insurance, maintenance, and/or gas
- Compensation days—for unpaid overtime/business travel time
- Country club or health club membership
- Accidental death insurance
- Deferred compensation
- Dental insurance—note deductibles and the percentage that is employer-paid
- Employment contract and/or termination contract
- Expense account
- Financial planning and tax assistance
- Life insurance
- Medical insurance—note deductibles and percentage that is employer-paid
- Optical insurance—note deductibles and percentage that is employer-paid
- Paid sick leave
- Pension plans
- Personal days off

- Profit sharing
- Short- or long-term disability compensation plans
- Stock options
- Vacation

Handling References when a Job Offer Arrives

A few words here on handling your references when an offer is imminent. When references get checked, employment dates and leaving salary are always verified; don't think of fudging, as it is cause for a dismissal that could dog your footsteps for years. Beyond that, your immediate past manager is the one most likely to be checked. Depending on the company and your level, coworkers and other past managers can also be contacted.

Call potential references, describe the job you have been (or are about to be) offered, explain why you think it is a good opportunity and why you believe you can be successful (omit these details when talking to exact peers unless the offer is already in the bag). Ask if he or she thinks it would be a good fit, and why.

You can then, if appropriate and time allows, tell the reference some of the questions he or she might be asked. These might include the time you have known each other; your relationship to each other; the title you worked under (be sure to remind your reference of promotions and title changes); your five or six most important duties; the key projects you worked on; your greatest strengths; your greatest weaknesses; your attitudes toward your job, your peers, and management; the timeliness, quality, and quantity of your work; your willingness to achieve above and beyond the call of duty (remind him of all those weekends you worked); whether he would rehire you (if company policy forbids rehiring, make sure your reference will mention this); your earnings; and any additional comments the reference would like to make. This whole list may be an overwhelming amount of information to unload on a colleague, so pass on questions tailored to your situation.

If you have any doubt about the quality of a pivotal reference, take the precaution of having a friend do a dummy check on all references just to confirm what they will say when the occasion arises. Of course, this only works if that friend is a consummate professional capable of carrying it off! This way you can distinguish the excellent references from the merely good.

Better yet, go to *www.allisontaylor.com*, the leader in the reference-checking business. For a modest fee (about $60 for a basic reference check), they verify references on your behalf. That way you'll know in advance just who will be your best spokespeople.

Offer Letters, Employment Agreements, Relocation, and Stock Options

Never resign an existing job until you have an acceptable written offer in hand. The rule is: if you don't have an offer in writing, you don't have an offer. When that offer letter or employment agreement does arrive, you are in the final stages of negotiation. This is the time when you'll see if the written offer reflects your understanding of previous conversations, and you'll see if there are some things still to negotiate.

An offer letter should include specifics about your compensation package, start date, benefits, policies and procedures, and relocation issues; an employee handbook detailing everything you are entitled to as an employee may well accompany the offer letter.

Employment agreements become more common the higher up the corporate ladder you climb, and the more critical your work becomes to the success of the corporation. An employment agreement is a more restrictive document that goes into greater detail about what you can and cannot do as a result of employment with the company.

In the employment agreement, you'll find everything you would in an offer letter, plus issues such as assignment of inventions, non-disclosure, non-compete, severance, and relocation, all of which are all likely to be addressed in detail. Any stock option agreement will probably be in a separate document but presented to you at the same time as the formal offer. As these contracts can be extremely limiting and even affect your employability after you leave the company, you may wish to consult with counsel. An employment lawyer can review and advise you on the specific implications of each clause and help you with revised and less restrictive wording. As you will have a solid understanding of the issues, you will be able to phrase your questions succinctly and control the costs of any such legal consultation.

Assignment of Inventions

If you design or create anything in your work that is eligible for copyright, trademark, or patent, you can expect an assignment of inventions clause in your agreement. It will request as a condition of employment that you turn over anything you create during your employment with the company. This is very likely to include work you do on your own time if it in any way relates to your duties with the company. Companies do pursue this particular issue with some persistence, so you will need to address any personal projects in advance to get appropriate waivers into the employment agreement.

Non-Disclosure

A non-disclosure clause is intended to prevent your discussing company business with any outside source and blabbing the company's secrets to the competition. The wording is likely to be general, and therefore more restrictive to you. The more specific the language about what you can and cannot say about your work, the better it is for you. You obviously don't object to protecting the integrity of your employer, but you would like to be able to talk intelligently about your responsibilities and achievements to a future potential employer.

Non-Compete

The employer will likely present you with very general language restricting you from working for any competitor for a specific and probably extended period of time. Accepting this clause without careful analysis could restrict your employability when you leave the company, either by layoff or your own volition; after all, who is most likely to hire you? Someone in the same line of business, of course! By making this clause more specific, you will also make it less restrictive. Negotiate to specify by name which direct competitors you wouldn't be able to work for in that specified time frame. An employment lawyer's advice will help you.

Severance

Negotiate for as extensive a severance package as you can—say, a month's salary for every year of employment or every $10,000 of salary, with outplacement/job search assistance. Since outplacement is only as good as the person giving it, it is preferable to negotiate a dollar amount so that you can spend the money in the way you think most suitable to your needs and with the consultant of your choice.

If you sign a non-compete clause, request that your severance extend through the entire period of your non-compete restrictions. This is a perfectly reasonable request that should be accommodated without trouble.

Relocation

When job-related relocation comes around, we all find ourselves in an ocean of unexpected expenses. So once the overall offer is acceptable to you, key in on relocation issues. Many companies expect to pay all or part of your relocation costs, unless you live within fifty miles of your new workplace, in which case you are usually on your own. Since the employer regularly addresses these issues, you should not be reticent about negotiating them.

Relocation packages vary enormously from person to person and company to company. However, if they want you badly enough, employers will usually try to accommodate reasonable requests.

The higher up the corporate ladder you climb, the more relocation services you are likely to receive. On the low end, you may get offered reimbursement for a moving truck and a few hundred dollars for incidental expenses. While the employer expects to bear the cost of your relocation, every dollar spent affects the bottom line of the HR department. So no matter where you stand on the corporate ladder, getting above and beyond the standard offer will require your asking for it.

For example, companies know your relocation costs will be treated as taxable income, but they won't say anything about it unless you do. Explain that the taxes you expect to pay can amount to 30 percent of the monies spent, and that this would place a heavy burden on you financially. With a typical executive relocation running around $50,000, the tax implications of relocating to accept a new job could come as a nasty shock. Ask that the company pick up the personal income tax burdens you incur as a result of your move.

Only some aspects of your relocation are tax deductible. For example, the costs of moving your personal belongings and one trip to the new location are deductible, but house hunting trips and the costs of temporary accommodation are not.

Other things you can ask the company to help or reimburse you for include:

- House hunting trips before you start. After all, it is in the best interests of the company to have you settled as quickly as possible.
- Temporary housing costs while you find a suitable permanent residence. Again, most companies will comply with at least thirty days, sometimes as many as ninety to 120 days.
- Shipping of autos, boats, and so on.
- Costs of a professional moving company packing, shipping, and delivering your household goods.
- Costs of selling and buying a house, if you are a homeowner.

- Job-search assistance for a working spouse. Try to get a dollar amount so that you can choose your service provider. Come to knockemdead.com for more advice on coaching services.
- Help in finding schools for the kids.
- Orientation programs for the new community.

It will help your negotiating position to estimate these costs in advance. You can pick up the phone and request estimates, or you can visit Web sites like *www.homefair.com* and *www.homestore.com*, which have electronic calculation tools and cost-of-living comparisons. The latter will help you evaluate how far a dollar will go in the new town in comparison with where you live today.

When it comes to offer letters and employment agreements, the employer naturally hopes that you will accept them as they are presented, but you are under no obligation to do so. Every aspect of the offer is negotiable, and as these are largely issues that have not arisen in the interview cycle, the employer will expect a savvy professional to address them.

Negotiating Stock Options

Stock options, while typically handled in a separate document, will be offered at the same time as your other benefits. It is usually best to address the stock issue once all the others have been settled.

In good economic times, employers turn to stock options as an effective recruitment and retention incentive. Options give you the right to purchase a set amount of stock in the company at a predetermined price (usually attractive), and over a fixed period of time. In exercising your options (buying the stock), you need to remember that stocks can and do decrease in value, sometimes dramatically.

There are several types of stock options, each with its own specific tax ramifications. However, as an employee, you are most likely to be offered "incentive stock options." Fortunately, with this type of option, you only have to pay taxes on your gains when you sell the stock; if you keep the stock for at least a year after purchase, you will not have to pay capital gains tax.

When negotiating stock options, always bear in mind that they are a gamble. The employer is going to talk about the offered stock options as if they were money in the bank, but they are not. Don't get bamboozled by rosy descriptions of the company's future; stay focused instead on the current market value of the stock. This is especially important if you are being asked to accept options as part of your overall compensation package. In some instances, you can be asked to accept options in lieu of cash. If the options you are offered are in any way to replace salary, think carefully, as you can't eat stock options.

If you are accepting a job with a publicly traded company, learn the value and performance of that stock by obtaining public records. On the other hand, if the company is privately held, you'll have to rely on the information that is provided to you by the employer. In this instance, consider market segment, business strategy, operations, liquidity, and senior management track record. In effect, you are evaluating your faith in the company, the imminence of their going public, and whether or not the company is a start-up or a well-established entity.

Of course, if the stock options do not impact your take-home pay, it can't hurt to get as many as you can. There is a big difference between getting the options and actually exercising your right to buy and sell them. Your considerations will include: what the purchase price will be, when you can exercise your options, and the restrictions on when you can buy the stock and when you can sell it. These matters will all be laid out in the separate options agreement furnished by the employer at the same time as the employment agreement, so read it carefully before you start negotiations in this area.

Everything to do with stock is negotiable, so you don't have to accept whatever you are offered without question and negotiation. Naturally, you will ask for more options than you are initially offered. You may not exercise those options, but having them available is in your best interests.

Your stock options will have a vesting period—the length of time you must work for the company before you can exercise your options. The employer, who is using the options as a retention tool, wants the vesting period to be as long as possible, thus tying you to the company with the lure of the stock. You, on the other hand, want to shorten the vesting period and, if possible, get an "incremental vesting schedule."

An incremental vesting schedule allows you to buy a few shares every month or quarter, probably getting you fully vested in the same period of time, but in smaller, more frequent steps along the way. Another reasonable request is to ask for "accelerated vesting" in the event of the employer merging or being bought by another company. This way, you become fully vested at the time of the acquisition.

Your agreement will also limit the time period in which you can exercise your options—not only when you can first exercise them, but also the point at which your option ends. For your financial flexibility, you will want to negotiate to extend this period as far as you can, even after you leave the company. For example, if you have a non-compete clause, you are essentially still tied to the company for a specific period of time, so it is reasonable to ask if you can exercise your options through the same period of time covered by your non-compete and non-disclosure clauses.

If you are not offered a "cashless exercise provision" you should certainly negotiate for it. A cashless exercise provision allows you to buy stock without spending any of your hard-earned money. The way it works is that when you buy a block of stock, you are simultaneously allowed to sell as many shares as are required to cover the costs of buying the stock; hence it becomes a cashless exercise, leaving you with the stock but not out of pocket.

Getting the stock options is one thing. Exercising them is another step that you will not want to take without professional financial counsel.

Hopefully, you will be able to negotiate an agreement that is acceptable to both parties; you will then need to write both an acceptance and resignation letter. A career spans upward of half a century, so you don't want to burn bridges today that you may need to cross again tomorrow. Take the time to craft professional documents. One of the companion volumes to this work, *Knock 'em Dead Cover Letters*, will help you create powerful, professional letters for all occasions. The book is full of examples and has specific sections on acceptance, rejection, and resignation letters.

Evaluating the Offer

Once the offer has been negotiated to the best of your ability, you need to evaluate it—and that doesn't have to be done on the spot. Some of your requests and questions will take time to get answered, and very often the final parts of negotiation—"Yes, Mr. Jones, we can give you the extra $10,000 and six months of vacation you requested"—will take place over the telephone. Regardless of where the final negotiations are completed, *never accept or reject the offer on the spot.*

Be positive, say how excited you are about the prospect and that you would like a little time (overnight, a day, two days) to think it over, discuss it with your spouse, whatever. Not only is this delay standard practice, but it will also give you the opportunity to leverage other offers, as discussed in the next chapter.

Use the time you gain to speak to your mentors or advisers. First, a word of caution: In asking advice from those close to you, be sure you know exactly where that advice is coming from—you need clear-headed objectivity at this time.

Once the advice is in, and not before, weigh it along with your own observations—no one knows your needs and aspirations better than you do. While there are many ways of doing that, a simple line down the middle of a sheet of paper, with the reasons to take the job written on one side and the reasons to turn it down on the other, is about as straightforward and objective as you can get.

You will weigh salary, future earnings and career prospects, benefits, commute, lifestyle, and stability of the company, along with all those intangibles that are summed up in the term *gut feelings*. Make sure you answer these questions for yourself:

- Do you like the work?
- Can you be trained in a reasonable period of time, thus having a realistic chance of success on the job?
- Are the title and responsibilities likely to provide you with challenge?
- Is the opportunity for growth in the job compatible with your needs and desires?
- Are the company's location, stability, and reputation in line with your needs?
- Is the atmosphere/culture of the company conducive to your enjoying working at the company?
- Can you get along with your new manager and immediate work group?
- Is the money offer and total compensation package the best you can get?

Notice that money is but one aspect of the evaluation process. There are many other factors to take into account as well. Even a high-paying job can be less advantageous than you think. For instance, you should be careful not to be foxed by the gross figure. It really is important that you get a firm handle on those actual, spendable, after-tax dollars—the ones with which you pay the rent. Always look at an offer in the light of how many more spendable dollars a week it will put in your pocket.

Accepting New Jobs, Resigning from Others

Once your decision is made, you should accept the job verbally. Spell out exactly what you are accepting: "Mr. Smith, I'd like to accept the position of engineer at a starting salary of $82,000. I will be able to start work on March 1. And I understand my package will include life, health, and dental insurance, a 401(k) plan, and a company car." Then you finish with: "I will be glad to start on the above date pending a written offer received in time to give my present employer adequate notice of my departure. I'm sure that's acceptable to you."

Notify your current employer in the same fashion. Quitting is difficult for almost everyone, so you can write a pleasant resignation letter, walk into your boss's office, hand it to him or her, then discuss things calmly and pleasantly once he or she has read it.

Notify any other companies that have been in negotiation with you that you are no longer on the market, but that you were most impressed with meeting them and would like to keep communications open for the future. (Again, see the next chapter for details on how to handle—and encourage—multiple job offers.)

It bears repeating that your resignation is not the time to air your grievances, you have simply been presented with a great opportunity and are thankful for the skills this job gave you. This same person may be checked for a reference down the line and you want the recollections to be positive.

MULTIPLE JOB INTERVIEWS, MULTIPLE JOB OFFERS

RELYING ON ONE interview at a time can only lead to anxiety, so you must create and foster an ever-growing network of interviews and, consequently, job offers.

False optimism and laziness lead many job hunters to be content with only one interview in process at any given time. That severely reduces the odds of landing the best job in town within your chosen time frame. Complacency guarantees that you will continue to operate in a buyer's market.

The recommended approach is to generate as many interviews as possible in a two- to three-week period. Interviewing skills are learned and consequently improve with practice. With the improved skills comes a greater confidence, and those natural interview nerves disperse. Your confidence shows through to potential employers, and you are perceived in a positive light. Because other companies are interested in you, everyone will move more quickly to secure your services. This is especially important if you are unfortunate enough to be unemployed. Being out of work is when you need money the most and is the time when the salary you can command on the open market is substantially reduced. The interview activity you generate will help offset this.

By generating multiple interviews, you bring the time of the first job offer closer and closer. That one job offer can be quickly parlayed into a number of others. And with a single job offer, your unemployed status has, to all intents and purposes, passed.

Immediately, you can call every company with whom you've met, and explain the situation. "Mr. Johnson, I'm calling because while still under consideration with your company I have received a job offer from one of your competitors. I would hate to make a decision without the chance of speaking with you again. I was very impressed by my meeting with you. Can we get together in the next couple of days?" End, of course, with a question that carries the conversation forward.

If you were in the running at all, your call will usually generate another interview; Mr. Johnson does not want to miss out on a suddenly prized commodity. Remember: It is human nature to want the very things one is about to lose. Your simple offer can be multiplied almost by the number of interviews you have in process at the time.

A single job offer can also be used to generate interviews with new firms. It is as simple as making your usual telephone networking presentation, but it ends differently. You would be very interested in meeting with them because of your knowledge of the company/product/service, but also because you have just received a job offer—would it be possible to get together in the next couple of days?

Relying on one interview at a time can only lead to prolonged anxiety, disappointment, and, possibly, unemployment. That reliance is due to the combination of false optimism, laziness, and fear of rejection. Those are traits that cannot be tolerated except by confirmed defeatists, for defeat is the inevitable result of those traits. As Heraclitus said, "A man's character is his fate." Headhunters say, "The job offer that cannot fail will."

Self-esteem, on the other hand, is vital to your success, and happiness is found with it. With it you will awake each day with previously unknown vitality. Your vigor will increase, your enthusiasm will rise, and a desire to achieve will burn within. The more you do today, the better you will feel tomorrow.

Even when you follow this plan to the letter, not every interview will result in an offer. But with many irons in the fire, an occasional firm "no" should not affect your morale. It won't be the first or last time you face rejection. Be persistent and, above all, close your mind to all negative and discouraging influences. The success you experience from implementing this plan will increase your store of willpower and determination, affect the successful outcome of your job search, and enrich your whole life. Start today.

The key to your success is preparation. Failing is easy—it requires no effort. It is the achievement of success that requires effort, and that means effort today, not tomorrow, for tomorrow never comes. So start building that well-stocked briefcase today.

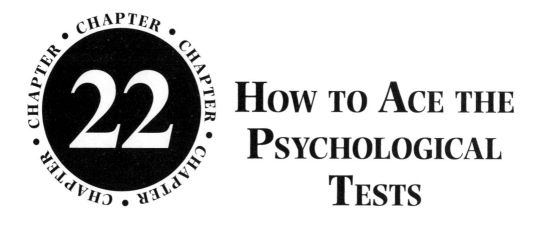

HOW TO ACE THE PSYCHOLOGICAL TESTS

CAREFUL! ANSWERING THESE questions casually can be hazardous to your professional health.

In late 1989, Congress banned most private-sector applications of the polygraph test, voice-stress analysis, and other electronic screening methods. While many government personnel (for instance, those involved in drug interdiction activities) are still subject to these tests, many private employers have had to change their ways, and are increasingly turning to psychological testing to weed out what they consider to be undesirable job applicants. These tests may be known as aptitude tests, personality profiles, personnel selection tests, or skills, aptitude, and integrity tests, but in the end they are all the same thing: an attempt to find out if you show signs of being a "risky" hire.

Although the 1989 legislation led to new popularity for psychological tests, they have been around for decades. Psychological exams come in two flavors. One is a face-to-face meeting with a psychologist, and the other (far more common) is a written test, often multiple choice.

In any discussion of this issue, we should bear in mind that psychology is, by the admission of its own practitioners, an inexact science, and that few of the tests used in employee selection were designed for that purpose. While these tests cannot be regarded as a definitive litmus test on your potential employability, many companies are grafting the imprecise discipline of psychological testing onto the equally imprecise one of employment selection. The result is cheap and easy to administer. Those seeking employment are often asked to answer "a few routine questions" that end up being anything but routine. The tests, which should not be used as the sole basis for a hiring decision, are nevertheless often used in a pass-or-fail way and have a huge effect on people's livelihoods. In your case, let's do everything we can to make sure they don't have a negative effect on your job prospects.

It isn't surprising that many of the companies using the tests are concerned about the honesty of prospective employees. Each year, American industry loses an estimated $40 billion from employee theft. While honesty is often one of the behavioral profiles examined, the tests can also examine aptitude and suitability for a position. Often, the exams are geared toward evaluating the amount of energy a person might bring to the job, how he or she would handle stress, and what his or her attitudes toward job, peers, and management would be.

Unfortunately, answering a psychological test with complete personal honesty may very well threaten your chance of being offered employment. That's the bad news. Here's the good news: you can ace the tests without having to compromise your personal integrity.

Not long ago, I did an in-house employee selection and motivation seminar for a large corporation. When asked for my opinion on the subject of psychological testing, I replied the tests were often used inappropriately as a pass-or-fail criterion for hiring, and anyone with half a brain could come up with the desired or correct answers. "The question is," I concluded, "how many people who could have served you well will you miss out on because of a test?"

The managers assured me they had a test that was "virtually infallible" in helping to identify strong hires and certainly not subject to the machinations of the average applicant. They asked if I would be prepared to take it. I not only agreed but also promised to prove my point. "Let me take the test twice," I said. "The first profile you get will tell you to hire me; the second will say I'm a bad risk."

I took the test twice that day. "Applicant #1" came back with a strong recommendation for hire. "Applicant #2" came back with a warning to exercise caution.

How was this possible? Well, none of us is the same person in the workplace as in our personal life. Over a period of time at work, we come to understand the need for different behavioral patterns and different ways of interacting with people.

Sometimes our more considered, analytical, and logical approaches pass over from our "professional self" into the personal realm. However, in the world of work, we are not expected to override the "corporate way" to do things according to our personal preferences. When this happens, and personal preferences take precedence over existing corporate theories of behavior, we get warnings and terminations. In other words, as professionals, we are inculcated with a set of behavioral patterns that enable us to be successful and productive for our employers.

Did I really "fool" the test? No. I was completely honest both times. The "winning" test was the one in which I viewed myself—and, thus, described myself—as a thoroughly professional white-collar worker in the job for which I was applying. The "losing" test was the one I used to describe myself as the kind of person I see myself as in my personal life.

This was not a hoax perpetrated by a smart aleck. I am that person they would have hired, and I possess a strong track record to back up my claim. I simply learned the behaviors necessary to succeed, adopted them, and made them my own—just as you have undoubtedly done, or are in the process of doing.

Many of the tests lack an awareness of the complexity of the human mind. They seem to miss the point when they ask us to speak honestly about our feelings and beliefs. They do not take into account that our learned behaviors in our professional lives are, invariably, distinct from the behaviors we display in our personal lives.

If you understand what you are likely to face, you can prepare and present yourself in the most effective way, and you can do it without compromising your integrity.

How to Prepare for, Read, and Answer the Tests

There are five different types of tests, designed to plumb different aspects of your doubtless troubled psyche:

- Personality
- Personnel selection
- Aptitude
- Skills
- Integrity

Let's take a look at each of these.

Personality Tests

Are you a people person? Do you get upset easily? Are you quick to anger? Employers are using tests of general personality more frequently these days to screen job candidates. They use these tests because they believe that certain personality traits are required for success in a particular position.

There are two basic kinds of personality tests: projective and objective.

Projective Personality Tests. The projective tests ask you to tell a story, finish a sentence, or describe what you see in a blob of ink. These tests, in some form or other, have been around for decades, and psychologists use them a great deal to help understand how we deal with tough issues.

One popular test shows you pictures of a scene and asks you to describe what's going on. The psychologist may ask you to "tell me more about it." These areas of your mind are also accessed through the use of incomplete sentences, where you are given the beginning of a sentence and have to fill in the rest of it on your own. So, for instance, you may be asked to complete a sentence such as "When I am at work, I . . ."

In an employment-selection context, these tests are generally looking for leaders, achievers, and winners. They search for analytical and system thinking skills, and look at decision-making and consensus-building styles.

Objective Personality Tests. Objective personality tests ask dozens, sometimes hundreds, of questions using some sort of rating scale, like strongly agree to strongly disagree, true-or-false, or yes-or-no. These tests usually have good reliability and validity. They were not designed to be used for employee screening, although they often are.

Knowing the names of the most common tests can tip you off to the type of screening being done. Tests you might run into that screen personality include:

- *NEO Personality Inventory*: measures adjustment, extroversion, openness, agreeability, and conscientiousness
- *16 PF*: measures sixteen personality factors, including a lie scale
- *California Psychological Inventory*: measures twenty personality scales such as empathy, tolerance, responsibility, and dominance. (This is a good personality test, but it can be expensive for an employer, so it isn't used as often as some others.)
- *Minnesota Multiphasic Personality Inventory*: a very long, heavy-duty test of major psychological problems, often (wrongly) used in employee selection

Personnel Selection Tests

Personnel selection tests are personality tests designed specifically to screen job candidates. These tests measure psychological behaviors such as trustworthiness, reliability, and conscientiousness. Some of them also psychologically screen you for potential alcohol or substance abuse. Tests you might run into that examine these areas include:

- Hogan Personality Inventory
- Employee Reliability Inventory
- PDI Employment Inventory

Aptitude

If you don't have the skills it takes to do the job, do you have the aptitude to learn? In a work world where the learning curve for new skill development becomes increasingly interesting to potential employers, we can expect to see the use of aptitude tests on the upswing. Judging your ability to develop skills in general or skills in a particular area is the premise behind these aptitude tests.

Some of the aptitude tests you might run into that examine these areas include:

- Wechsler Adult Intelligence Scale—Revised
- Raven's Progressive Matrices
- Comprehensive Ability Battery
- Differential Aptitude Tests

Skills

If the job calls for typing seventy-five words per minute, you may be given a typing test. If you are a programmer, you may be asked to take an objective test of programming skills or asked to debug a program. There are tests to measure every possible skill: filing, bookkeeping, mechanical comprehension, specific computer programs, math, credit rating, and so on. Some of them are typical paper-and-pencil written tests. Newer tests present the information using a software program.

It's hard to argue against some of these tests. After all, if the job calls for you to type letters and reports all day, the employer wants to hire the best typist. If you're supposed to use Microsoft Word on the PC all day, the employer will look for the person with the best knowledge of that program. As long as the employer is measuring an important skill, testing skills makes sense.

Integrity Tests

Integrity tests are increasingly popular. Some companies are leery of personality tests, so they turn to integrity tests to screen out liars, cheats, and thieves. Some tests measure honesty, or integrity, whereas others measure other psychological traits.

The problem with these integrity tests is that they don't work. A psychologist wrote that in one case using an integrity test would eliminate 2,721 honest applicants so that 101 potentially dishonest applicants would be denied employment. I should point out that the integrity test itself actually is okay; it's just that so few people actually steal that the use of the test eliminates a heck of a lot of good applicants. Another major study found that 95.6 percent of people who take these tests and get a failing score are actually incorrectly classified!

Here are a couple of integrity tests in consistent use today:

- Personnel Selection Inventory
- Personnel Reaction Bank

So listen carefully and apply what you learn in this chapter so that you don't become an incorrectly classified statistic.

Getting to Know Yourself and Acing the Mind-Readers

Born independently wealthy, very few of us would be doing the jobs we do. But we are doing them, and we have learned certain sets of skills and behavioral traits that are critical to our ability to survive and succeed professionally. The first thing you must do, then, is identify and separate the professional you from the personal you.

✎**Step One:** Never answer a test question from the viewpoint of your innermost beliefs. Instead, use your learned and developed professional behavior traits and *modus operandi*. Ask yourself, "How has my experience as a professional taught me to think and respond to this?" To do this effectively (and to understand ourselves a little better in the process), we need some further insights into the three critical skill sets that every professional relies on to succeed:

- Professional/technical skills (whether you're a secretary or a senior vice president)
- Industry skills (such as—if you happen to be in banking—your overall knowledge of the world of banking: how things work, how things get done, what is accepted within the industry, and so on)

- Professional behavior traits (the traits, discussed in Chapter 11 of this book, that all employers look for and that will get you ahead once you are on the job)

✎Step Two: Look at yourself from the employer's point of view. (Review "The Five Secrets of the Hire" and "The Other Side of the Desk" for some helpful ideas.) Evaluate the traits that enable you to discharge your duties effectively. Examine the typical crises/emergencies likely to arise: What supportive behavioral traits are necessary to overcome them? As you do this, you will almost certainly relive some episodes that seemed to put you at a disadvantage for a time. When it was tough to do things the right way, you had to buckle down and see the problem through, even though doing so did not necessarily "come naturally." The fact is, though, you overcame the obstacle. Remember how you did so, and keep that in mind as you answer the questions.

Conversely, you will want to look at those instances where a crisis had a less-than-successful outcome. What traits did you swear you would develop and use next time?

Highlighting such traits constitutes your acknowledgment of the supremacy of learned behavior in the workplace. It does *not* constitute lying. (Why do you think so many professionals strive to keep their business lives separate from their personal lives? What is the point of such a separation if the two lives are identical?)

✎Step Three: Think of people you've known who have failed on the job. Why did they fail? What have you learned from their mistakes and made a part of the "professional you"?

✎Step Four: Think of people you've known who have succeeded on the job. Why did they succeed? What have you learned from their success and made a part of the "professional you"?

Once you have completed this exercise in detail, you will have determined how a professional would react in a wide range of circumstances and identified the ways in which you have, over time, developed a "professional self" to match that profile.

Getting Ready for the Test

Any test can be nerve-wracking, but when it comes to these tests your livelihood is in the balance, so tip the odds in your favor with these tried and proven techniques:

- The tests instruct you to answer quickly, offering the first response that comes to mind. Don't. Following this path may cost you a job. Instead, look at the test in terms of the exercises outlined above; provide reasoned responses from the viewpoint of the "professional you."

- Time limits are usually not imposed. On the contrary, those administering the test will often begin the proceedings with a soothing "take your time, there's no pressure." (Except, of course, the minor pressure of knowing a job offer is on the line!)

- If there is a time limit, find out how much time you have. Figure out about how much time per question or section you have. Pacing yourself helps, because you won't panic when you realize you've only got five minutes to complete the second half of a fifteen-minute test. Of course, you'll bring your watch.

- When in doubt, guess. Some of the really sophisticated tests you may have taken to get into college nailed you if you guessed wrong, but skill tests usually work differently. They add up all your right answers to get your test score. So, when in doubt, eliminate any of the obviously wrong answers, and take your best shot.

- With skill tests, ask for a warm-up or practice section. One computer-typing test has an optional practice session. Ask about it. If the test is on a computer, adjust your chair, keyboard, and monitor before the timer starts.

- For paper and pencil tests, make sure you have enough desk space and sharp pencils.

- If the test is going to be done with other applicants in a group situation, stay focused on what you are doing. If you have to sit in the front of the room so no one else distracts you, do it. If the test will be long and there's no break, make sure you won't get hungry (take a power bar) or have to use the bathroom.

- No matter what, use all your allotted time! Check your answers, and make sure they are written in the right places. Depending on your remaining time, review every other, or every fourth, question. Of course, if you can recall at the end which questions you were unsure about, review those first.

- You may not even realize you're taking an integrity test until the direction of the questions gives it away: "Have you ever stolen anything?" "Have you ever felt guilty?" "Have you ever told a lie?" Avoid the temptation to respond impulsively with something like "Lies? No, I prefer to chop down the damned cherry tree." The truth is, we have all done these things in our lives. When you are asked, for instance, whether there is anything you would ever change about yourself, or whether you think everyone is dishonest to some degree, the overwhelming likelihood is that your own honesty is being tested: the best answer is probably "yes."

In fact, if you never admit to these behaviors, you could be pegged as a faker. While fakers may be kept in the running, they've earned a question mark. Fakers are sometimes viewed as being eager to please or simply a bit out of touch with their true feelings.

Many of the better tests in use today also use lie scales that can detect when someone is faking. How do they do this? One way is to include questions like "I always tell the truth" or "I never have a negative thought about a coworker." When the test is developed, hundreds or thousands of people take it, and the researchers figure out what the typical response is to these questions. Anyone who deviates from the average response on enough of these faking questions is also flagged as a faker.

If you must answer questions about ethics in a face-to-face encounter, explain your answer, placing it far in the past where appropriate, and explain what you have learned from any negative experience. If such questions must be answered on paper, the best approach is to follow the dictates of your own conscience and try to bring the issue up after the test. You might say something like this:

"Gee, that question about lying was a tough one. I guess everyone has told a lie at some time in the past, and I wanted to be truthful, so I said 'yes.' But I'd be lying if I didn't tell you it made me nervous. You know, I saw a show on television recently about these tests. It told the story of someone who lost a job because of answering a question just like that; the profile came back with an untrustworthy rating."

This may reduce the odds of your being denied the job in the same way. If the test does come back with a question about your honesty, you will at least have sown seeds of doubt about the validity of such a rating in the interviewer's mind. That doubt, and your disarming honesty, might just turn the tables in your favor.

Be careful, and take a balanced approach as you answer integrity test questions. Honesty is the best policy:

- In a face-to-face meeting with a psychologist, use the same techniques we have discussed throughout *Knock 'em Dead* to qualify the questions before answering them; when you suspect a trap, employ the tricks that will help you clarify things and buy time.
- The written tests may contain "double blinds," where you are asked a question on page one, and then asked a virtually identical one thirty or forty questions later. The technique is based on the belief that most of us can tell a lie, but few of us can remember that lie under stress, and are therefore likely to answer differently later. This is held to show the potential for untruthfulness. The problem isn't that one answer is likely to deny you employment; the questions are asked in patterns to evaluate your behavior and attitudes on different topics.

- Read the test through before you start answering questions! (There's "plenty of time" and "no pressure," remember?) Review the material at least three times, mentally flagging the questions that seem similar. This way you will be able to answer consistently.

- Resist any temptation to project an image of yourself as an interesting person. These tests are not designed to reward eccentricity; think sliced white bread. You are happy at work and home. You enjoy being around people. You don't spend all your evenings watching movies. You don't spend your weekends with a computer or pursuing other solitary pastimes (unless you are a programmer or an aspiring Trappist monk). You have beliefs, but not too strong. You respect the beliefs of all others, regardless of their age, sex, race, or religion.

- Relax. One part of the Wechsler test (a developmental aptitude test) asks you to repeat back a string of numbers to the psychologist. If you're too hyped up, you'll get flustered and blow it. These tests measure intelligence plus your test-taking behavior. And you can certainly improve your test-taking behavior!

- Learn to visualize success in advance. Picture yourself at the test. Go through each step: you hear the instructions, the examiner says to begin. You read the test questions and realize you will do well. You get to a really tough part of the test. Visualize your success, and visualize your setbacks. Realize that you can and you will pull through okay because you have a clear vision of the professional you. When you finish the test, read through your answers a few times. If you don't like any answers, change them.

- Remember to use your professional, working mindset when you take these tests. Answer as you would if you were on the job and your boss were asking the questions.

◆ ◆ ◆

Everything I have said here takes for granted that the overriding goal of the employer is to determine whether or not you are suitable for the job. If you can give an accurate, affirmative answer to that question, the approach you take in doing so is—to my way of thinking—of little consequence. If you have learned and applied what it takes to prosper in your profession, it is your right to provide an honest profile of your professional self, in whatever forum you are to be evaluated.

IN DEPTH

THIS SECTION PROVIDES you with the skills you'll need to navigate specific crises.

WHAT IF THINGS AREN'T CLICKING? On some days, it may look like there are considerably more obstacles to your campaign than anything else. Lethargy and discouragement can set in. What's more, bills maintain a most inconsiderate habit of requiring payment, which can be tiresome even if you are still employed—and downright crushing if you're not.

Similar obstacles, of course, can arise on the job. Careers get stalled, promotions fail to materialize, jobs demand change. While there's nothing particularly amusing about career problems, bear in mind that your biggest potential asset and liability in the search is the person staring back at you from the bathroom mirror each morning. That person is a walking, talking advertisement—pro or con—of your professionalism. If the face you see is drawn, pale, aggravated, or simply tired, you need to stop and take stock. You may be short-circuiting your own efforts.

In this section of the book, we'll look at some techniques for making the financial pinch you may be feeling throughout your job search a little more bearable. We'll also examine the best ways to manage your career once you actually get the position you want.

CONDUCTING A JOB SEARCH WHILE YOU'RE STILL EMPLOYED

DO WHATEVER IS necessary so that you don't get your walking papers before you decide to walk.

Looking for a great way to get fired? Leave the original copy of your résumé in the office photocopier. It was bad news five or ten years ago, before the downsizing boom. Today it's like signing your own death warrant. Who would you lay off, the guy who really wants to work at the company or the one who has demonstrated his intent to leave?

Most prudent people conduct a job search while they're still employed. In fact, if you suspect a layoff is imminent (see the next chapter, "When You See Clouds on the Horizon," for some of the early warning signs), you must start looking or get caught in a glut when 500 others get the pink slip. Maybe you have a dead-end job, are employed in an industry that's doomed in the technological age, or suspect you have more professional potential than your current employer can tap. Maybe you took a lesser job to put food on the table and keep a roof over your head. No matter what the reason, if your job doesn't seem long for this world, now is the time to start looking around.

Just don't get caught.

Before you start looking for a job while you're still employed, look at your motives.

If you intend to use a job offer from the outside to get a counteroffer from your current employer, forget it. Even if you get a raise, you will likely only profit in the short term. Sooner or later, the fact that you strong-armed your employer is likely to catch up with you, when the next round of downsizing comes along, as we both know it will.

Home Is Where the Office Is

Use your home rather than the office. You won't be tempted to leave your résumé in the photocopier, and you can work in privacy.

Set up your home-based office as though you were running a business. Designate a room as yours, and allow no phone calls, TV sets, visitors, or other distractions during work hours.

When job hunting while you're still employed, the last thing you want at your current job is inquiries from potential employers. So you must have a means to take calls from potential employers that will present you in a fashionable light.

You might be able to talk your spouse into taking on the role of receptionist. Or you can have a special hotline installed and give that number exclusively to prospective employers. Keep an appropriate message on your answering machine for the duration of the job search, and make sure that family members and roommates answer the phone professionally at all times.

Stick to It

You might be working for yourself in an informal environment, but there are still some rules. You're in charge of setting them and implementing them.

Once you've established a plan for your job search, stick to it. Decide what your work-at-home hours will be, whether it's thirty minutes before dinner or two hours before bedtime each night, and set the schedule in stone.

Since your job search probably won't be a matter of public record, work to keep yourself motivated. Reward yourself for your successes. Decide on a movie you'll see—or a restaurant you'll go to, or whatever works for you—to celebrate sending out the twentieth, fiftieth, or hundredth batch of letters, going on your first interview, and so on.

Be persistent. I remember, years ago, my friend Dennis had a hook for his jacket on the back of his office door. When he put it on every evening, the last thing he saw was a message that read, "Keep Writing." It was a reminder for him to continue his job searching campaign when he got home. When the going gets tough, remember your goal—a more interesting job, better pay, increased job security, and so on—and don't let anything deter you!

Get Organized

Since you have a job already, you don't have the luxury of spending forty hours a week on a job search. So you have to make the most of every moment.

Take some time to research everything you've been wanting to know about the industry you're working in but haven't had time to find out recently. See who the important players are, which companies are prospering, and who's been promoted. Catch up on old contacts. Contact or join trade organizations and associations, and make friends throughout your industry. Attend trade shows and conventions. Or, if you prefer, learn all you can about an up-and-coming industry that might make for an interesting career move, and find out how your skills might be applied toward it.

Stretching Your Job Search Hours

To maximize your time, you might want to engage the services of employment agencies. (Use employer-paid services only—see pages 75–77.) That way you can have headhunters do some of the legwork for you—and it always helps to have job search allies.

The key to stretching your job search hours is to make the most of every moment you do have available instead of lamenting about the time you don't have. Use lunch hours, weekends, holidays, personal days, and any other off-the-clock time you have available to conduct research. The Internet is a great place to conduct an after-hours job search.

Check out job fairs and college or alumni offices for job listings. You might also try your hand at writing (and publishing) magazine articles related to your profession, or securing public-speaking engagements to boost your exposure to large groups of people in your field. The easiest way to get started with either of these tactics is to become an active member of your professional association. That gives you access to trade newsletters, magazines, meetings, and so on.

Market Yourself

Because job-hunting while employed is less frantic, you will have time to learn about companies and contacts through your research, and you can learn where each company is headed and what each really needs. Use this information to send a perceptive and powerful cover letter with your résumé. You dramatically increase your odds when you have someone to approach by name. When you identify and approach employers directly in this way your more personalized approach will make you stand out. (For more information about cover letters, see *Knock 'em Dead Cover Letters*.)

How to Keep Your Job While You're Looking Elsewhere

Do whatever is necessary so that you don't get your walking papers before you decide to walk:

- Don't let anyone in the office know that you're looking for another job, if you can help it. Even if you tell no one besides your best friend, you've told one coworker too many. Word has a way of getting around, and if management finds out, you've had it.
- Make sure everything seems the same. When you're at the office, dress the way you've always dressed, contribute to meetings just as you've always contributed, keep the same hours, and so on. Don't let anybody suspect you're meeting recruiters during lunch hours, losing interest in your job, or taking time off for interviews. Everything should go on as before. If anything, do your job better than you have before, and become an even more valuable worker.
- Keep office items at the office. Don't pack up your belongings, even if they're personal things such as photographs, until you're ready to leave.
- The great advantage of looking for a new job while employed is the relative lack of urgency. You have time to research companies and people, time to rebuild your résumé, time to craft *Knock 'em Dead* cover letters, time to become part of your professional community. You will be more focused and informed. The result will not always be a better job but will certainly be a more career-buoyant you.

How to Resign

Once you've accepted a job offer and you're ready to resign, do it graciously. Now is not the time to pay back your employer for years of grief; save the bridge burning for your fantasies and go about the business of severing relations professionally. You never know when you'll run into your former employer or when you'll need the old so-and-so again.

Although employees who are terminated are expected to clean out their desks and leave immediately, resigning workers are generally required to give proper notice. Helping make a smooth transition for your remaining colleagues builds bridges for the future. You can even offer to hire and train a replacement—and you can promise to be available to answer questions even after you leave. Follow through if you do so.

An important tip: it's okay to be happy, but keep your mirth under control while you're in the office. Save the rip-roaring celebration for family and friends. Even your closest colleagues can resent your good fortune, so don't do anything to encourage them to believe you might be gloating. Remember, those you offend on the way up could very well show you the way down sometime in the future.

WHEN YOU SEE CLOUDS ON THE HORIZON

CHAPTER · CHAPTER · CHAPTER · CHAPTER · CHAPTER · CHAPTER ·

24

CONTINUED EMPLOYMENT NO longer depends on company loyalty but rather on your ability to change with the times.

Yes, it *can* happen to you.

In today's changing economy, any—repeat, *any*—employee can be laid off. Anytime. Anywhere. Make no mistake about it, if your number comes up it will in all likelihood be time for you to begin looking for another job somewhere else. Despite any delicate layers of euphemism that may accompany your notice, your employer will almost certainly not, as in the past, be calling you back. In virtually every sector, the competition for available jobs is stiffer than it was a decade ago. So you have to ask yourself: Where would a layoff leave you?

At one time, businesses absorbed employees hungrily and even created jobs based on incoming talent rather than existing need. However, the guillotine eventually began to fall, enacting sweeping cuts worthy of *A Tale of Two Cities*. The American Management Association's annual survey on downsizing found that over a five-year period, two-thirds of its sample had downsized at least once; 43 percent had downsized at least twice; and 24 percent had downsized three times or more. In a recent twelve-month period, the average number of positions eliminated in a layoff was more than double that of the previous survey (317 compared to 133).

In other words, heads have rolled—and not solely as a result of general recessions. Today's business climate and technology have changed forever the nature of our work force. Today's markets are ultracompetitive, geared toward sudden technological shifts, and increasingly international in nature. For these and other reasons, all companies—even those showing record profits—are streamlining their organizations. When there are mergers and acquisitions, the elimination of duplicate employees is now the first order of business. An infusion of "new blood" is typically accompanied by a decision to purge the "old blood."

If that weren't disorienting enough, companies have begun rethinking whether much of the work they do even requires employees in the first place. More and more, non-core business functions are being contracted out and eliminated from the corporate structure. Areas in the direct line of fire include such former "untouchables" as accounting and finance, information systems, and human resources. There is increasing talk of paring down to an "irreducible core" of permanent employees and supplementing cyclical needs with temporary or contract workers.

Yes. All of this is depressing. But for the companies involved, these changes are often unavoidable. In many cases, keeping the guillotine sharpened is the only alternative to shutting the doors and laying *everyone* off.

Your ability to keep your head—and keep yourself employed—will depend on your ability to accept some facts about today's work and world. First, you must acknowledge that the idea that you will work for one employer for the bulk of your career is no longer viable. Check the demographics yourself: employers have shown no hesitation in laying off mid- to senior-level managers short of retirement by a few years, months, or even days. Continued employment no longer depends on company loyalty but on your ability to change with the times.

A Watchful Eye

By continuously assessing the health of your company, you can make informed decisions about what kind of changes you must make. In some cases, the company is so troubled that looking for another job before the ax falls is the best course of action. In other situations, adapting to a new way of doing business may be a sure-fire way to be among those valued employees in the irreducible core. Only you will be able to tell.

While restructuring does not necessarily mean that a company is planning a major layoff, it's a pretty darned good indication. Call it better-than-even odds that the one follows the other. Once you see evidence of unspecified "big changes on the horizon," your diagnosis of the situation—and your ability to adapt to it—should come into play. As corporations flatten their structure to become more efficient, employees are asked to work and think in new ways. Those who are unable to adapt to the new structure, or whose roles are found to be untenable in the new organization, will be the first to go.

Unfortunately, many people (particularly those with a long history at the company) ignore what is going on right under their noses. Witness the case of the flight engineer who worked for a major airplane manufacturer. He saw his own name on a list of people the organization had determined it could do without—and refused to believe it. When he was handed his pink slip, he was speechless with shock.

As an employee, you probably have as much access to information as you need to make an informed judgment about what's on the horizon. When it comes to your own corner of the organization's universe, you know as much as the CEO and probably a good deal more. An accountant can see that revenues are not meeting expenditures. A salesperson knows when quotas aren't being met. Think carefully about the events that affect your department or position, and (discreetly, of course) investigate them further whenever you can.

On the brink of a disaster? Or poised for explosive growth to which you can contribute? You must discover into which category your company falls. Some changes in the company may be difficult to interpret. For instance, your company might use attrition—simply not filling vacated positions—as a way to cut costs. The next step might be to reduce administrative or support staff. You have to determine whether the company is sincerely attempting to improve efficiency and productivity, or whether these actions are leading to deeper staff cuts.

The signs will differ depending on the size of your employer, and you may have to put on your Sherlock Holmes hat to get the type of information you need. Learning more about your company, your industry, and your market will also make you a better and more valuable employee. More important, it will enhance your career buoyancy.

Let's say you work for a publicly held corporation. By watching the price of your employer's stock over a specific period, you should be able to get an idea of the firm's performance and standing in the marketplace. It's simple enough to check the price of your company's stock (and, for comparison, that of its competitors) in a daily newspaper. Your firm's annual report may have similarly useful information, such as long-term plans and recent successes and failures. Has the company consolidated any of its operations? This may be a clue to future downsizing plans.

The Internet provides access to a variety of company profiles; you can use this resource to learn more about your company. Is the information you find positive or negative in tone? Does it relate, directly or indirectly, to your work? Read about your employer's competitors as well; you'll be in a better position to understand your company's moves. Trade and business publications are excellent sources of information about your company and its competitors, and they will also give you an indication of the overall condition of the market.

Knowing the strategic advantages your company holds in the market can also be helpful. If you see these advantages disappearing (either because of new technology or other unexpected developments, such as sudden demographic changes or a natural disaster), collapse may be inevitable. If this is the case, you are well advised to start looking for another job *now*. Don't talk yourself into believing that things will eventually get better: they almost certainly won't.

Unfortunately, the downward spiral of a large corporation may be slow and subtle. In many cases, you may have to do more than read the trade papers. By successfully building a network of contacts throughout the organization, you may be able to find out what is going on in departments far removed from your own. Developing a strong ally or two in the human resources department is often a good first step; people in this area know in advance about any work force changes. By knowing and understanding what the company's plans are for the next one to five years, you will be better able to judge your employer's stability.

If you work for a large corporation and you find that the firm is planning for next year, next quarter, or next month, but has no idea where it is going in five years, a red flag should go up. There's a problem somewhere. Either management is inept, flying by the seat of its collective pants, or it is in a firefighting mode, living from one day's crisis to the next. You will have to make your own judgment as to whether or not the people at the top can get their act together.

What about a smaller or mid-sized organization? Some clues are bound to be more obvious in a close-knit environment, where people often wear several hats. Look for bills that don't get paid, new work that doesn't come in, and old contracts that end without renewals or new work to take their place. You should also keep an eye on your workload and that of your fellow employees. If the company is shuffling people around more than usual, or if job responsibilities are changing significantly or frequently in a short period of time, there may be trouble ahead.

With work wrapping up on the two key projects in which he was involved, a highway engineer found himself shuffled between southern California, Milwaukee, and his home office in Phoenix several times in one year. He knew that when things were going well, he rarely traveled because he had enough work to keep him in the office. From these clues, he deduced his number was up. Not long after the new travel pattern emerged, his employer asked him to take early retirement.

Dramatically increased or decreased travel can be one sign that new initiatives affecting you may be on the way, but there are others. A sudden change in your performance evaluations may indicate some behind-the-scenes politicking—or a more straightforward attempt to discredit you and justify your dismissal.

Similarly, any indication that your boss's position is shaky may mean that your job is at risk as well. Changes in top leadership often mean a shakeup of philosophies, standard operating procedures, and staffing levels. Your value to members of the "old guard" may prove of little consequence to the "new guard." However, proving yourself valuable to the organization in general may help stall your demise—and buy you the time you need to look for another job. (It may also provide you with better referrals, or a chance to be redeployed elsewhere in the company.)

The Hammer Falls

Some layoffs are unavoidable. Perhaps the company is no longer involved in the part of the business in which you have worked, or it cannot support more than the most elementary operations.

If you are asked to leave, it's in your best interest to keep your cool. Resist the temptation to blow up at your employer. Sure, it's unlikely you'll ever be asked back to your job, but remember that saying about burning bridges? Concentrate on getting the best severance package (and future references) you can.

Ready for a surprise? You might be in a good negotiating position when it comes to that severance package. There are a number of reasons for this. First, it's likely the employer is feeling guilty about the layoff. Second, other employees will watch how you're treated when you leave. It's bad for company morale if you're treated unfairly at this stage, and the employer knows it. Finally, who knows where you'll find yourself after you leave the company? Someday, when you make it to the top, your former boss may even approach *you* for a job!

When a severance package is presented to you, listen calmly. Once the details have been laid out, you will probably want to ask for more. Unless the company's employee handbook clearly details the benefits you are entitled to, it is almost certainly to your advantage to attempt to negotiate a higher severance figure. How and when you ask are the key.

You may want to take more time to think about a severance package before signing anything. By then, you will have had time to think clearly, assess your situation, and figure out your financial needs. (See Chapter 25, "Keeping the

WHEN YOU SEE CLOUDS ON THE HORIZON | **317**

Financial Boat Afloat," for more details on this.) Taking a little extra time also allows you a "chill-out" period, which will reduce the likelihood that you will come across as angry and irrational when you present your arguments.

Whether or not you decide to ask for time to think about the severance offer, you should approach any attempt to increase the severance package in a non-threatening manner. Begin by saying, "I'm certain that you're making every effort to be fair." Summarize your contribution to the company so the employer knows exactly why you deserve the increased consideration.

Try for benefits that are already in the company's budget, such as magazine and newspaper subscriptions or professional association membership renewals. You might even be able to talk your former employer into continued use of a company car for a time.

As helpful as it may have been in helping you forecast the rough weather you are now negotiating, the human resources department, with its rulebooks and set policies, is unlikely to be your ally in this cause. Try to avoid negotiating your severance package solely through this office. Instead, co-opt your former supervisor, who is likely to feel much more guilt. Granted, the meeting may not be one you look forward to with great enthusiasm, but this is not about getting mad or becoming vindictive; this is about survival. The best recipe calls for generous amounts of calm objectivity and carefully measured doses of despair.

The Emotional Costs

Take time to mourn the loss of your job, as you would any other loss. Don't tough it out. Admit that this hurts. The degree to which you effectively work through the shock will determine how quickly you can get back on your feet and mount a successful job search.

The aftereffects of job loss are similar to the stages of grieving that follow divorce or the death of a loved one: denial, bargaining, anger, depression, and acceptance. Dealing with these can be difficult and may require more time than you would think.

Finding support is crucial to your success in landing another job. Consider joining community job search clubs or meeting with an *ad hoc* group of other people in your situation. (Perhaps there are others who were laid off at the same time you were at your old firm.) By following these steps, you will expand your opportunities and maintain some perspective on the situation.

When you're ready, turn this horrible experience into a growth opportunity. Assess the experience and be honest with yourself. Did you inadvertently contribute to the situation? Was there anything you might have done differently? Did you learn anything that you can apply in your next job?

Keeping the Financial Boat Afloat

HOW TO MAKE the best choices in tough times.

For too many of us, it actually takes losing a job in tough times to illustrate how close to the economic edge we usually live. To be sure, we take on financial obligations of our own free will—but the media, the society we live in, and, yes, our erstwhile employers all encourage standards of consumption we quickly learn to take for granted.

If you are reading this in a state of shock because you have recently been terminated, have a seat and take a deep breath. Things are probably not as bad as they seem right about now, but you still need to keep your wits about you. Rash decisions, decisions made in desperation, are the ones we end up regretting. Take some time to decompress.

When Still Inside the Building

If, on the other hand, you are lucky enough to be reading this before your termination has been finalized, be careful how you approach matters. It goes without saying that you should check your instinct to settle old scores or to lash out at the firm that is letting you go, but there are other important pieces of advice you should follow as well. Most of what follows is meant for those who have fallen victim to staffing cuts, but some of the ideas can be adapted to those who are terminated under less than favorable conditions—especially Rule Number One.

Rule Number One is simple: *Don't sign anything* until you are convinced you have everything the law, ethical considerations, and good old-fashioned guilt can elicit from the employer.

Ask about outplacement services. Outplacement firms are companies that provide you with job search assistance ranging from a one-day seminar to "as-long-as-it-takes" counseling. This type of program is increasingly common; don't feel guilty about asking for it.

Negotiate the best possible severance package. A week's severance pay for every year of service is the standard, inadequate though it is. Whatever you are offered, try to wheedle a little more. Point out that times are tough; if the unemployment rate is high, say so, and use actual numbers if you can. Remember, guilt works. Those who don't ask, don't get.

Find out what your benefits will be over the next months. Murphy's law, which states that whatever can go wrong will, applies with double force to the unemployed. Under the current insurance laws, you can continue the health plan your employer provided for you at a subsidized rate for up to eighteen months, after which time you can continue on the same plan at a (much higher) personal rate.

Determine the company policy on providing references. Sometimes companies will give no more than salary and dates of employment to those who call asking about your tenure there, regardless of your level of performance, which can adversely affect your job search. If you learn this is the policy in your case, get a written letter to that effect to show to potential employers. If possible, obtain a written testimonial from your manager before you sign anything or leave the company.

You and I know, of course, that a reference is essentially the same thing as a letter testifying to your character. If you run into "company policy" trouble here, you can point out that you are not asking for an official reference, but the supervisor's personal evaluation of you as one professional discussing another.

The fact that the personal reference need not appear on company stationery is usually a plus in obtaining the letter.

Request that the employer tell callers that you are unavailable, rather than unemployed, and that you will return all calls. Obviously, you won't be able to make this last forever, but you may be able to maintain at least the appearance of gainful employment. Every little bit helps.

If it isn't part of your outplacement package, try asking for desk space and telephone cost reimbursement for your job search. Of course, this is only feasible if you work in an appropriate office environment. Asking for desk space and telephone time in, say, a retail setting will do nothing but brand you as a head case. Assuming the circumstances are favorable for such a request, you may be able to get two or three months' worth of help, or perhaps a flat cash payment. You certainly shouldn't rely on this, but it is worth asking about.

Ask for professional financial counseling. In case the employer hasn't thought of this (a good bet), call an accountant for an estimate of the amount of money involved. Say, "I've just been laid off; I'm married, with two kids and a mortgage. I want to know how much you'd charge to help me create a live-able, pared-down budget." Then go to the employer with the figure. If a number of people are being let go, you may be able to get the employer to spring for a seminar for everyone. Prioritize the requests you want to make from this list then, in conversation with your employer, start at the top and work your way down.

Once You've Left the Building

The time for all of the above has passed. You and the employer have parted company, and you must make some sense of the financial picture before you. If you don't face up to the financial problems of unemployment in a timely fashion, you may end up losing everything except the shopping cart. So face the facts early—and if you didn't do it early, do it now. Immediate action will help you reach the point where problems are rectified all the sooner. Procrastination can only worsen your situation.

If you have stocks or stock options, you may want to consider cashing them in. In some instances there will be a specific time frame in which you must exercise your options or lose them, you should also be prepared to pay a capital gains tax on your profits. If you have a vested company-sponsored pension plan, this will merit your close attention, as well. I have heard of employees who had to sue to get money owed them through these plans, but this problem generally arises only with smaller employers. Check with an accountant or financial adviser for all the details.

You may have the option of having your severance money paid out to you on a regular basis, approximating the payment pattern of your wages, or in a lump sum. Some feel that it is to your advantage to have the payments spread out because this defines you as being on the payroll and, therefore, at least technically employed. Others argue that such a ruse is of marginal aid and point out that in a time of severe financial stress, you should at least earn some interest on your money.

Your best course is probably to ask to have the money paid out over a period, if you see a realistic prospect of an offer on the horizon and if that offer will be aided by your being able to claim, legitimately, that you are still on someone's payroll. Otherwise, bank it all. If you do choose to deposit all the money, look at your calendar before the check is cut. For tax reasons, you will almost certainly want to avoid receiving huge sums late in the year.

That lump sum can be dangerous if you're not used to dealing with large amounts of cash; beware of the Payday Millionaire Syndrome. Now is not the time to use "all that money" to refinish your basement or get a new car. Be prudent with your cash. Strike that: Be *miserly* with your cash. Bear in mind that some authorities estimate it will take you, on average, one month of job searching for every ten thousand dollars of yearly salary in your desired job. This is a much-repeated but inaccurate statement, as the length of your search will depend on the intelligence and effort you put into its execution. That said, the higher up the corporate ladder you have climbed the fewer the opportunities, so it is only circumspect to economize between paychecks!

No matter how bad things get or how tempted you may be, avoid cashing in any IRAs you have—you will pay huge tax penalties. Instead, look into a loan against your IRA or any other tax-deferred annuity.

If you consider refinancing your home mortgage, take into account not only the new interest rates you will pay and your likelihood of moving within five years, but also any closing fees you will encounter. Closing costs on refinanced mortgages can run from a few hundred to thousands of dollars. There may also be tax issues to consider, and these could add to the cost of refinancing as well. You may end up pursuing savings that are illusory, so check with a qualified financial adviser before refinancing.

Get a handle on your credit card use. *This is a vitally important point.* It is natural to avoid the unpleasant, and no one enjoys the business of downgrading one's lifestyle expectations. But as bad as the picture may be, it can't be half as depressing as turning a blind eye to your problems. Avoid, at all costs, maintaining a false standard of living by pushing your credit card limits to the upper ionosphere. As detailed later in this chapter, your best course for now is simply to cut all existing cards (but one) in half.

Getting into credit difficulties will undermine your confidence, strain your personal relationships, put a big dent in your morale, and, most important of all, *prevent you from getting hired!* Virtually all professional interviews these days are preceded by an application form with a space for your signature beneath a block of minute type. In that unreadable thicket of words, required by the Fair Credit Reporting Act of 1972, is an authorization for the employer to check your references and your credit history. Employers are usually content to process your application if they have your résumé, your name, your address, and your signature on the application form. This signature, they will tell you, is simply something they "need for their records."

Uh-huh.

Credit agencies make a business of marketing their files to corporate employers, who use them as tools for evaluation of potential employees. The service is popular because credit information is seen as an indicator of future performance. This, of course, is based on the premise that knowing how a potential employee handles fiscal obligations provides a preview of that person's likelihood of stealing from the company, acting irresponsibly, or otherwise compromising the employer. Whether or not you agree with this idea, understand that a bad credit rating has the potential to blow your candidacy out of the water—and it can do so even if *all* of the other variables point to a successful outcome for your job search.

You can find out more about your credit rating by contacting the major national credit rating bureaus:

TransUnion—*www.transunion.com*
Equifax—*www.equifax.com*
Experian (formerly TRW)—*www.experian.com*
CSC Credit Services—*www.csc.com*

Credit bureaus are legally obligated to update reports containing factual errors, so be sure to notify the appropriate companies immediately if you find any mistakes. Even if you do not find outright misstatements on your report, you have some options. Many experts recommend that you send the credit bureau a letter explaining that your late or incomplete payments resulted from the loss of a job—a temporary state of affairs that is a world away from simple fiscal irresponsibility.

Starting Over

If you are in or are getting into debt as a result of losing your job, you should by all means face the problem squarely.

Sit down (with your family, if this is applicable) and review the situation. Air any unresolved issues, and thoroughly examine your situation. Then work out your current monthly financial picture.

Once you know where you stand, there comes the dreaded task of taking action.

I said a little earlier on that you should, if you find yourself in financial difficulties while conducting your job search, simply cut your credit cards in half—all but one of them, at any rate. The one exception is to allow the member of the family who is conducting the job search to have some flexibility in obtaining stationery supplies, strategically selected interview wear, printing services, and the like. But even this carries with it a warning: make your plastic job-search purchases prudent ones! This is not the time to update your entire wardrobe on the vague conviction that you'll be going on lots of interviews and will therefore need lots of great clothes.

Treat your remaining credit card with the wary respect you would accord an adversary who has become a temporary ally—someone who still very much bears watching. It is misuse of credit cards, more than anything else, that is responsible for plunging the professional into hopeless levels of debt.

If your financial situation is giving you cause for concern, consider contacting the nonprofit National Foundation for Credit Counseling (*www.nfcc.org*) at 301-589-5600. They have been providing free and low-cost counseling to people in financial hot water for over thirty years. With branches throughout the country, they can assist you in creating a workable budget and realistic plans for debt repayment, and they can even contact creditors on your behalf.

If Things Don't Look Good

You might want to consider a debt consolidation loan. This is an arrangement whereby a loan is taken out to pay off all debts, giving you just one simple bill to deal with per month.

Such a loan looks like a great hassle eradicator, but it can cause more problems than it solves if you're not careful. Some people have taken out consolidation loans and gotten everything shipshape—only to use the new "breathing room" they've won to charge their credit cards back up to the limit and push their home equity lines to dangerous levels. The result is not a reprieve from financial woes but a doubling of their severity.

Whatever you do, watch out for the "credit repair" companies that offer to "fix" all your credit problems for a substantial but (considering the stakes) seemingly reasonable fee. The Federal Trade Commission has been all over these fly-by-night outfits, and with good reason. The overwhelming majority does nothing but take your money, dazzle you with words, and baffle you with B.S.

If the situation deteriorates to the point where bankruptcy seems to be a realistic prospect, I recommend you contact creditors to negotiate even smaller payments than the ones you've been making. You may be surprised at their eagerness to work with you. Tell them what you can pay; if it's interest plus something, there is probably a deal to be worked out. Using the legitimate threat of bankruptcy to get creditors to offer you more favorable settlement arrangements is a powerful tool, and credit card companies have been known to accept a fraction of what is owed them under these circumstances. Once you go into bankruptcy, the creditors are likely to get nothing whatsoever from you. (By the way, this maneuver is one you can use but once in a lifetime. Sadly, it cannot be employed as an annual cost-cutting measure.)

For more information on personal bankruptcy, consult your attorney or contact the local bar association, which is listed in your phone directory and can refer you to a bankruptcy specialist in your price range.

On a more positive note, remember there are many steps you can take to generate some interim cash that will see you through the tough times. You can:

- Rent out a room in your house.
- Get a part-time or temp job.
- Take out an ad in the local pennysaver promoting your services as a repairperson (if you've always been good with your hands).
- Sell your professional services as a consultant.
- Turn a hobby into a profitable occupation. A friend of mine lost her income and, being an artist, started an after-school art program for kids. Now she has three employees, is looking for more space, and is making over $60,000 per year. Very wisely, she contacted SCORE, the Service Corps of Retired Executives, for free counseling on how to start and operate her business. SCORE is sponsored by the Small Business Administration and has offices just about everywhere. For women and minorities, there are numerous low-interest loan programs available through the Small Business Administration. Contact your local office.

Debt Collectors

If you're seriously considering talking to an attorney about filing for bankruptcy, chances are you are also being dunned by debt collectors, a fearsome species. People in this profession generally do not attend charm school as part of their training, so don't be surprised if you are addressed in a way that oversteps the social niceties. On the other hand, you should know when these people overstep their legal bounds.

The Fair Debt Collection Practices Act of 1977 protects you and your loved ones from illegal, rude, unfair, and unreasonable collection practices. Some of the specific limitations under which the debt collection industry must act are listed below:

- Debt collectors are forbidden to ask you for your telephone number, salary, payment dates, or place of employment. (But they may still use their own best efforts to locate you, and they can be depended upon to come after you when you find a new job.)
- Debt collectors can only speak to others about you in the context of determining your whereabouts. They cannot discuss with anyone the nature of their business with you unless you give them permission to do so.
- Debt collectors can contact you in person, by phone, or by letter—but only at times and places convenient to you.
- Debt collectors cannot harass or abuse you or anyone connected with you (such as a spouse or other family member) about the collection of your debt. This means telephone harassment, abusive language, and threats of violence are all out.

In all fairness, debt collectors have a job to do and bosses to pacify just like everyone else. Treat them with respect and they will probably return the favor. If you keep the channels of communication open, you probably won't have to worry about any of the abovementioned horrors. If you do have problems in any of these areas, don't hesitate to talk to a lawyer.

The Second Time Around

Time passes. (It always does.) Life continues, crises recede. This is a tough stretch, but it won't last forever. Once you make it through to the other side—and you will—take a look around and prepare yourself for a surprise. You will probably be a better person for all of this. The next time you're on a career roll, you will likely find it easier to forget the myriad admonishments we all receive to "live up to our income." The next time, you might be perfectly positioned to live up to your dreams instead.

CONCLUSION:
THE GLITTERING PRIZES

All victories have their foundation in careful preparation, and in finishing *Knock 'em Dead*, you are loaded for bear and ready for the hunt.

Your winning attitude is positive and active—dream jobs don't come to those who sit and wait—and you realize that success depends on getting out and generating interviews for yourself. At those interviews, you will maintain the interviewer's interest and attention by carrying your half of the conversation. What you ask will show your interest, demonstrate your analytical abilities, and carry the conversation forward. If in doubt about the meaning of a question, you will ask one of your own to clarify it.

The corporate body recognizes that its most valuable resource is those employees who understand and contribute toward its goals. These people have something in common: they all understand their various jobs as series of challenges and problems, each to be anticipated, met, and solved. It's that attitude that lands jobs and enhances careers.

People with that attitude advance their careers faster than others because they possess a critical awareness of universally admired business practices and value systems. They then leverage their careers by projecting the personality traits that most closely complement those practices and values.

As I said at the beginning of this book, your job search can be seen as a ritualized mating dance. The name of that dance is "attitude." Now that you know the steps, you are ready to whirl away with the glittering prizes. There is no more to say except go to your next interview and knock 'em dead.

INDEX TO THE QUESTIONS

Do you think grades should be considered by first employers? See page 252.

Do you think people in your occupation should be paid more? See page 275.

Explain your role as a group/team member. See page 197.

Give me an example of a method of working that you have used. See page 208.

Have you done the best work you are capable of doing? See page 175.

Have you ever been asked to resign? See page 184.

Have you ever been fired? See page 183.

Have you ever been refused a salary increase? See page 273.

Have you ever had any financial difficulties? See page 223.

Have you ever had difficulties getting along with others? See page 250.

Have you successfully worked with a difficult person? See page 229.

How did you get your last job? See page 230.

How did you get your summer jobs? See page 247.

How did you pay for college? See page 248.

How did your boss get the best out of you? See page 196.

How do you feel about your progress to date? See page 174.

How do you get along with different kinds of people? See page 193.

How do you handle rejection? See page 224.

How do you handle tension? See page 182.

How do you manage to interview while still employed? See page 199.

How do you organize and plan for major projects? See page 177.

How do you regroup when things haven't gone as planned? See page 200.

How do you stay current? See page 221.

How do you take direction? See page 191.

How does this job compare with others you have applied for? See page 188.

How have you benefited from your disappointments? See page 208.

How have your career motivations changed over the years? See page 200.

How interested are you in sports? See page 196.

How long have you been looking for another position? See page 183.

How long would it take you to make a contribution to our company? See page 175.

How long would you stay with the company? See page 175.

How many hours a week do you find it necessary to work to get your job done? See page 177.

How many other jobs have you applied for? See page 188.

How much are you looking for? See page 273.

How much are you making? See pages 95, 101.

How much do you need to support your family? See page 273.

Were you ever dismissed from your job for a reason that seemed unjustified? See page 184.

What are some of the problems you encounter in doing your job? See page 227.

What are some of the things about which you and your supervisor disagreed? See page 195.

What are some of the things that bother you? See page 194.

What are some of the things you find difficult to do? See page 228.

What are some of the things your supervisor did that you disliked? See page 195.

What are the broad responsibilities of your job? See page 172.

What are the reasons for your success in this profession? See page 170.

What are you looking for in your next job? See page 179.

What are you making now? See page 272.

What are your biggest accomplishments? See page 176.

What are your future vocational plans? See page 247.

What are your outstanding qualities? See page 178.

What are your pet peeves? See page 194.

What are your qualifications? See page 176.

What are your salary expectations? See page 273.

What are your salary requirements? See page 273.

What area of your skills/professional development do you want to improve at this time? See page 219.

What aspects of your job do you consider most crucial? See page 173.

What can you do for us that someone else cannot do? See page 179.

What college did you attend, and why did you choose it? See page 248.

What did you dislike about your last job? See page 173.

What did you like about your last job? See page 173.

What difficulties do you have tolerating people with different backgrounds and interests from yours? See page 202.

What do you feel is a satisfactory attendance record? See page 227.

What do you hope to be earning two to five years from now? See page 275.

What do you know about our company? See page 251.

What do you think determines progress in a good company? See page 252.

What do you think of your current/last boss? See page 191.

What have you done that shows initiative and willingness to work? See page 249.

What have you done that shows initiative? See page 194.

What would you like to be doing five years from now? See page 176.

What would you say about a supervisor who was unfair or difficult to work with? See page 198.

What would you say if I told you your presentation this afternoon was lousy? See page 232.

What would your coworkers say about your attention to detail? See page 201.

What would your references say? See page 180.

What's your idea of how industry works? See page 251.

When do you expect a promotion? See page 201.

When you joined your last company and met the group for the first time, how did you feel? See page 208.

Which of the jobs you have held have you liked least? See page 247.

Who else have you applied to? See page 188.

Why aren't you earning more at your age? See page 222.

Why did you leave your last job? See page 226.

Why do you feel you are a better _____ than some of your coworkers? See page 199.

Why do you think you would like this type of work? See page 251.

Why do you think this industry will sustain your interest over the long haul? See page 251.

Why do you think you will shine in this profession? See pages 187 and 251.

Why do you want to leave your current job? See page 226.

Why do you want to work here? See page 171.

Why do you want to work in this industry? See page 187.

Why have you changed jobs so frequently? See page 225.

Why should I hire an outsider when I could fill the job with someone inside the company? See page 223.

Why should I hire you? See page 179.

Why were you fired? See page 183.

Why were you out of work for so long? See page 224.

With hindsight, how could you have improved your progress? See page 218.

Would you like to have your boss's job? See page 191.

Wouldn't you feel better off in another firm? See page 231.

You have a doctor's appointment that conflicts with an emergency meeting. What do you do? See page 199.

AGE DISCRIMINATION IN A YOUTH-ORIENTED CULTURE

Concerned about age discrimination? No matter how young you feel inside, it is self-defeating to believe that no one is going to notice that you look nearer to sixty than to thirty. It seems like only yesterday that Abbie Hoffman said, "Never trust anyone over thirty"—and I laughed. Now I am the establishment, and if you are reading this you are probably part of the same club. This appendix is intended for that person who still has the need to compete and who intends to fight a vigorous rearguard action, minimizing the negative impact of age discrimination. In talking about ways to minimize the impact of age discrimination on your job search, I may offend the personal convictions of some about growing old gracefully. I intend no offense; I am simply offering actions you may or may not wish to consider in your personal discrimination battles.

So let's face some of the not-so-pleasant facts.

- We live in a youth-oriented culture, and none of us look as young as we used to.
- The higher we climb professionally, the fewer the opportunities and the tougher the competition.
- We engage in a constant struggle to do our jobs, have lives, and continue our professional education to avoid obsolescence.
- With age and experience we continually cost more.
- We can be seen as know-it-alls and as potential management problems, especially to younger managers.
- We can be seen as lethargic and without drive.

What can you do about age discrimination? Ever since Title VII of the 1964 Civil Rights Act, it has been illegal to discriminate in employment against someone because of his or her age. Nevertheless, it happens. Let's address some things we can impact, short of launching a time-consuming and difficult-to-win lawsuit.

Sometimes interviewers seem to have an irrational (and some would say immature) bias against maturity. Sometimes we cause problems for ourselves with our manner, our appearance, and with the way we handle questions. You hear about age discrimination and you see it with your own eyes. When you feel intimidated and become defensive, this only draws attention to the issue. Defensive mannerisms in a job interview can be misinterpreted to mean you're someone with an attitude problem who could present an unwanted management challenge.

With age—if we are lucky—comes maturity, but with it can also come a blind spot to the insecurities we once felt in youth. That younger interviewer may very well be intimidated and defensive, too. Now we have two people feeling uptight and neurotic! Use your maturity to be sensitive to this issue, both in dealing with your own feelings and being alert to the possible discomfort on the interviewer's side of the desk.

Interviewers do have some legitimate concerns: Are you a management problem, and are you current with the changes that technology continually delivers to the workplace? It's a fine line you tread: Yes, you want to demonstrate your knowledge and experience as a front-rank senior professional; and no, you can't afford to come across as a know-it-all and thereby a potentially disruptive force.

In such a fast-changing business climate, coming across as a know-it-all has another potential problem: The interviewer may see you as rooted in the past rather than the present. Being current requires more than formal, ongoing professional education classes. It also requires staying connected to your profession. The best way to achieve and maintain this professional currency (pun intended) is to be an active member of one or more professional associations. If you are not currently a member of a professional association, type "_____ associations" into an Internet search engine, replacing the blank with your profession; or, visit the Internet resources page at *www.knockemdead.com*. Take out membership in at least one association and get involved with the local meetings; the activity will keep you professionally vibrant and connected. Attending regular local meetings is also good practice in establishing a rapport with fellow professionals in strange environments.

In your interviews, strive to subtly give the impression that you are constantly learning and looking for opportunities to learn—not only from ongoing professional education, but from every professional encounter. If appropriate, you might add that this attitude and breadth of experience enable you to recognize the potential in new and unusual approaches. Again, be ready with an illustrative example.

Being perceived as a know-it-all raises the specter of a management problem, and manageability is an issue for every job candidate regardless of age (never more so than with executives). You may well be asked questions about management and manageability, how you handle input and criticism, and how you give the same. Consider your approaches to these questions in advance (see the entire interview section), and rehearse how you will handle them.

Another way we can avoid giving the impression of arrogance is with our attitude and the way we answer questions. Here it helps to monitor your body language when you're talking (see the body language chapter) and maintain eye contact to show you are an active listener. Smile—not continually like some gibbering bliss ninny, but enough to give yourself an amiable posture. You should also mirror the interviewer's smiles, pleasantries, and witticisms. They are efforts at friendliness, and you should respond in kind.

Illegal Questions about Age

As it is illegal to discriminate against a job candidate because of age, many questions about age in an interview can be considered illegal. However, that doesn't stop them from being asked, so the question is how to handle them.

You could say, "That's an illegal question, and I'm not going to answer it." Of course, a response like this isn't going to get you a job offer; you sound like a troublemaker already. As I discuss throughout the interview chapters, the best way to answer any question is to demonstrate that you understand what is behind it, and at the same time, make a positive statement about yourself in the response.

So what is behind these questions? Understand, perhaps surprisingly, they usually mean that the interview is going well—the interviewer is looking at you favorably, probably thinks you can do the job, and is just showing an interest in you as a human being.

Let's step back from a job interview, just for a moment, and imagine ourselves at a barbecue. You meet a stranger and make small talk, "Where are you from? You married? Kids? You have grandchildren? I'm surprised, you don't look old enough. How old are you?" Questions we have all asked at one time or another, yet if asked during a job interview every one of them could be interpreted as illegal. All too often, these questions at an interview are just the result of someone showing interest in you as a person, like at the barbecue.

So here's one way we could answer the age question: "I'm forty-nine." That's okay as far as it goes, but it doesn't do anything to advance your candidacy, so let's drive straight on to the next and best option, where you answer the question and show that your age adds a plus to your candidacy.

"It's interesting you should ask. I just turned forty-nine. That gives me _____ years in the profession, and _____ years doing exactly the job you're trying to fill. In those years I've seen mistakes made and learned from them [be ready with a couple of examples if asked]. I guess the great benefit to my experience and energy level is _____." Finish with a benefit statement about what you bring to the job.

There are some people who believe (and I am one of them) that even if the question remains unspoken, it is asked nevertheless. In my coaching practice, I tell clients they may consider answering the unspoken question themselves at that point when the interviewer asks, "Well, do you have any questions?"—if not before. I suggest they use this same second answer, but with a fresh introduction. Something along the lines of:

"Well Jack, when I sit in your chair looking at a seasoned pro, I'm considering issues like energy, manageability, and professional currency, so let me tell you something about my. . ." You can then proceed, as in the above example, with the benefits of your experience and maturity as they relate to the job under consideration. In other words, you show yourself to be perceptive, up-front, and to the point, and you'll make some other pluses besides.

Discrimination in a youth-oriented society is something that will not go away. We need to do everything we can to stack the odds in our favor. That means facing the facts and doing whatever we feel is appropriate to maintain an air of vibrancy about our appearance. So on this important appearance issue, the key is to educate yourself and act on the information. You can only look and feel better about yourself as a result.

The Consulting Option

We have looked at how appearance and attitude during an interview can affect the outcome. I want to address an approach to job search that has special relevance to seasoned professionals.

I spent an evening with Dave Theobald, the founder of Netshare (http://netshare.com), a career site exclusively for successful professionals. As we compared our various aches and pains, we also talked about the very real issues of age discrimination and what a man or woman can do about it, above and beyond the issues we have already discussed in this appendix. Here are the salient points of our conversation (captured on the tablecloth and later transcribed).

1. For those over fifty-three, we think a mass mailing to recruiters is a waste of time and money. The only time a recruiter is going to present a candidate in the mid-fifties is when he or she has an excellent relationship with the client and can say, "I know he is fifty-six, but I want you to interview him anyway because I think he is an excellent candidate."

2. Contract/project recruiters are a different story. "Gray is in." (See—in some instances, you don't need to dye your hair any longer.) There are some real advantages for the mid-fifties people looking for contract jobs. First, the job can be anywhere. Second, you can size up the company just as the company is sizing up you—evaluating the culture, chemistry, philosophical fit. Third, it may turn into a full-time job.

3. The disadvantages of contract work are: (a) no benefits, medical in particular, and (b) no security. (This disadvantage is somewhat moot because there is really no job security today anyway.)

4. A big advantage to contract work is that if it doesn't work out beyond the agreed-upon period, say six months, your ego isn't bruised, and you can talk about recent consulting assignments in subsequent interviews.

Of the senior-level companies, IMCOR is probably the biggest and best contract search firm.

The idea of contract and consulting may come as culture shock to an executive raised with decades of corporate identity and teamwork. However, unending corporate employment is no longer the only option, nor necessarily the norm, as you will see. Dave of Netshare illustrates this in a way that I know to be true from my own observations and writing on entrepreneurial matters.

Dave says, "A 'test' I have given a number of people in their fifties is to pick ten people your own age. These can be people you went to grade school or college with, or worked with at the peer, subordinate, or superior level, just so long as they are your age. If you are fifty-four to fifty-five, perhaps up to three are still working in traditional corporate jobs (with benefits); if fifty-six, between two and three; if age fifty-seven to fifty-eight, no more than two; if fifty-nine to sixty, one at best is still in a traditional corporate job." Dave finishes, "When I have done this, I have yet to be challenged and told I am wrong."

This is an important message for the professional man or woman in their middle years. It says that corporate jobs at the level you were used to are likely to become increasingly scarce. In our middle years, we need to put those hard-earned skills toward other endeavors. Yes, we'll continue to pursue that full-time job with benefits, but, yes, we'll also consider contract employment as a viable alternative that gives us more flexibility. It also means that we can adapt another version of that résumé to position ourselves as consultants and apply the very same techniques we use for job searching toward landing consulting assignments. The structure of our corporations has changed so much in recent years that there is far more discretionary money for outsourcing services than ever before. The fifties are also the decade that breeds a surprising number of successful entrepreneurs

We don't live in an either/or world, and there is nothing to stop you pursuing full-time employment just as you pursue consulting/contract assignments and consider buying or setting up your own business. You can make the same money (or better money), keep more from the tax man (write-offs), and have far more freedom in your life. The work is largely the same, the approaches for getting it are pretty much identical, and you are at that point in your career when you can offer real value as an outside authority. It is well worth your consideration as a parallel activity in conjunction with your job search.

For More Information

You can send me your comments and questions about any of the *Knock 'em Dead* books through my Web site at *www.knockemdead.com*, or by:

> E-mailing me at *martin@knockemdead.com*
> Or writing to me at:
> Martin Yate
> c/o Adams Media
> 57 Littlefield Street
> Avon, MA 02322

The best of luck to you in your job search, and throughout your career!

INDEX

339

The bestselling job-search series that will help you land the job you want!

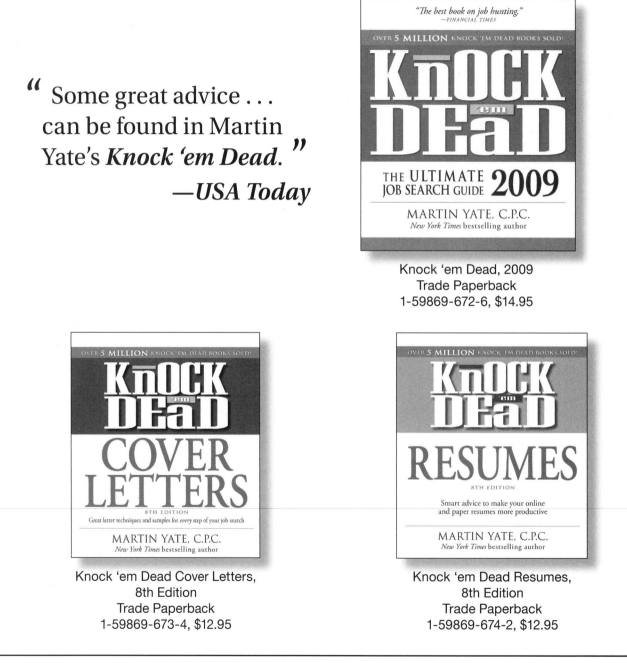